T0301586

Surviving the Sanctuary City

Tina Shrestha

Surviving the Sanctuary City

Asylum-Seeking Work in Nepali New York

University of Washington Press / Seattle

Surviving the Sanctuary City was made possible in part by the University of Washington Press Authors Fund.

UNIVERSITY OF WASHINGTON PRESS / uwapress.uw.edu

LIBRARY OF CONGRESS CATALOGING-IN-PUBLICATION DATA
Names: Shrestha, Tina, author.
Title: Surviving the sanctuary city : asylum-seeking work in Nepali New York / Tina Shrestha.
Description: Seattle : University of Washington Press, 2023. | Includes bibliographical references and index.
Identifiers: LCCN 2022060194 | ISBN 9780295751511 (hardback) |
  ISBN 9780295751528 (paperback) | ISBN 9780295751535 (ebook)
Subjects: LCSH: New York (State)—New York—Social conditions—21st century. |
  Nepali people—New York (State)—New York. | Marginality, Social—New York (State)—
  New York. | Part-time employment—New York (State)—New York.
Classification: LCC HN80.N5 S537 2023 | DDC 307.3/362097471—dc23/eng/20230314
LC record available at https://lccn.loc.gov/2022060194

Contents

Surviving the Sanctuary City

Introduction

SUFFERING AND SURVIVING

Once a week every Sunday, from morning until early evening, one can observe a continuous flow of working men and women, usually in small groups, making their way from Roosevelt Avenue and Seventy-First Street toward Woodside Avenue to the Adhikaar office. Tucked away in a fairly quiet residential street of a middle-income migrant neighborhood in Woodside with an elementary school in front and a Korean church next door, this grassroots community center is not exactly conspicuous to visitors and attendees unfamiliar with noncommercial parts of Queens, New York City. Indeed, as many of my Nepali-speaking participants from the English for Empowerment (formerly called English as Second Language, or ESL hereafter) class and new volunteers mentioned on more than one occasion, if it were not for the recently painted main door in bright red and *Adhikaar* (figure 1) written in Nepali, they would not have been able to locate the community center. Moreover, the center offers somewhat of an intriguing contrast to the bustling marketplace of Jackson Heights only few blocks away. Popularly known as "Little India" among predominantly South Asian New Yorkers and tourists alike, the commercial center of Jackson Heights—with its never-ending avenues full of colorful shop fronts displaying saris and *lehengas*, restaurants catering to South Asian customers (Indian, Pakistani, Bangladeshi, Tibetans, and Nepalis), large hoarding boards advertising the latest Bollywood films and actors, and music stores blasting the latest Bollywood film songs— overpowers the quiet presence of Adhikaar as well as its community members and attendees, the newly arrived Nepali-speaking migrants primarily from the Indian subcontinent.

The community center offers an escape, if temporarily, from the hustling and

FIGURE 1 Adhikaar,
Woodside, New York City.
Photograph by the author.

nonstop consumer-related activities in this part of Jackson Heights. The men and women making their way discreetly to the single-story community center are here to attend one of the several ESL classes facilitated twice a week by six to seven male and female volunteers, including myself. Through its ESL classes, the community center offers a variety of migrant workers' rights–related lessons and workshops, including information sessions on changing immigration laws and policies, minimum wage, health care, and benefits. Because the majority of student-participants and attendees in these classes are workers in the service sector, including restaurant, domestic work, and nail salon industries in the tristate area of New Jersey, New York City, and Connecticut, Adhikaar has been influential in large-scale organizing, advocacy, and mobilizing. In association with the National Domestic Workers Alliance (NDWA), in particular, Adhikaar plays a key role in national and city-wide protests (figure 2) and movements throughout the country, including several marches to Albany and Washington, DC. Besides being a meeting place for the newly arrived and second-generation Nepali-speaking migrants and citizens, like myself, Adhikaar is an important space for grassroots activism—made possible by the vibrant gathering of multiethnic and multilingual people from the Himalayan diaspora, with their differently situated experiences of labor, legality, and struggle to survive in the United States.[1]

Equally important is the work of two individuals—Luna and Narbada *didi* (figures 3 and 4). Luna, a visionary activist and recently naturalized US citizen with a passion for social justice and workers' rights, cofounded Adhikaar with only a US$500 award from her university after obtaining a master's degree in public administration from a prestigious college in the Northeast. As a prominent activist of an emergent migrant community, Luna often spoke of the fight for social justice being central to her effort in the advocacy and organizing of Nepali workers. She explained to me on a number of occasions that one of the main challenges facing the community was the "lack of information" and awareness about immigration laws and workers' rights policies. According to her, direct services offered at the community center attend to immediate relief related to workplace disputes, such as exploitative working conditions, long hours, withholding of wages, or compensation for injuries, et cetera. Realizing the mission of Adhikaar for her also entailed "raising awareness in our community about existing [US immigration] laws and policies, creating mechanisms for seeking redress when rights are violated," a significant aspect of the work she and her fellow community activists performed on a regular basis.

If Luna was responsible for Adhikaar's vision and mission for grassroots activism, Narbada didi played a critical role in realizing that vision for its members through advocacy and the work of community organizing and mobilizing. "Bahini, America ma baseka Nepali haruko barema bujhnako lagi, Nepali haru yahan aayera kasari afno dukkha ra peedha bechara, kehi naboli, basekachan bhanne kura bujhna jaruri cha." (Sister, to *know* about Nepalis living in America, you have to first *understand* how Nepalis have been surviving here by selling their suffering, silently.) These were Narbada didi's first words of wisdom to me when I met her a year (2008) before starting fieldwork in the city. At the time, I simply thought that Narbada didi, like every Nepali I met in the city, was merely sharing her opinion about who and what Nepalis were becoming in the United States. A charismatic presence among several middle-aged community leaders, Narbada didi, originally from Kalimpong, India, is often the first person one

FIGURE 2 Adhikaar along with the Domestic Workers United (DWU) at the Domestic Workers Bill of Rights support campaign, New York City, 2010. Photograph by the author.

FIGURE 3 Narbada didi at the Domestic Workers Bill of Rights support campaign, New York City, 2010. Photograph by the author.

FIGURE 4 Luna at the Domestic Workers Bill of Rights support campaign, New York City, 2010. Photograph by the author.

meets at Adhikaar, as she gives lessons to a team of young organizers, visitors, and volunteers-in-training. She is well known in the larger migrant communities for her activist knowledge, wit, and dedication to assisting migrant women since the inception of the organization in 2005.

If Adhikaar stood for making sense of migrants' social world, then asylum institutional spaces—asylum offices, law firms, and human rights agencies—where I provided English-Nepali interpretation, represented everything the community center and Queens did not.[2] Nepali migrants and asylum claimants navigated these latter spaces with ambivalence, fear, and anxiety while going through the asylum legalization and awaiting decisions.[3] The majority of the working-class, non-English-speaking Nepali migrants, former refugees, and asylum seekers do not access pro bono legal counsel upon immediate arrival, and those who do receive pro bono legal counsel through the human rights agency go through meticulous screening interviews and documentation processes supporting their asylum claim. The few whose cases succeed at the human rights agency and attain a spot for pro bono legal representation at a private law firm must pass through the protracted interpretation and witness-preparation sessions to ensure the credibility of their claims and a more pronounced form of labor incorporation.

Interpretation for claimants and their legal advocates mainly took place in conference rooms, lobbies, and nearby cafés and restaurants of private law firms throughout New York City. More in-depth conversations and interviews with former claimants (several of whom I did not provide interpretation) took place in the privacy of their homes, hospitals, parks, and cafés in their neighborhoods in Queens and Brooklyn. I rarely met with claimant-interlocutors outside the human rights agency or private law firms while providing interpretation unless they specifically requested. It was only after my role as an "interpreter" and their position as an "asylum seeker" ended with the filing of their claims to the asylum offices or immigration courts that I formally interviewed them about their experience of going through the process. I found myself advocating for them once my role as an interpreter ended.[4] It was not something I had planned.

Crucially, in bringing together specific asylum claims and claimants' reflections of their asylum-seeking experience, I have chosen to employ, after Kirin Narayan (1999) and Jason De León (2015), what Michael Humphreys and Tony Watson have called a "semi-fictionalized ethnography" that "restructur[es] . . . events occurring within one or more ethnographic investigations into a single narrative" (2009, table 2.1). For instance, if the asylum institutional spaces became an important, if accidental, ethnographic site during the asylum documentation, interpretation, and witness preparation sessions, the process of interpretation itself gradually became indispensable in gathering "data" about Nepali New Yorkers.[5] Rather than pretend to position myself as a neutral participant, I have therefore tried to not remove myself from the entangled circumstances that I found myself in while interpreting for claimants and their human rights advocates and lawyers. These interactions and exchanges were never simply a dialogue between claimants and me. Rather, these were ongoing three-way conversations, where my role as a cultural mediator and interpreter did not end. For it was often in the messy, intense, and inexplicable three-way engagement, including the awkward glances and abrupt silences, that many things were revealed to me most clearly. It was also where my role as a participant-*interpreter* would be more pronounced, dominating the conversation and giving me little chance to do any observation.

At the outset, firstly, interpretation seemed like everything that ethnographic research was not supposed to be. If participant-observation required one to be a perceptive observer, first and foremost, and gradually interpret one's intentional or accidental participation into a given situation as part of a broader sociocultural phenomenon, then participant-*interpretation* required me to act, or rather speak, first and observe and reflect on my participation later. I was to be heard, literally, as an echo for both parties once each party finished completing their statement—whether a complete sentence or a running thought—no matter how fragmented or obscure. "It is up to us, as an asylum claimant's lawyers, or the claimant himself/herself to ask for clarification and further explanation if we do not understand each other. It is not your responsibility," one counselor had politely but firmly asserted. "You *simply* interpret," another had instructed me during an asylum interpretation session. Yet there were lawyers who expected me to become a cultural interpreter and, sometimes, a document translator, while others would specifically ask me to intervene if claimants started broaching subjects tangential to their asylum claim. In retrospect, it was precisely this unpredictability, a range of random and incompatible expectations, and contingency of my immersion, as an interpreter, into asylum institutional spaces during each asylum assignment that made interpretation itself an ethnographically enriching experience. The involuntary participation during interpretation allowed me to become a more engaged ethnographer—a distant insider (among Nepali asylum claimants) and simultaneously an informed outsider (for human rights advocates and, later, pro bono lawyers in private law firms).

Second, and equally important, it enabled me to observe and participate in the processual stages of suffering coconstruction within the less understood asylum institutional spaces. This, in turn, allowed me to identify, map, and ultimately analyze the importance of "the asylum backstage" work in claimant testimony. More broadly, through my extended immersion in the asylum interpretation, I was able to document suffering as an object of socio-legal practice with its own terms and conditions and internal contradictions. It revealed dimensions of interpretive limits and possibilities of suffering emergence that need to be addressed if one is to fully understand the implication of moving away from a "suffering subject" as a sociopolitical category in anthropological analyses.

Finally, each asylum interpretation session would simply last too long—anywhere from two to six hours—and in a period of six to twenty-four months, these sessions would be as sporadic as once or twice a month to as frequent as three or four times a week. Naturally, both claimants and I would be too exhausted after an interpretation session to continue any conversation, let alone discuss specifics of their claims. In a strange way, these interpretation sessions themselves became a "deep hanging out," notwithstanding the guided and controlled conversation that one could imagine ensuing between me and my interlocutors. My responsibilities neither began nor ended with providing legal interpretation per se. Although I primarily provided language interpretation assistance and, at times, translated documents, it was often the beginning of a highly complicated and convoluted asylum process that I inadvertently became part of. Or, rather, it became part of me. One claimant-interlocutor, Purnima, aptly said, "Lau aba timi pani mero jeevan katha ko bhaag bhayou" (Now, you too have become part of my life story), after being asked by her lawyers to verify, cross-check, and sign the Nepali translation of one of the English documents, as they were not able to locate another native Nepali speaker.

While it was not possible for me to loiter in the lobbies or conference rooms of private law firms and human rights agencies, I seemed to be doing nothing but loitering in Jackson Heights, facilitating English classes and volunteering with various workers' rights programs and workshops at Adhikaar. Queens was also where I lived. There, I spent most of my time waiting for, and sometimes waiting with, former and current claimants—some of them were my ESL student-interlocutors and their relatives and close associates—discussing the recent developments in their asylum claims and related activities. Through weekly ESL facilitation at Adhikaar and the English-Nepali asylum interpretation in private law firms, the entanglement of suffering and survival strategies of Nepali New Yorkers was gradually revealed to me.

This brief sketch of these varied spaces in New York City where I conducted twenty-four months of continuous fieldwork (between 2009 and 2011) and follow-up visits, intermittently (2012–2014), illustrates the range and scale of ethnographic possibilities and limitations—from brief encounters to sustained dialogues, and fleeting interactions to meaningful engagement, and distant observation to in-depth participation in the working lives of Nepali-speaking men and women. It is also evidence of the immediate and extensive process involved in constructing suffering as an object of social cohesion, its interpretive limits and possibilities, and norms of sociality among people in the greater Nepali-speaking migrant community. Despite the visible differences of these spaces, my interlocutors all shared a common concern for what they interpreted, and I gradually learned, as their social world of suffering, a substantial and enduring consequence of surviving rather than thriving in America that they internalized to be crucial to the work of legalization and becoming precarious workers. The book, thus, traverses between these interconnected contexts, comprising for my interlocutors the crossroads between their precarious lives and temporalization of labor inseparable from and exacerbated by protracted legality since migrating to and "integrating" into US society for a decade or more. I situate these discussions within the literature on critical asylum and refugee studies, informed by well-established claims in the anthropology of suffering and the growing interest in "migrant suffering" and survival strategies, more broadly.

TOWARD A/POLITICAL SUFFERING

Two fundamental theorizations of suffering in anthropology drive the work on critical refugee and asylum studies: first, a phenomenological approach that centers on suffering as an existential inquiry and experience juxtaposed against the structural conditions and, second, the concept of "social suffering" that takes into account the broader political context and subjective capacities capturing the "dialectic quality of experience" (Kleinman 1998, 288).[6] Liisa Malkki (1995a), for instance, in her seminal work *Purity and Exile* usefully problematizes the "universalization of the figure of the refugee" as one whose corporeal wounds speak louder than words; political history is rendered irrelevant (9–10). She also (1995b) puts forward a far-reaching critique of the concept of "refugee-ness," the driving argument behind which is that the dehistoricization of the refugee status and identity-making emanate from the "de-historicization" and "de-politicization" of violence and suffering, ironically, displacing and silencing refugees. This victimization and silencing stems not only from the institutional patterns of identification and construction of testimonies but also from deeper contradictions of people's own situated historical narrations about violence, memory, and displacement. "The elaboration of legal refugee status into a social condition or a moral identity does not occur in an automatic or predictable way, and that even people who fled originally from the 'same place' can, and often do, come to define the meaning of refugee status differently, depending on the specific lived circumstances of their exile," Malkki argues, drawing on the distinction between "historicizing conditions" of people living in camps and experiences of those resettling in towns (1995a, 380).

Yet Malkki's summation of the myriad voices outside the liberal process and politics of suffering downplays the more subtle ways in which it is precisely the entanglement between shifting criteria (along with visual and documented *imaginaries*) associated with recognition of "genuine" refugees and suffering of asylum seekers, performances of ethno-national identities, and highly individualized and contextualized lay accounts in people's "native" languages that produce the paradox of suffering visibility. This experience of the paradox was a familiar thing among Nepali New Yorkers, as they reflected on their migration trajectories into the legible account and legitimate model of "immigrant America" in order to find a collective voice, as they relied on and participated in the low-wage precarious labor for their livelihood, as they attempted to *make papers* through suffering claims before state authorities, employers, and private citizens who periodically and arbitrarily questioned their moral deservingness.

There are many ways in which Malkki's important work draws the anthropology of suffering into debates in critical asylum and refugee studies and extends a broader analysis of structure and agency into its inquiry.[7] Importantly, the conceptual move away from resurrecting a "suffering subject" as a sociopolitical category for an object of institutional knowledge production in these approaches has generated insight into the global regimes of refugee and asylee as well as state-level management, including legal-judicial and bureaucratic consequences, for those categorized as refugees and asylum seekers. While reconceptualization of a suffering subject has disappeared from the purview of anthropological discourse, popular visual and textual representation of "refugees as a miserable 'sea of humanity'" still persists (1995b, 377). Thus, the steady empirical growth of scholarship on renewed theorization of subjectivity and ever-expanding critique of social and institutional, including humanitarian, ethics, productions, and politics have not resulted in a better understanding of suffering emergence and recognition in the contemporary immigration enforcements and asylum systems (see, for instance, Fassin 2012; Griffiths 2012; Bohmer and Shuman 2018; Gibney 2006).

While studies incisively scrutinize the ahistorical construction of "suffering-subject" by showcasing how "politics of suffering" materialize, the significance of its constructed-ness has gone largely undisputed, contributing, inadvertently, to understandings of suffering as static, interpretable, imaginable even, in asylum accounts (see Zarowsky 2004; Shuman and Bohmer 2012). Furthermore, and interrelatedly, the critique of asylum "suffering narration"—coherent or fragmentary—produced within the institutional framework has, paradoxically, bolstered reliance on "culturally" specific scripts, narrative styles, interpretations, and performances assumed to match lived experience of people from distant times and places (see Blommaert 2001; Maryns and Blommaert 2001; Johnson 2011; Bohmer and Shuman 2015; Beneduce 2015). Finally, suffering itself is reconceptualized to be a distinct, individualized, recallable past with an increasingly narrow construal of ethical worldviews and moral consciousness.

Didier Fassin, Matthew Wilhelm-Solomon, and Aurelia Segatti's strikingly original "Asylum as a Form of Life" analyzes the asylum as a field of power, contradictions introduced by the immigration enforcement policies and asylum politics, and, following Wittgenstein, the tension between "a particularly shared world and a universal human condition" (2017, 160). They assert that the state production of the paradoxical condition for asylum seekers, whereby their existence is inextricably linked to everyday forms of legal enforcement, constructed a trap from which their interlocutors could not escape: "Their existence is conditioned by the prevailing legal, political, and bureaucratic indeterminacy. Their life is not regular but irregular. They are outside the law. Yet they are defined by it through their permit of lack thereof" (166). For Fassin, Wilhelm-Solomon, and Segatti, the central value of this paradoxical existence as "a form of life," what their informants describe as "*as'lem*," lies in the creation of the asylum system that is "enmeshed in the life, survival strategies, and existential conditions of asylum seekers, which in turn shapes the politics of asylum" (167).

Notwithstanding this influential claim in disrupting series of binaries, including universalism/particularity or victimhood/agency, a closer interrogation of everyday suffering and survival practices among Nepali migrants and asylum claimants shows that the wider migrant community in practice plays a critical rather than ancillary role in the emergence and circulation of such a condition in the contemporary political moment. That long-term investment into and anticipated logic of precarity inherent in "the work of making paper," while navigating the asylum system, indicate that neither is the unpredictability of seeking asylum experienced uniformly across communities nor does the juridical and bureaucratic indeterminacy dissuade people from entering and becoming entangled in such paradoxical circumstances. Moreover, there exist moments in which migrants and asylum claimants—at times one and the same and, at other times, one or the other depending on the situation at hand—draw on their larger social network, kinship, and friendship circles for support, knowledge, and resources to counteract discrimination and persistent violence in the liberal state. As such, their reluctant participation in the asylum "form of life," navigating (in)visibility, and the institutionalization of paradoxical conditions also give rise to new collective existence and new meaning-making processes with new discourse about what suffering and survival strategies, or "life form," could and ought to be.

Fassin, Wilhelm-Solomon, and Segatti's central point is that "asylum as form of life" is more "dialectical than ontological"—universally recognizable, culturally indexed, and socially constructed—that asylum would not function as such without a sustained dynamic between institutional indeterminacy and people's contingent engagement with, even reification of, and appropriate response to a given time and place. Without undermining the much-needed force with which this insight has reopened discussion in critical asylum and refugee studies, I suggest that asylum seeking has long involved a struggle to balance dictates of liberal subject-making and mundane bureaucracy with the disciplinary measures of changing immigration, labor, and asylum policies and the new demands of survival strategies.[8] The challenge for those of us interested in the collective world of people bounded together but not strictly circumscribed by their asylum-seeking experience in a liberal state is to understand how this struggle continues and continues to be productive of durable structures of "unequal access to the means of existence" (Ticktin 2011, 223); suffering narrations are also deep resources for strategic collective consciousness, albeit short-lived, that nonetheless challenge the liberal logic of suffering recognition altogether.

Miriam Ticktin has taken up the role of apolitical suffering as the transformative link between the legitimacy of undocumented migrants, or *sans-papiers*, and the disciplinary regimes of care in France: "When confronted with large groups of immigrants . . . the suffering was suddenly visible as a collective experience, part of a larger context. And with groups of sans-papiers in public spaces, the issue became racialized" (2011, 123–24). Adopting Paul Rabinow's notion of "biosocial," Ticktin illuminates in the case of France that the liberal notion of a suffering subject and the mobilization of undocumented migrants' eligibility for the illness clause became increasingly linked to a "new 'biosocial' space": a migrant community of practice created not only by shared illness but also by using "biology as a flexible social resource" (193).[9] In this collective self-disciplining through biological marking in the liberal governance, the proliferation of apolitical suffering played a significant role, which was predicated upon its new dichotomy as a space for pro-immigrant organizing, but also as a political space upon which the notion of a passive (migrant) suffering script was to be founded and in which the "suffering body" was formulated. Expanding Malkki's work on the "refugee corporal wounds," Ticktin contends, "For the modern liberal subject, biology is fluid, open to choice. . . . Yet for immigrants . . . biology is seen as their very essence."[10] According to Ticktin, the paradox of (in)visibility and migrant suffering—governed in France "by a regime of truth that understands them as simply immutable biological bodies" (2011, 213)—directs our gaze to the liberal state's inclusion of people under unequal conditions. The liberal categories of "victimization" and "liberation," "subjugation" and "recognition," "morality" and "politics," and "refugees" and "migrants" are interdependent and coconstitutive binaries. In the modern forms of life, biological or morally legitimate "suffering bodies" have no meaning outside the immigration and asylum politics, and "antipolitics" cannot be understood except through reference to the political: "The subjects produced by the antipolitics of care have inequality literally inscribed on their bodies. . . . Regimes of care are grounded in a politics of universality, but they produce a stratified, anti-Enlightenment universality—one that sets suffering bodies against explicitly rational, enterprising, and political beings. Immigrants are stripped of their legal personas when identified solely as suffering bodies, and as such, they cannot be protected by law; they are rendered politically irrelevant" (218).

This project owes a critical debt to the questions Ticktin asks and the pathways she has identified for addressing them. She makes a compelling argument for the joint study of immigration and asylum politics in a liberal state, suffering-subject making and techniques of recognition: "Understanding that [the] suffering [body] is always produced by and a part of social and historical contexts gives us a place from which to ask when and for whom the body becomes the primary form of access to universal personhood" (2011, 15). Perhaps most importantly, then, Ticktin's major contribution to these issues has been to reorient the discussion by asking "the embodied forms of suffering that are considered legitimate as well as what exceeds this legitimacy. . . . Who gets to embody this paradoxically privileged position as the most disenfranchised, the most wretched of the earth. . . . And what political realities are reproduced or dependent on the figure?" (11–12). Yet for Ticktin, apolitical suffering in France is about "a particular biological form with affective resonance—enough to compel moral action" (13), which should be understood as a form of "new humanity"—"not an Enlightenment, reasoning humanity . . . [but one that] assumes a lower status" (16). This project attempts, by tracing the relationship between emergent concepts—"suffering" and the work of "making paper" (i.e., *dukkha* and *kaagaz banaune*, discussed in detail below and in subsequent chapters)—and transformations in practice by people's survival strategies in the liberal state, to propose the various pathways by which people themselves negotiate the limitations and opportunities of liberal recognition of suffering. As several of my ESL students' and claimant interlocutors' stories of labor and legalization will demonstrate, these pathways do not consistently result in the construction of a self-governing subject but more often than not involve creation of a parallel space, language, and inhabitation of suffering characterized by collective accounts, observations, and silences. Such intersubjective engagements of partial independence, the diverse migratory trajectories and overlapping suffering narrations in the wider migrant community, are important sites for articulation of inequalities that challenge the liberal recognition of immigration and asylum politics, and of "suffering community" formation itself in the contemporary moment.

The US immigration and asylum politics have long propagated self-identification of/as a suffering subject as a functional, even coveted, status for undocumented migrants while it dictated unequal conditions whereby asylum legal and juridical discretion would be exercised. Through conversion of suffering accounts into asylum templates in human rights agencies, testimonial coconstructions in the documentation and the witness-preparation sessions in private law firms, and victimhood frames in upholding juridical arbitrariness, the liberal US state has mobilized some issues to prominence (i.e., culturally interpretable suffering performance infused with claimants' industriousness as taxpaying worker-subjects) while disabling articulations of other issues (i.e., the continued and exacerbated suffering linked to legal limbo status and precarious production of migrants and asylum seekers). As such, the liberal state provides opportunities for making suffering claims that do not counteract labor productivity at the same time it restructures the pathway, realms, and unequal conditions upon which those suffering claims cannot be substantiated. Many of my Nepali interlocutors, for instance, expressed partial ownership of their individualized suffering accounts and collective moral practice, and because of this often hesitated in pointing to a singular cause of their protracted legal and labor precarity.

Changes in the immigration and asylum policies in the post-2001 political moment had changed which suffering claims would withstand the arbitrary, inconsistent, bureaucratized asylum system. Several of my interlocutors' asylum testimonies as well as their subsequent identities as claimant-*workers*, while legally represented through the dual lens of a "hard-working migrant" and "credible claimant," stood a better chance if and when their suffering was categorized as apolitical. Yet moments of uninterpretable and unimaginable suffering articulations that my interlocutors expressed in silence and visible discomfort during their participation in or the aftermath of asylum seeking render visible what can equally be called apolitical or depoliticized suffering. This is a somewhat different picture of apolitical suffering than Ticktin (2011) observes in the case of France, and suffering-subject formation is crucial because of its inverse relationship to the liberal recognition: "One must remain diseased to stay in France and to eventually claim citizenship" (198), and subsequently, "being part of the formal economy of illness requires that [undocumented migrants] remain part of the informal labor economy" (215).

The wider context of "the work of making paper" among Nepalis, initiated through but not restricted to their participation in the asylum process presented in this book, provides a closer look at the relationship between the making of the paradoxical and precarious worker subject, the extraneous suffering articulations, and the visibility of a marginalized community, in which apolitical suffering is undoubtedly dominant, thriving even; however, its use and significance depends upon contingency, struggle, and uncertainty, exceeding the liberal interpretation, legitimacy, and political recognition. Suffering, then, might be best seen not through the frameworks of a universally imaginable or particularly experienced human condition but, as proposed by Jason De León (2015), as "survival strategies and capacities" that have been institutionalized and normalized over a long period of immigration enforcement in the United States.

Crucially, interior immigration enforcement expanded to develop and configure asylum legalization with the strikingly similar logic of institutionalization and systems of labor regularization during key political moments. These moments also provide an important backdrop for understanding the context of migration and modes of legalization available to and inhabited by my interlocutors: the period between the 1980s and the 1990s marked the first legislative determination to grant asylum after Congress passed the Refugee Act of 1980, followed by the 1986 Immigration Reform and Control Act (IRCA), and although Nepali migration to the United States existed by this period, Nepalis were not the primary beneficiaries of the asylum provisions; the late 1990s through 2006 was a long decade for Nepalis, given the political unrest caused by the Maoist civil war (1996–2006), coinciding with the 1996 Illegal Immigration Reform and Immigration Responsibility Act (IIRAIRA), which facilitated immigration enforcement from the federal to the state level, and especially after the Patriot Act (Doyle 2002) in the immediate aftermath of the 9/11 events in the United States, making status and labor regularization neither appealing nor accessible for many Nepalis living in the United States, except for a relatively small number who embarked on the asylum process.[11] Post-2006, however, saw a rise in Nepali immigrant-community formations in several cities, including New York, and the number of people seeking asylum not despite but because of the interior immigration enforcement.[12]

Asylum as a relatively unpopular but potential status-regularization route is a key aspect of the contemporary US immigration architecture. The continuity of interior immigration enforcement from one political moment to another and the ways in which asylum legality itself has significantly expanded new, contradictory, and divergent forms of labor subjectivities to be operationalized is not a coincidence. Seen this way, asylum is a form of interior immigration enforcement that is an expression of liberal benevolence bestowed upon the most wretched population and simultaneously a part of a whole array of legal mechanisms that seek to identify, categorize, and discipline the *not*-yet-deported migrants into rightful, legal, temporary worker-subjects fit to be governed by the liberal state. This is yet another reason this book examines asylum legalization within its legal-juridical institutional space and beyond in the wider contexts of immigration politics and society within which it is embedded.

Political recognition of suffering, in Ticktin's account, seems to be a force of uniform governance and social control; however, past decades of interior immigration enforcement and asylum policies unfolding across the Western liberal states have brought into limelight the unsustainability of truth and care regimes, and it is also unclear at this moment whether the liberal recognition of the suffering subject will continue to provide any kind of temporary or permanent relief for those identified as suffering, undocumented migrants and asylees. Perhaps by grounding apolitical suffering in the language of legitimacy and universality—"apprehended through medical and scientific techniques and rationales," "recognized as morally legitimate," "exemplified by the sick body" (3–5)—Ticktin's analysis also adds to the *imagination* of suffering as something to be embodied by the victims of the liberal state's violence, recognized then by their benevolent advocates, and inevitably made interpretable. As part of a larger conceptual approach toward the political formation of suffering of undocumented migrants and asylum claimants and its logics, this forecloses important questions about the relationship between apolitical suffering and the paradox of visibility, if what it does is shift attention from the liberal state to the logic, organization, and recognition of nonstate actors and institutions (i.e., medical humanitarianism or transnational regimes of care).

Keeping analytical focus grounded on the collective perspectives and self-reflexive critiques of a particular community, however narrowly construed, makes it possible to see that what happens next offers a variation of the analytic of apolitical suffering that Ticktin thoughtfully provokes.[13] It also sheds light on the interconnectedness of suffering cultivations and survival strategies in the liberal state that recognize certain aspects of suffering while silencing others.

The perspectives of community leaders, activists, and former claimants who benefit from the opportunities afforded by the interior immigration enforcement and asylum politics are just as important to consider as differently marginalized experiences of those who do not benefit from "morally legitimate suffering" or are categorically silenced. The emergence of a migrant "suffering community" would not be possible without adherence to and engagement with the liberal logic of suffering recognition. At the same time, foregrounding spaces and languages of disengagement from, and not resistance to, liberal recognition—as in the moments of uninterpretable silences, however incomplete and unpredictable, in the ESL sessions or asylum interpretations—is a potential step toward "breath[ing] new life and legitimacy into political struggles that [do] look beyond the immediate present" and challenge the liberal limits of recognizability and visibility (Ticktin 2011, 223). For suffering remains a significant marker and powerful expression for the community and its class-based identity, increasingly irreconcilable with the homogenized construction of an ethnicized group, itself a dominant feature of liberal subject-making and identity in the United States (see, for instance, Dhingra 2007; Prashad 2001).

Moreover, the process by which un/documented and documentable migrant communities are reconstituted and acquire new knowledge, belonging, and temporary livelihood possibility as they continue to be available as an unrestricted supply of cheap and deportable labor is part of the classic immigrant story in America, and particularly of the liberal state. In order to examine this further, I attend to people's joint asylum labor and suffering as the paradox of visibility, in which migration and asylum narrations relegated to social and legal domains become a condition of possibility for interpretability and increasingly a prominent component of collective identification—creation of a suffering community. Even when individuals subscribe to the suffering logic prevalent among those engaged in the asylum-seeking work, enduring features of dukkha continue to drive their logic of becoming a member in the Nepali migrant community. Through Adhikaar's grassroots activism, advocacy, and community awareness, including English-language classes, multilingual and multiethnic groups from Nepal, northern India, and Tibet gradually found voice in their ongoing and disproportionate share of suffering in America.

Focus on suffering has long been critical in the study of a marginalized or migrant-community formation in liberal states. However, examining its current incarnation in the contemporary asylum politics of interior immigration enforcement requires seeing not only the interplay between emergence and transformation in the migrant-community formation but also the ways in which the liberal state's concepts, its certain truths as self-evident and undeniable, and its capacity have conditioned and seeped into its emergence alongside, and parallel to, intermediary sociocultural processes, rationalities, languages, and actors. Additionally, the larger story this project tells of "immigrant America" itself is one in which interior immigration enforcements—through its asylum system—and migrant-labor integration are by no means determinate, and the possibility for retraction, complete U-turn even, ever-present (see, for instance, Gonzales et al. 2018).

SUFFERING IMAGINARIES

In this book, I locate suffering as a cultivable behavior and a conscious practice among my interlocutors. I analyze the ways in which they explain their current socioeconomic marginalization, incorporation into precarious labor, and legalization in relation to asylum seeking, constituting both material and existential suffering. Grievances about unpredictable and temporalized work allowed me to understand how legalization and status regularization were entrenched in multiple and unequal distributions of suffering confronting the working-class and non-English-speaking Nepali New Yorkers. Asylum seeking undoubtedly came with a different set of challenges, lived experiences of suffering starkly different from the supposedly pre-asylum-seeking days for many, for it had its own terms and conditions, constraints and possibilities. I use the notion of suffering work to refer to the peculiar sociality and aptitudes acquired through a learned and simultaneously an accidental participation in—a sort of apprenticeship to—inhabiting a particular type of suffering. Indeed, adoption and transformation of people's lives, behaviors, attitudes, and characteristics in critical ways to presumably "'fit' a presumed legal requirement" to "move closer to deservingness for permanent residency or citizenship through naturalization" is a growing concern among scholars of the contemporary US immigration and migrant legalization (Menjívar and Lakhani 2016, 1823, 1820; see also Miller 2012; Bletzer 2013; Canizales 2015). Similar to these recent trends that emphasize people's agentive capacity in "civic spaces" (Batalova, Hooker, and Capps 2014; Bhuyan 2008; Chauvin and Garcés-Mascareñas 2012) to acquire practices and outlooks associated with being perceived as "deserving" members of society while distancing behaviors considered "undeserving" and illegitimate, my interlocutors' legalization experience and labor incorporation attest to the workings of the asylum enforcement that produce and, in turn, rely on people's identification as precarious claimant-*workers*.

Furthermore, suffering is analyzed not so much as a truth about the multitude and types of testimonies generated during the asylum interpretation, documentation, and witness preparation but as something people must adhere to as long as they chose to live in the United States. Suffering here is an emergent means through which testimonies as part of their lived experiences are reflected, reevaluated, and critiqued for their failure to accurately consider the moral and material consequences of the work performed throughout the asylum process. Rather than isolate suffering as a narrative or lived experience, then, this book traces the ways in which suffering works as a developable condition realized both at the moment (while going through various stages of the asylum documentation and the witness preparation procedure) and retrospectively (having participated in the construction of suffering testimonies). At the same time, asylum seeking did not necessarily obliterate parallel and preexisting material suffering or anxieties claimants expressed as undocumented workers. Instead, it magnified and forced them to acknowledge with certainty the precariousness of their suffering and the inherent contradictions of their existence—as migrants and claimants. As such, asylum seeking brought to the forefront moments when suffering was exaggerated and incomprehensible, as people gradually learned to orient their actions, evaluate their beliefs, and transform moral worldviews through imaginaries and structures provided by the asylum legal context, the circumstance of which was neither predetermined nor immediately graspable. Such a conceptualization of suffering allows me to capture well the productive ambiguity that informed Nepalis' asylum-seeking experiences at large. Claimants articulated asylum seeking in terms of suffering work and "making paper," wherein through the extensive critique of suffering enactment and orientation not completely with their own volition, they nonetheless facilitated their own active participation into labor precariousness, turning them into certain kinds of workers in contemporary America.

Thus, rather than attempt to choose or reconcile with one set of debates and insights offered by these perspectives, I draw on them to illuminate the multilayered experience of suffering, seeking asylum, everyday shared dilemmas of labor and livelihood, material practice in the work of legalization, and collective consciousness. Nepali migrants and claimants did not see suffering (dukkha) coming into conflict with the continuous and concrete act of ongoing suffering caused by asylum seeking and legal documentation therein, or in the words of my informants, kaagaz banaune. Rather, in conversations and in-depth interviews, usually in the postasylum context, claimants identified asylum testimonies required of them as a key site for realization of a lived experience of suffering and simultaneously finding concrete expression of their collective suffering. Yet "making paper" is widely regarded as suffering-work running parallel to and often interrupting their working lives. This association marks Nepalis as hardworking migrants and claimants, simultaneously, an attribution that is the object of critique but also affirmation of a shared sociality—the self-conscious process by which people inculcate suffering practices and articulate survival capacities. Toward these ends, the strategy I employ here delineates points of view from which suffering practice and politics are interconnected, although not always causal of each other. One of the goals is to demonstrate through ethnographic analyses how suffering is mediated and documented by familiar and unfamiliar social terrains among claimants and their encounters with advocates, human rights activists, and pro bono lawyers. In so doing, I document how people go through a learning curve to make certain (familiar) experiences unfamiliar in the process of seeking asylum in the United States. I am not suggesting that Nepalis simply fit into given categories of "suffering migrant" or become passive asylum seekers. Rather, I attend to the formation of crossroads where it becomes simply impossible to interpret across multilayered sociocultural and legal contexts of irreconcilable narrations, versions, *imaginaries* of suffering.

The question of suffering Nepalis seeking asylum in the United States is one such crossroads. For interlocutors enmeshed in different stages of the protracted asylum legality, inhabiting the "work of making paper" entailed participation in a wide range of activities in the asylum backstage. Those in the midst of the asylum documentation and witness preparation described the process as a form of labor disrupting their lives, whereas those awaiting decisions reflected on the period of "making paper" as having replaced their working lives altogether: from locating resourceful individuals in their networks to learning their asylum story, from memorizing details to coherently recounting their stories, from practicing delivery of their testimonies in courtrooms to waiting after the hearing. The suffering migrant and claimant-*worker* produced in the asylum institutional spaces illustrate the ongoing cultural dynamics, unpredictability, and inherent contradictions that can neither be captured in the familiar trope of the universalized category of "migrant suffering" or "asylum claimant" nor be dissected as a culturally specific code of acting and becoming. When asylum claimant, though contextually dependent, is understood to translate into a universal category of either victim or agent, certain (visible) behaviors and sensibilities are interpreted as characteristics of a suffering individual. In the cases I discuss and elaborate in later chapters, one would end up finding Nepalis as nonsuffering claimants and suffering migrant workers of the asylum system, simultaneously.

My purpose of examining these differential conceptions of suffering is to problematize attribution given to it as an *exclusively* existential human condition—a taken-for-granted category—to reorient interrelated debates on truth and intersubjectivity in asylum rather than foreclose an inquiry into "migrant suffering." Through the book, I direct attention to how suffering as a lived experience and a narration of asylum-seeking experience enabled people to articulate the incompatible and unequally shared terms and conditions of survival. In exploring the role that asylum-seeking experiences of Nepalis played in the formation of suffering narrations among the claimants, and ultimately the formation of suffering-selves and collectives, I suggest considering the relationship between suffering and survival that might result in a more productive discussion of suffering in anthropology and beyond.

For one, the material of this project demonstrates that dynamics of suffering imaginaries within and outside the asylum context—the screening and the eligibility interview process, the documentation and the witness preparation, and juridical arbitrariness—have far-reaching consequence for the migrant community in question, its negotiations of socio-legal recognition, and the intensification of their *habitual* suffering and survival strategies. The case of Nepalis serves to illuminate the extent to which these dynamics matter for migrant suffering recognition in the United States today, and their rationale reveals a set of assumptions about what it means to identify with and/or differentiate from asylum claimants, institutionalized and generated through enduring interior immigration enforcement and asylum politics. Exploring suffering outside the asylum context and beyond the liberal recognition of assumed coherence between embodiment and interpretability involves understanding suffering anew: wide-ranging articulations, moral ambiguities, and emergence and transformation in the migrant community that underwrite the liberal conditions at the same time as it signals a particular survival strategy to navigate the shifting relationships between labor and illegality, a strategy that straddles resistance and recognition.

In the remainder of this introduction, I sketch the discourse and practices of suffering in the Nepali diasporic formation and, specifically, the embeddedness of an emergent community-formation and collective consciousness in the city. I portray the force of suffering as a discourse of self-reflexive critiques of people's everyday survival strategy and legalization in the city by offering a few vignettes from my interlocutors in Nepali New York communities. Throughout, I highlight my dual positionality as an ethnographer and participant-*interpreter* while employing dialogical ethnography, paying attention to the pedagogical nature of most of my encounters, interactions, and conversations.[14]

DUKKHA (SUFFERING) AND KAAGAZ BANAUNE (MAKING PAPER)

From the beginning of my attempt to insert myself in the community and everyday working lives of activists, volunteers, and student-participants, I needed to constantly reflect on my own (relatively privileged) positionality in the emergent Nepali migrant communities in the city. Yet the kind of academic language I was learning, which had informed my own politics, was proving inadequate, time and again. The self-reflexivity turns in ethnographic research and anthropological scholarship, inspired by postcolonial theory and critical liberal politics, which had shaped my own academic training, socialization, and orientation, seemed elitist, imperialistic even, in its reach and reinforcement of a narrow articulation of liberal politics and the conceptualization of the political confined to academic debates, many of them initiated by anthropologists.[15] The imperialistic forms of knowledge production inherent in anthropological and wider social science approaches, moreover, became particularly evident to me during my early conversations and interactions with colleagues, interlocutors, and fellow volunteers.

During a workers' rights training workshop, Narbada didi began her speech by passionately declaring:

Saathiharu ho, "bolne ko pitho bikcha, nabolne ko chaamal pani bikdaina" bhanne ukhan ta sunnubhako hola ni. Haamile afno dukkha afai sanga rakchaun, kasailai bhandai nau. Kaslai ghata huncha yesto garda, bhannus ta? Haami afai. Yahan hamro nimti haami afaile bolnu parcha. Haamile bolenau bhane arka le hamro nimti boldainan. (Friends, the proverb "one who *speaks up* can sell flour, and the one who does not cannot even sell his rice" is something with which all of you must be familiar. We tend to keep our *sufferings* to ourselves; we do not *share* them often enough. Tell me, who loses when we do that? We do. Here [in America] we must *speak* on behalf of ourselves. If we do not, no one else will.)

These statements may be interpreted as a standard speech act not atypical of communicative performance and strategy in grassroots activism to encourage mass participation by specifically invoking cultural distinctiveness and the question of belonging, one through which activists, community leaders, and social mobilizers seek to shape and sway people's opinions and behaviors. Without necessarily disregarding this possibility, however, I would like to redirect our reading of these comments by drawing upon a set of internal debates and concerns—prevalent among Nepali community activists and volunteers working closely with migrant workers and asylum seekers—quite distinct from those often associated with assertions of diasporic identity construction and belonging. In this alternative interpretation, Narbada didi's remarks can be read as a reflexive critique and pedagogical tool for self-transformation and orientation of one's behavior, conduct, and action to align with the practicalities of living and working in the United States. More important, Narbada didi's instruction to attendees of the training to share their suffering was not followed up with any detail about either its presumed form (physical, emotional, psychological, mental, etc.) or the audience with whom they were supposed to share. The volunteers and community members vigorously nodded in agreement. No question was asked.

Fascinated and confused by her use of the analogy to encourage workers to speak of their troubles and hardships, I asked Narbada didi what specifically she meant. All the participants were gone, and we were having tea in the living room of the office. She explained to me that what ails Nepalis is their hesitancy in actively promoting their suffering. As a way of elaborating on one particular form of suffering, this is what she had to say:

In all these years that I have worked with Nepalis, I know who has really suffered and who has not. When people suffer, they rarely share with others unless they can trust you. But when you don't have any choice or your suffering is too much, people need to share their dukkha even with strangers. There is no time to think about what is right and what is not. Some *make papers* easily and others cannot. Not everyone has the same luck, you know. There is enough suffering already for many of these people who come to the community center. They live in someone else's house, working six days a week and not finding time to even grieve for their families back home. Many of them do not understand their employers because of the language problem. They should not have to suffer just to work and survive.

That evening, Narbada didi shared with me her own experience of going through asylum seven years ago, which entailed, in her own words, "selling suffering." She shrugged and continued, "You know every Nepali has [the] same dukkha in this country. Everyone needs to *make papers*." Following her logic in this context, in persuading others "to speak up" (as in a sales pitch) and to self-promote, literally, Narbada didi was employing the proverb metaphorically to explain the importance of voicing one's grievances and making his/her suffering heard in the fight for survival as a new migrant worker who may also be going through the asylum legalization. The shared cultural logic is that consuming rice, associated with a more privileged social standing and a symbolic marker of middle-classness in Nepal, is more expensive than flour and is rarely consumed by the poor. Convincing someone to buy rice requires much more "talking" than convincing them to buy flour. Among other things, the work of the community organizers, activists, and volunteers at Adhikaar is centered on direct services, assisting newly arrived migrants to negotiate difficult workplace situations and navigate immigration bureaucracy and documentation. ESL classes, workplace negotiation strategies, lessons on employment rules and minimum wage, nanny-training skills, and workshops are all intended to arm people with information, preempting a wide range of workplace scenarios that many found themselves navigating. Because Adhikaar is a community center for participants and volunteers from all walks of life, organizing and mobilizing talks of fair employment and workplace injustices quite naturally opened up a space for people to share grievances in day-to-day life. As the quote above insinuates, Narbada didi is one of those fortunate people who after having "made papers" easily are assisting those unnecessarily suffering "just to work and survive."

"Kaslai farak parcha ra? Hami sabai saranarthi bhayera ya asylum garekaharu jastai ta baseka chainau ra yahaan kaagaz bhai sake pachi pani, aakhirma?" (What difference does it make? Or, more accurately, To whom does it really make a difference?) She responded in her usual upbeat and disarming manner, though with a hint of defeat, when I inquired why only a small percentage of Nepalis were "making paper" and others had either remained undocumented or were waiting for their employers to sponsor their work visas. Having worked closely with her for a little over five months at the time, I had become used to, anticipated even, Narbada didi's tendency to retort in a form of rhetorical hyperbole. More importantly, she was asking me to reflect on my own question, first and foremost, and then adding this punch line—"Aren't we all living like refugees and asylum seekers even after having made papers in the end?"—drawing me into a deeper conversation beyond the mere informational and statistical data about asylum numbers, variation in claim types and duration, and often ethical binary between "bogus refugees and asylum seekers" and "suffering migrant workers." It was a decisive moment of a dialogical encounter. With this poignant remark, Narbada didi invited me to expand on my own question and, by extension, my position on the issue of people "making paper." She was simultaneously making her own position explicit on the subject while assessing mine. Questions surrounding the politics of recognition, interpretive possibility, and collaborative work it simultaneously entailed preoccupied me throughout the fieldwork, data collection, and analysis periods and, ultimately, the writing of this book. As indicated by Narbada didi's remark, a shared predicament, almost always articulated as a riddle, existed widely among my interlocutors.

For Narbada didi was not alone in her theory of silently suffering Nepalis but was one of the few people who, while distinguishing herself from those she worked with and provided direct services to, was highly perceptive of her own contradictory position as a former asylum seeker. Her concern about the interconnection between suffering and "making paper" through asylum legalization was shared by community organizers, ESL volunteers, and student-participants I met through Adhikaar.

Once Pelki didi, one of the ESL student-participants, casually declared that she did not work as hard as she had done when she first arrived in the United States. At the time, I automatically assumed that she was referring to her particular work situation and followed up with questions about possible long working hours, inadequate wages, withholding of payment, days off, sick leave, or other issues related to workers' rights violations that she might have experienced in her previous job. Without responding to my follow-up inquiries about her remarks, she and her sister-in-law Sanju didi started speaking among their friends in Hyolmo, a language foreign to me and other participants in my class. After almost fifteen minutes of back-and-forth between my student-interlocutors, Pelki didi responded in the following way: "No. I still do the same job of cleaning house and bathrooms and get paid the same as I did years ago. But I worked hard to make papers." Again, I understood her to be referring to various forms of paperwork—from applying for a social security card to filling out various employment forms, such as an I-9, from opening a bank account to obtaining W-2 forms for filing taxes—that many newly arrived migrants at Adhikaar shared as part of their learning experience and settling into the new society. For I was aware of the constant fear and anxiety caused by such bureaucratic paperwork and documentation for people who did not speak English and/or had little or no formal education in Nepal. As I started to steer the day's conversation to related topics about filling out different paperwork and employment documentation, she mumbled under her breath, "Tapaile bhujnu bhayena, bahini. Kaagaz banauna dui barsa lagyo mero ta. Dherai kaam garnu pareko thiyo. Dherai dukkha pani khayen." (You do not understand, younger sister. It took me two years to make paper. I had to *work* hard. We suffered a lot.) Her remark generated a momentary silence until Sanju didi followed up by explaining to me that as previously undocumented workers, they had few options in terms of employment, primarily as live-in maids and domestic workers. Pelki didi further went on, "Tara kahan cha time hami sanga dukkha liyera basna? Hamro dukkha ta hami sangai chan ni. Hami ta khali chup laagera dukkha matra sahana sakchaun." (Who has time to dwell on our sadness or grief? Or, accurately, Do we have time to obsess over our suffering? Our suffering will remain with us. We simply suffer in silence.) Sanju didi then added a rejoinder with a laugh, "That's why we talk a lot in your class, Tina Miss." Participants, thus, often engaged in and worked out contradictions of what counted as dukkha in relation to kaagaz banaune and why, after all, they needed to "make papers."

My retelling of the incident with fellow ESL volunteers that Sunday was met with dead silence and exchange of hesitant smiles. One of the volunteers, Reema, discreetly asked me if I had "made paper" and, if so, how long it took me. If I had made it by myself or had gone through lawyers. Without waiting for my response, she asked, "Tapain ko green card bhaisakeko ho?" I told her that I had a US passport and that my paternal uncle, a US citizen, sponsored my family in the late 1980s, and we migrated on the family reunification scheme twenty years ago. "Oh, tyasaile tapainlai yo kuro anoutho lageko" (Oh, that is the reason all this sounds peculiar to you), she said with a gentle smile and added, "You are one of the lucky people. Even my green card is being processed. But it is not easy for these people." She pointed to a group of students in another ESL class next to where we were having our lunch. "So do you want to do policy work or go into teaching after finishing your studies?" Because I did not respond in time, she took the opportunity to advise me on various possibilities. For obtaining a higher education degree in the United States and not doing anything practical with it, as in policy or advocacy work, seemed such a waste, Reema explained to me. A sociologist by training, Reema tried to pursue a master's degree when she arrived in the United States thirteen years ago. However, being a single parent responsible for raising her son meant she needed to find full-time employment.

She ended up working two jobs, as a day care worker during weekdays and a live-out nanny on weekends. She did not get a chance to pursue further education. After her son started college, she began volunteering at Adhikaar, providing nanny training workshops, facilitating ESL classes, and engaging in curriculum design and development.

"Any research that does not result in some kind of social policy is of no interest to me," Luna had made clear to me during one of our early conversations, after I expressed my interest in volunteering at Adhikaar as an entry point to undertaking research among Nepalis in the city. "I do not believe in people parachuting and conducting research in the community and leaving once they are done," she had confided. "I have done it myself in the past and did not like it." As someone with a master's degree in public policy from a private, elite US institution like myself, she explained her disillusionment with academic knowledge production. Pointing me toward her bookshelf, which housed a wide-ranging collection of books by postcolonial writers, she asked, "What is the point of learning to speak and write in a convoluted manner that people you are claiming to *speak for* can neither understand nor relate to?" The question was clearly not a personal attack, although directed at me, and I found no reason to disagree with her. Curiously, I also felt no need to either defend or doubt the exceptional scholarship and political potential of "the postcolonial turn" within and beyond academia. It was clear to me, in that very instant, that our shared academic socialization had given us the language to articulate, ironically, our different approaches and relationships to research itself. More important, it provided an opportunity for us to engage, question, reflect, and critically assess our shared predicament of working in "our community," employing divergent methods for achieving the same end. After some time, I said, "Perhaps people do not know or care that they are being *represented*, or perhaps it is a particular kind of intermediation or representation that is facilitating people's marginalization, even silencing many."

Luna's eyes brightened, and she redirected our conversation to her experience of working in the field of human rights and social justice and myriad issues confronting the Nepali-speaking communities in particular. She spoke in some detail about workers' rights projects through which she and her fellow South Asian and Asian American activists engaged with the disenfranchised and marginalized people in various communities only to realize the ongoing issue around organizing, mobilizing, and advocating for people based on their regional and racialized identities, even working-class backgrounds. Having previously worked with South Asian activists, organizing and representing South Asian immigrants, she declared, "Most Nepali-speaking migrants cannot be lumped together because they are working for many South Asian American households; [the] majority of their employers are Indians and Pakistanis." Referring to a well-known case of an Indian diplomat, who had brought their Nepali maid from India to New York City, held her passport, and withheld her salary for years, Luna discussed Adhikaar's work on filing this lawsuit an important step toward acknowledgment of diversity and inequalities within South Asian communities throughout the country. "As you know, many of the problems facing Nepali working-class migrants are [more] similar to the experiences of working-class Latino and Mexican migrants than Asian Americans," Luna stated. At the same time, she voiced her concern that as an activist of an emergent migrant community, her work of translating Adhikaar's vision and communicating the significance of the work performed by community organizers—Narbada didi and Reema included—depended on navigating two different worlds. She explained that while finding allies and collaborating with other activists with similar political agendas and working with migrant communities across racial, ethnic, and class backgrounds was necessary, it was equally important to redirect conversations about shared political visions so that they can ultimately materialize into concrete changes on the ground—turning into specialized services and facilities required for the majority of the newly arrived Nepali-speaking migrants.

Our conversation that day ended with her frank prediction that my ongoing volunteer work at Adhikaar would be an important first step for doing research and getting my PhD like hers was when she obtained her master's degree in public policy. In her activist conceptualization of politics, she was echoing Nicholas De Genova that social science research is intricately tied to social relations, forming the very basis of our knowledge production.[16] But what we do with our degrees obtained in the United States, she gently advised me, is ultimately up to us. Our friendship developed gradually, over time, on the basis of mutual respect for the possibilities afforded by our differently situated worldviews and disciplinary limitations yet our shared political orientation. Community-based research with definable policy implications beyond the confines of academia, for Luna, was critical to her activist outlook and politics. The rich intersubjective engagement with people like her and others in the city, for me, encompassed the "ethnographic dialogical encounter."

These early encounters and conversations in a wide-ranging context with my Nepali interlocutors, including ESL students and asylum claimants, persistently and powerfully drove home that parallel to suffering accounts, people regularly engaged in different forms, scales, and practices of silence. Whether partaking in the periodic silence practiced by my ESL student-participants, interpreting the knowing silent gazes of the fellow ESL volunteers, witnessing in silence the work of community activists and organizers who were impacting deeply the lives of people they encountered, observing self-censorship performed by economically mobile Nepali Americans, or simply resigning in silence with claimants as the absurd demands of the asylum documentation and witness preparation unfolded, I found that silence was prevalent everywhere. Yet, as Luna had indirectly warned me, I could not simply parachute in and do research and leave. But like Narbada didi stated matter-of-factly, people "should not have to suffer just to work and survive"; exactly how people were involved in these two activities had to be a critical starting point for me, as well. I had to further ask difficult questions about what was at stake in producing knowledge about the community I was gradually becoming a part of not because of our common origin or language but because of our shared ethno-racialized yet distinct socioeconomic and legal positions in the US nation-state. From my early encounters and exchanges with people within and outside Adhikaar, questions about what I "really" wanted to know, how I was going to learn, and more important, how, if at all, my research could prove useful for people I worked with and/or assisted in asylum interpretation inevitably became a critical part of my relations and continued engagement.

Toward these ends, I follow Audra Simpson's (2007) conceptual move from the disclosure of collective knowledge to the recognition of "the collective 'limit,'" meaning that my interlocutors' avowal to remain silent is a significant declaration of a collective predicament that many I came to know and worked with shared.[17] However, rather than isolate silence—whether as periodic interruption in claimants' testimonies or as a practice of censorship among participants at Adhikaar that redirected our conversation to tangential accounts of people's work grievances—as a literal act and *absence* of speech, I consider it as a *presence* beyond speech, a verbalization of suffering generalities, and an asylum testimonial documentation. Thus, I have no intention of producing a representative account of "Nepali migrants and asylum seekers' suffering" nor of establishing Nepalis as "authentic refugee and asylum subjects" through objectified interpretation that renders legible the normative US immigration and legal frames of deservingness demanded of its ethno-racialized migrant communities. Rather, my aim is to interrogate suffering imaginaries in US immigration enforcement and asylum legalization as well as its logics of operation from the vantage point of the working lives of Nepali migrants and claimants.

For one, the Nepali case does not neatly fit into "migrant suffering" or asylum and refugee studies per se, as people represented themselves as sympathizing with the general plight of their fellow Nepalis notwithstanding the actual knowledge of what or how that suffering may be lived, experienced, and interpreted by those they regarded as neighbors, coworkers, and acquaintances. Yet if one lived in one of the Nepali neighborhoods in Queens and was exposed to asylum-seeking activities, either through direct assistance in providing legal interpretation and translation services or working closely with migrants on a range of issues related to labor and legality at Adhikaar, as I was doing, the ongoing discussions, reflexive critiques, even contradictions around suffering would quickly become part of one's social world. In this context, it is logical that people attempt to make finer distinctions about the forms and practices of suffering in order to survive. Hence, Narbada didi's telling observation—"how Nepalis are *surviving* here [in America] by *selling suffering*, silently"—indicates what everyone in the greater Nepali community knows or gradually learns, as I eventually did.

ONE / Locating Nepali New Yorkers

DUKKHA IN THE DIASPORIC IMAGINATION

"Ours is a growing community [*baddho samudaya*] in America; unless we demand *to be counted* in this country, no one will recognize our dukkha and respect us as people," announced a prominent figure in the Nepali community during a meeting at Adhikaar well attended by several leaders and members from ethnically and linguistically diverse Nepali migrant communities throughout the tristate area. Expressing this widely shared sense of being invisible as people, the community leader had emphasized its direct connection to Nepalis' collective experience of suffering, much like Narbada didi had been pointing out to me. In urging his fellow community members and volunteers to mobilize Nepalis in their different neighborhoods and communities to partake in the Census 2010, his message was simple: *to be counted*, literally, as people was the only way for Nepalis and their suffering *to be* visible. Or put another, not so far-fetched, way: becoming *visible* is inseparable from making one's suffering count. This message has different implications and meanings for people variously positioned in the Nepali community in New York City and in the United States at large. Evocation of suffering was used as a call for a diasporic identity, community formation, and political recognition—rather than conventional categories based on nationality, ethnicity, region, race, gender, class or, say, language and religion.

This chapter contextualizes Nepali diasporic formation and the making of Nepali-speaking communities in the United States since the latter half of the twentieth century. It first introduces the long-standing theme of dukkha in the emergence of the Nepali diasporic consciousness and, more recently, in the contemporary narratives of low-wage Nepali migrants elsewhere. Second, it provides a brief overview of the interconnection between US imperialism and the history of Nepali migrant mobility to attend to the divergent migration trajectories and socialization of Nepali-speaking migrant communities in the United States. In particular, it highlights postwar America's initiatives and development projects instigating the migration of middle-class Nepalis (between the 1950s and the 1990s). Here, Nepali migration to the United States is broadly categorized into three groups or generations: those arriving as postgraduate students and professionals in the development decade (1950–60), families and extended relatives of naturalized US citizens arriving since the 1990s through family reunification schemes and student and work visa sponsorships, and diversity visa lottery and refugee and asylum provisions due to the Maoist civil war (1996–2006) and the post–civil war reconstruction period (2006–14). Finally, the chapter concludes by locating Nepali New York communities in the twenty-first century and the wider context of the 2006 pro-immigrant mobilization protests in the United States and the visibility of suffering migrants and asylum claimants, simultaneously.

The Nepali diaspora has been documented widely in terms of varied migration trajectories, settlement patterns, transnational lives, labor, and identity formations.[1] The construction of a cohesive "Nepali" diasporic identity long intersected with the development of "common experience, shared sentiments, and a single language" among Nepali nationalist intellectuals in India in the late 1930s (Hutt 1997, 117; see also Onta 1996). Not surprisingly, Nepali language as a symbol of a unified nation yielding a sense of shared history, belonging, and consciousness first appeared among the diasporic nationalist intellectuals and residents in Banaras, West Bengal, and Darjeeling (Hutt 1997; Subedi 1989; Subba 2008). At the same time, people from the Himalayan region did not consider themselves "Nepali" until the late nineteenth and early twentieth centuries (Whelpton 2005). Indeed, contemporary works continue to draw on this important distinction and highlight the Himalayan region and the non-Nepali-speaking ethnic communities in their study of diasporic cultural (trans)formation, mobility, and belonging in New York City (Hangen 2018; Craig and Gurung 2018; Gurung et al. 2018; Sherpa 2019; Craig 2020; Gurung et al. 2021). This study adds to this growing work on New York Nepali and Himalayan migrant and diasporic communities by exploring the dual experience of everyday labor and legal precarity through the lens of suffering.[2]

The centrality of discursive practices of dukkha in the Nepali diasporic imagination—particularly related to people's migration experience and labor—goes as far back as the letters of Gurkha soldiers serving in the British Indian Army during the First World War (Onta 1994) and much of the early twentieth-century diaspora literature (Hutt 1997). In contemporary studies of Nepali labor outmigration, dukkha has been explored as a normative role of speech, performance, and action to indicate affective states of migrants, for example in their lives in the labor camps of Qatar (Bruslé 2012), their experience with brokerage and recruitment mediation for jobs in Malaysia (Shrestha 2018), in the constrained choice of female workers in New York City (Gurung 2009), and in neutralizing accounts of agency (O'Neill 2007). Thus, using suffering as an organizing category, rather than the conventional construct of the "homeland-belonging-identity" nexus, has broader implication for understanding the significance and (trans)formation of an "evolving diaspora" (Shrestha 2022) across space and time.

US-NEPAL "ENCOUNTER": A BRIEF OVERVIEW

The United States first "encountered" Nepal through interrelated institutions of diplomacy, development aid, and democratization in the 1950s—a peculiar history of economic and political experimentation (see, for instance, Joshi and Rose 1966; Hoftun 1999; Whelpton 2005). It is productive to read this history as one of imperial formations/margins and unequal relationships, as one where a sovereign nation-state is not merely a priori but pragmatic and, thus, a necessity.[3] Nepali territorial sovereignty and independence was compatible, even critical, to the United States' geopolitical interest in the region at the time, resulting in the arrival of American government officials, diplomats, and civilians in Nepal.[4] The eventual overthrow of 140 years of autocratic Rana rule in 1951 and the reinstatement of the Shah monarchy proved coterminous with the growing US global power and postwar policy intervention around the world.[5] Yet a sustained US influence in much of the global South in the Cold War era entailed neither military base nor market liberalization but, as in the case of Nepal, experimentation of "development programs to modernize health, transportation, agriculture, land use, and family structure" (Robertson 2018, 928; Robertson 2016). Consequently, a new diplomatic relationship was forged in Nepal that deepened US influence in the country's social, economic, and political development affairs.[6]

With the advent of the "development decade," the newly formulated United States Agency for International Development (USAID) in Nepal was established in 1961. That same year, the Fulbright Commission was introduced, followed by the US Peace Corps Volunteer program.[7] These US state agencies were crucial in setting the precedent for recruitment, and the subsequent arrival, of various US delegates, government officials, and civilian experts for long-term development work. Indeed, American experts included engineers, scientists, economists, development planners, and anthropologists, many of whom also worked as researchers and consultants for the US Operations Mission (USOM)/USAID Mission in Nepal.

The consideration of this convoluted, if less understood and understudied, historical relationship should be a prerequisite to examining the contemporary organization and governance of mass migration of Nepalis to the United States. Studies concerned with Nepali migration that overlook this historical exchange and encounter, based on asymmetries of power underpinning long-standing diplomatic relations and development intervention, influencing the country's economic and political infrastructure, risk reducing Nepali experiences of migration and legalization to those of another group of "migrants and asylum seekers" and participate in the erasure of both a distinct production of migrant subjects and the legal conditions of possibility for their (il)legality and labor precarity upon arrival to the US nation-state.

CONSTRUCTING A NEPALI DIASPORA
IN THE UNITED STATES

Not surprisingly, the first generation of Nepalis, primarily men, arrived in the United States in the mid-1950s to obtain professional degrees in fields like medicine and engineering; others came to obtain graduate degrees facilitated through the then newly established US-Fulbright program, which eased them into the faculties of the university and the civil service upon their return. They possessed a blend of nostalgia for the newly reinstituted monarchy, a sense of national belonging to the nation that was theirs. Few had any intention of remaining in the United States after their graduate studies or professional training, for they primarily belonged to the upper-class echelon, which afforded them various material comforts at home. More important, to not return home was akin to failure to fulfill their moral obligation of "developing" an "underdeveloped" nation, their nation.

For this early generation of Nepalis, the United States began as a rite of passage much like for other immigrants from the Indian subcontinent in the 1960s (Khandelwal 2002; Kurien 2001; Shukla 2003). As is true in many such cases, this group navigated against white American nationalism through an affirmation of their sociopolitical belonging either to a wider continental, if externally imposed, category of "South Asian" or to an unequal hyphenated category of "Asian

American." Many, however, saw this as an American configuration and instead continued to assert their own distinct national heritage and cultural identity. If there was only one fact they liked to repeat to themselves and others, then it was that their nation is not India, never was a part of India, and had never been (formally) colonized by the British or other European colonial powers.

This generation of Nepalis deeply held, even tried to inculcate in their children, the belief that they, among others from the Indian subcontinent, were unique. They were not Tibetans. They were certainly not "desis" (originally indexing a linguistically distinct Hindi- and Urdu-speaking immigrant group primarily from India and Pakistan but increasingly a generic sociopolitical, working-class, South Asian identity). They were Nepalis. The overall impression one gets from this generation of immigrants in the United States is that Nepali cultural heritage and national belonging are often fractured along diverse ethno-linguistic (Bahun, Chettri, Newar, Gurung, Tamang, etc.), regional, and socioeconomic lines and, more recently, divided according to loyalties and affiliation toward political parties in Nepal. What most of them have in common is an urban upper- and upper-middle-class background, an education in an elite, English-medium school of Kathmandu, and a self-identification as Nepali with learned dispositions and flair in harmony with the mainstream American ways and sensibilities. Many take pride in their white-collar professional identity, reinforcing and re-fueling the wider American and Asian American imagination of a prototypical model minority and desirable "Asian," who is a hardworking, entrepreneurial, and socioeconomically mobile subject attaining an American dream. They are professionals who owed their educational and professional trainings to the US state given that they had the available means, resources, and capital accumulated through long-term socialization in their new home of settlement.

TRANSNATIONAL MIGRATORY NETWORKS
AND THE CIVIL WAR PERIOD (MID-1990S TO 2006)

The rising inflation and unemployment and the establishment of the multiparty democratic system in Nepal in the 1990s coincided with the 1996 IIRAIRA in the United States, which laid groundwork for legal exclusion of "undocumented immigrants" yet expedited inclusion, through the naturalization process, to convert "legal permanent residents" into US citizen-subjects.[8] Through "the free market of citizenship," the US state reconsolidated migrant labor and legality by temporalizing migration of predominantly working-class people as workers, refugees, and asylum seekers.⁹ As a result, Nepalis arriving to the United States in the 1990s were primarily middle class from Kathmandu who had families and extended relatives settled in the United States and were engaged in transnational community networks in their hometowns in Nepal (Sijapati 2010, 35–36). Two major migratory pathways during this period, thus, entailed family reunification or sponsorship by US citizens and student visa sponsorship. While many began arriving with their families in major US cities, from DC, Boston, New York, and New Jersey in the East to San Francisco and Seattle in the West to Atlanta, Austin, and Dallas in the South, a steady flow of urban middle- to upper-middle-class students continued to arrive to pursue tertiary education and professional training.

The abrupt collapse of the multiparty democratic system and the beginning of the civil war in 1996 fueled the mass exodus from Nepal. Beginning as rural uprisings against the Nepali state in the western districts (Rolpa and Rukum), the Maoist guerrilla war spread throughout the countryside and resulted in a nationwide civil war claiming thousands of lives. The protracted civil war and political instability in Nepal had decisive and irreversible infrastructural and human damages. The spread of the Maoist movement from rural to hill areas made the capital of Kathmandu increasingly porous and interconnected with the rest of the country.¹⁰ The Nepali civil war reached its peak of brutality in 2001–2, including the Royal Massacre in 2001, coinciding with the aftermath of the September 11, 2001, events in the United States, which brought Nepal into the limelight of international media.¹¹ The reentry of the Maoist Party in the mainstream political scene in 2008, controlling the Nepali state government, further spawned a difficult "reconstruction" and postwar period. In no time, national and international collaborative projects, initiated by a number of human rights nongovernmental organizations (NGOs), including the International Center for Transitional Justice (ICTJ), addressing issues of "reintegrating" war "victims" and "perpetrators" and promoting local notions of justice and healing appeared.¹² The sociopolitical landscape of "new" Nepali society—framed within the globalized language of national development, economic policies, ethnic identity politics, and human rights—increasingly made possible new forms of sociability and afforded once again opportunities for many, but not all, Nepalis. It facilitated migration of urban, educated, middle-class Nepalis to Australia, the United Kingdom, and the United States. This much longer, contested history of political development, and the process of building a "new Nepal" with the assistance of international framing, lays the very foundation of the contemporary migration from Nepal to the United States. For the question of who or what Nepalis/Nepali-speaking communities ought to become in the United States is intrinsically linked to what place the Nepali state and Nepali-speaking migrants occupy in the contemporary sociopolitical imagination of the US state.

If being "Nepali" meant "seeing [oneself] as a citizen of an underdeveloped country" two decades ago (Pigg 1992), it increasingly meant seeing oneself as a *suffering* subject of an uncertain state whose national identity was suspended since the end of the civil war. Most people over the age of thirty living in the United States recalled quite vividly the change in the sociopolitical climate and the experience of realizing the precariousness of their lives if they were unable to leave the country. This is not to suggest, in any way, that migration from Nepal was solely dependent on unstable political or economic situations. But in popular consciousness among the Nepali diaspora in the United States, "suffering asylum seeker" best described the status of most Nepalis who left home, perpetually displaced, and were claiming political asylum at the turn of the twenty-first century. Becoming an asylum seeker, for many Nepalis at the time, was occupying a position of legal victimhood from which they were expected (and even instructed in some cases) to speak and, in turn, to be recognized for *suffering* immaterial to their specific asylum claims.

POST-2006 PRO-IMMIGRANT MASS MOBILIZATION AND NEPALI NEW YORKERS

The heightened visibility, media coverage, and politicization of migrant illegality in the post-2006 pro-immigrant mass mobilization made, for the first time, unsustainable what Susan Coutin has called "disjuncture between physical and legal presence" of undocumented migrants and their "spaces of nonexistence."[13] Immigration enforcement predictably centered on the systematic curtailing of migrant illegality, interchangeably used with migrant criminality or "enemy aliens," elimination of which was rendered synonymous with restoration of law and order.[14] Migrant criminalization and detentions within the United States proliferated with "crisis of national security" rhetoric, and the "enforcement practices contributed to an unprecedented expansion of the plausible grounds for migrant 'illegality,' and prefigured subsequent legislative efforts to render procedural technicalities sufficient grounds for illegalizing otherwise 'legal' migrants" (De Genova 2007, 432–33). In other words, the post-9/11 decade witnessed a steady tapering of the conditions of possibility for pursuing immigration as a civil law issue, subsequently making it difficult to disengage the debate from the framework or logic of criminality. Not unexpectedly, local-level state police began playing a critical role in the surveillance, apprehension, and detention of undocumented migrants. The powerful discourse of law and order made migrant illegality interchangeable with migrant criminality and, over time, naturalized widespread interior immigration enforcement.

Extending this line of reasoning, the implications for decriminalization seemed equally important as, if not more urgent than, the demand for legal recourse for millions of undocumented migrants living and working within the United States, given the ever-increasing protracted legal vulnerability and the narrowing window for legalization pathways. Yet the 2006 pro-immigrant mobilization protests in public spaces were, above other things, an attempt to demonstrate to the state and the American public that "illegal aliens" were not "criminal aliens" but were hardworking migrants contributing to the economy and the US society at large. Aside from chanting popular slogan "Sí se puede!" the protesters, including labor activists, migrant-community leaders, and organizers, also held signs stating "We Are America," calling attention to the legacy of the United States as the "immigrant nation."[15] Despite the heterogeneity in socioeconomic status, immigration or visa status, and generational status among differently ethno-racialized participants in the protests, the mobilization brought to public attention the interconnected issues of "human rights, workers' rights, and immigrant rights" (see Heinskanen 2009). In their effort to move away from migrant criminality and demand the legalization of undocumented migrants, the proponents of the mobilization protests pointed out the necessity and the usefulness of undocumented migrants to the economy.[16] The opponents politicized the campaign as calculated "demonstrations by various socialist, communist, and even anarchic organizations," emphasizing "an anti-American, anti-imperialist message under the guise of an 'immigration rights' rally."[17]

Scholars studying immigrant rights movements have questioned whether the 2006 mass mobilization of undocumented immigrants that swept across the major US cities was an "ephemeral *moment* of spontaneous political action" rather than a sustained "long-term immigrant *movement*" (Bloemraad and Voss 2020, 684; see also Nicholls, Uitermark, and van Haperen 2019). Placing the mass mobilization within the national and historically uneven context of social movements and countermovements, they draw attention to the long-standing use of democratic institutions to pass anti-immigrant legislation targeting undocumented migrants. They point out the significance of labor unions' support in enabling the immigrant rights movement to reach to the multiscale and national level. And yet preventing or halting legislation from passing has been the primary activity of immigrant rights organizing, advocacy, and campaigns in the last thirteen years.[18] Others see the growing solidarity, coalition building, and partnership between local communities and immigrant rights groups leading up to the 2006 mass mobilization as promising despite lingering challenges (de Graauw, Gleeson, and Bada 2019).

Nicholas De Genova goes one step further and points out that the visibility of the mass mobilizations of undocumented migrants' physical and "deportable *presence*" in public spaces not only brought the question of "'immigrants' rights' into the forefront of 'domestic' US politics" but also enabled the state to function "as a broker of virtually indentured labourers" (2009, 451–52). Equally important, the previously "unspeakable question of immigration law and undocumented labour" was being "re-articulated" by immigrants themselves through their visible and "continuous presence . . . conditioned by their continuous (docile and ever-deportable) employment" (452). Such an "articulation of the unspeakable," as De Genova reminds us, has long involved undocumented migrants frequently challenging their own illegal status "as the iconic 'bad immigrant' by recapitulating its disabling normative logic: although 'illegal,' they were in fact hard-working, law-abiding, tax-paying 'good immigrants'" (2005, 85–91).

The "immigrant question" has repeatedly been invoked to bolster the liberal state's authority as well as to question it. Crucially, the issue of "immigrant legalization" has been at the center of political discourse and restrictive immigration laws; since the 2006 immigrant rights movements, migrant illegality and deportability moved to the forefront of the public debate, and the locus of controversy around interior immigration enforcement moved to the civic and bureaucratic spaces, including the asylum ad hoc institutions. Increasingly, legalization of undocumented migrants and asylum claimants meant, broadly speaking, temporalization and disciplining of a low-wage and racialized workforce into marginalized social spaces, variously marked as "ethnic enclaves," "immigrant-concentrated neighborhoods," and "minority community centers." The coalition building between the national pro-immigrant movements in several of the sanctuary cities, including New York, and the grassroots migrant advocacy groups like Adhikaar in the post-2006 era was meant to defend undocumented communities against the federal government's aggressive interior immigration enforcement of policing, surveillance, and deportation (figures 5, 6, 7). At the same time, the effects of these policies have been an increase in anxiety among people in the grassroots organizing and undocumented workers' rights leadership

FIGURE 5 May Day pro-immigration rally, New York City, 2010.
Photograph courtesy of Sonam Ukyab.

FIGURE 6 Adhikaar at May Day pro-immigration rally.
Photograph courtesy of Sonam Ukyab.

FIGURE 7 May Day pro-immigration rally, New York City, 2010.
Photograph courtesy of Sonam Ukyab.

and a growing assertiveness on the part of the national-level advocates (with greater financial resources, political capital, and established networks) to accommodate and manage, rather than contest, local immigration enforcements (Nicholls and Uitermark 2016).

By the time Nepali New Yorkers began seeking asylum in the early 2000s, there already existed sizable and established Nepali-speaking communities living and working throughout the United States for decades that had proceeded under different sociopolitical circumstances and immigration policies. The divergent yet restrictive visa categories, limited social capital, and economic conditions of the recently arrived Nepalis have made it difficult for people to hold on to or propagate loyalty toward a common, if imagined, nationalized past or present. In particular, the majority of Nepalis arriving in the post-9/11 United States do not neatly fit into a singular version of diasporic consciousness based on questions of belonging, identity, and shared linguistic heritage.

The Nepali population in New York City, for instance, went from 3,364 in 2010 to 6,744 in 2015, a growth rate considered to be much higher than the city's 4 percent increase and the 13 percent increase of its total Asian population.[19] Since 2010, the city has been home to 67 percent of New York State's (documented) Nepali

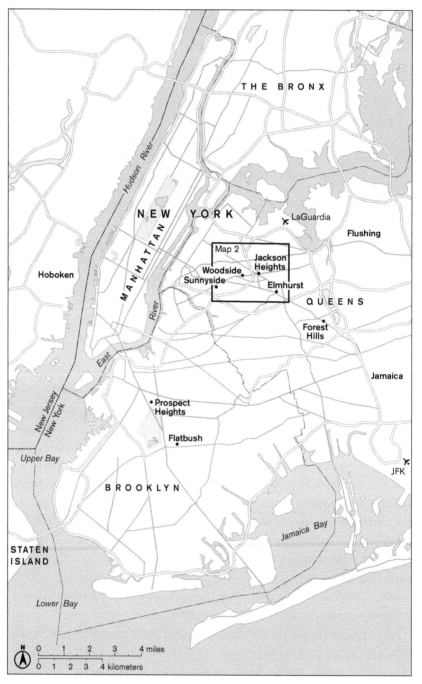

FIGURE 8 Nepali New York: Sunnyside, Woodside, Jackson Heights, Elmhurst, Forest Hills, Prospect Heights, and Flatbush. Map by Ben Pease.

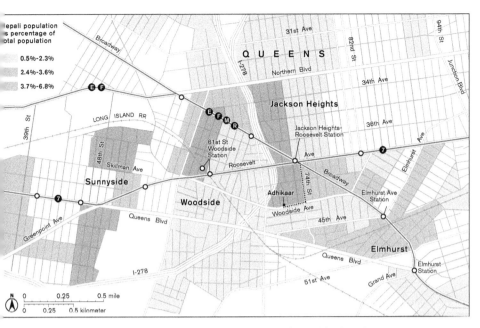

FIGURE 9 Map of Queens, New York City, showing Nepali neighborhoods in Jackson Heights to Adhikaar in Woodside. Map by Ben Pease.

residents. Queens—Sunnyside, Elmhurst, Woodside, and Jackson Heights—is the heartland of the multiethnic and multilingual Nepali diaspora in New York City, where 87 percent of Nepali New Yorkers live and work (figures 8 and 9). The rapid growth of the Nepali population in the city in the last two decades has resulted in the formation of several sociocultural and civil-society organizations (Hangen 2018), from pan-Nepali national organizations and ethno-linguistic identity-based organizations to youth political and party-affiliation organizations, as well as migrant grassroots organizations, like Adhikaar. However, membership in one category of organization does not prevent people from participating in another. Often people claim belonging to more than one organization. The transnational feature of these organizations has enabled sociocultural, economic, and political activities and events for people in the diaspora as well as continued participation in the changing society and politics in Nepal. Similar to other forms of transnational associations and organizations, people's participation in these organizations often accentuates not only points of connectivity but also divergent worldviews and diversity within the Nepali diasporic communities in the reconstruction of a Nepali cultural imagination that simultaneously draws on their lived experiences in the city.

For many Nepali claimants, postconflict Nepal, and suffering Nepalis in particular, was not simply a distant political reality at home. It was a powerful symbol for reorienting one's belonging anew and rendering meaningful social positions, individual and collective, as the ethnic leader (above) had done, through active engagement in the contemporary politics of suffering visibility and recognition in the United States. More precisely, the paradox of suffering narrations in recognition of Nepalis as asylum seekers was simply inescapable: the idea of "Maoist Nepal" held a powerful social imagination for Nepalis seeking asylum at a time when institutional forms and reconstruction work in postconflict Nepal were shaping the Nepali society itself. There were, of course, many interrelated sociopolitical and transnational histories behind this contradiction, depending on which part of history and social memory one focuses on and to what end. For my purposes, the suffering narrations among Nepali New Yorkers are situated within the convoluted context not only of the last two decades of Nepali sociopolitical history but also of the collective hardship and struggle people experienced upon arriving in the United States, which in turn allowed some to realign and reappropriate their suffering through asylum seeking.

If the war disrupted social lives among Nepalis, the postconflict and transition period had modified that disruption, facilitating new sociality among Nepalis in and outside Nepal, as in the case of recently arrived Nepalis in the city. As the war was officially over in Nepal, whether or not Nepalis could still appeal for asylum in the United States based on their experiences of continued suffering remained unanswerable for many. For Nepali New Yorkers I worked with and interpreted for, it was a source of constant anxiety. They were forever caught in the moral web of having to wish for political instability in Nepal to stabilize their legal statuses in the United States.

As one claimant-interlocutor, Tshering, succinctly put it to me, "Khai ke garne, bahini? Hamro desh ko haalat ramro bhako bhaye yahaan aunu parne thiyena. Aba yahaan ayera teen barsa pariwaar bina basisake ani dukkha paunu paisake pachi . . . tyahaan rajneeti byawastha ramro bhayeko khabar sunda kushi pani lagcha tara yahaan afno kaagaz bandaina bhanne daar pani cha." (Well, what to do, Sister? If our country's situation had been better, I would not have come here. Now that I have been here for three years without my family and have already suffered so much . . . I am happy to hear things are getting better there politically, but I am fearful that my papers may not be made here anymore.) This moral dilemma shared by Tshering was typical of many claimants awaiting their asylum verdict while toiling away every day without a sense of direction or secure future. The postconflict period and the changing political situation in Nepal, paradoxically, were also producing uncertainty for claimants that migrating to the United States was supposed to have resolved.

Likewise, the ESL participants and regular attendees of Adhikaar's workshops and other claimants I came to know intimately had minimal linguistic and cultural capital despite strong kinship networks. Migration, precarious labor, and the legalization experience left many skeptical of immigration policies and workers' rights laws despite my Adhikaar colleagues', activists', and organizers' efforts to rally, advocate for, and educate members on issues affecting their lives in the city. Their ambiguous legality was often accompanied by lower socioeconomic status, often considered deplorable by naturalized citizens and permanent residents, who were quickly joining the ranks of the newly prosperous and privileged group of South Asian model minorities in the United States.

People seeking asylum were also subjected to intense cross-examination at asylum offices and immigration courtrooms, causing more suffering and suspicion in wider migrant communities. "How have you been able to work in the US without proper documents so far?" a skeptical attorney almost always begins his/ her interrogation when meeting for the first time a prospective asylum seeker. Nepali claimants I came to know were hyperaware of how this dominant frame of suspicion surrounding asylum legality had penetrated in the Nepali migrant communities throughout the city and across the United States. On the one hand, it had resulted in a generalized negative stereotype of asylum seekers to which people continually subscribed, and on the other hand, active disengagement from the larger sociopolitical conditions of possibility for asylum legalities prevailed. Still, those who were staunch advocates of migrants' rights—Luna and Narbada didi included—acknowledged this reality in terms of their ongoing suffering. For those seeking asylum, the existence of this peculiar socio-legal hierarchy was apparent enough. Their awareness and hypersensitivity toward different socio-legal positions of people in the community was most clearly articulated to me by Kumar *dai*.

"Tyo ta sabhalai thahanai cha America ma sukkha pauna ko lagi dukkha ta garnai paryo ni, hoina ra, bahini?" (Everyone knows that to have a good life in America, one has to suffer, isn't it true, younger sister?) Kumar dai voiced his analysis of what primarily contributed to Nepalis' dukkha. According to him, typically there are two prime causes of constant grief and hardship for people.

"Most people either do not have work or they do not have proper papers. So basically, when you ask a person about his/her problem, and if he/she says he/she has not been to Nepal since being in the US, then you immediately know what he/she is looking for." We were sitting in Kumar dai and his nephew Rajesh's apartment in Jackson Heights. They had invited me for dinner to celebrate Kumar dai's successful merit hearing for asylum that put him finally on the legal path to obtaining a green card after five years of living in the city undocumented. We had ordered some *momos* from a nearby Nepali restaurant and were enjoying Kumar dai's *golbheda acchar*, or tomato sauce, which he had insisted tasted better than the restaurant's. We were making conversation about his asylum experience, since I was his interpreter during a series of prep sessions for the court hearing. I met Kumar dai, like other asylum claimants in the city, through sheer chance—"good luck," as he often liked to begin the story of his asylum-seeking days every time he would introduce me to his new friends in the neighborhood. Given that Kumar dai had mentioned only work and paper, I asked him how he would categorize second-generation Nepalis or those who had both. It seemed he had been waiting for that question, and he used the opportunity to argue that more Nepalis like me—who could understand Nepalis' dukkha and communicated to *kuires* (literally, foreigners, but in this case white Americans)—should be motivated to help those Nepalis like himself. Nepalis living in New York City are mostly employed in the service sector as domestic workers, cab drivers, nail salon workers, restaurant workers, and workers at local grocery stores, and some were beginning to open their own restaurants, owning small grocery shops in Queens. By contrast, the few who were fortunate like me were busy studying and making their own careers in the United States, Kumar dai explained. Their efforts to help Nepalis are always part of some volunteering training or employment connected to securing their own career either with state institutions, including hospitals and immigration-related law firms, or with nonprofit work and research (as I was involved in). I had come to appreciate Kumar dai's frank and unapologetic talk over the last several months I had known him.

DUKKHA AS COLLECTIVE CONSCIOUSNESS

Dukkha indicates both emotion and evaluation. It is a site of feeling and a practical moral state. The Nepali word *dukkha* has several connotations. Besides conveying pain, sorrow, grief, and sadness, it also symbolizes hardship or misfortune when used colloquially about one's state of mind and body. Nepalis often report that the feeling of dukkha may be associated with heartache, anxiety, fear, frustration, discomfort, and similar physiological and emotional phenomena. The term may be used coherently even in the absence of such states, since dukkha, when used as a moral concept, can be evaluative and a mode of sociability. In conversation between people, it conveys feeling sorry for oneself or someone else and empathizing with another person's dukkha.

Another meaning, and interesting for my analysis, is the intersubjective experience that the term *dukkha* conveys—that of sharing one's dukkha with another person, which can potentially open up an intimate space for creating new or reinforcing old relationships. To understand another's dukkha, however, is less about knowing the real cause of suffering than about allowing people to "work out" their individual suffering. Indeed, people often talk about being connected to those in their social networks by cultivating the capacity to empathize with another's suffering without direct knowledge, intervention, or even involvement. In this sense, sharing one's dukkha with someone, while being intricately linked to conveying moral conviction in that individual, is both an independent choice and a collective action. At the same time, the person who is a witness to others' suffering is also morally accountable. Dukkha as an individual experience and a shared moral practice, rather than adherence to an abstract situation, is central to the framing of suffering here.

Equally important, dukkha is about the collective consciousness and sensibility among my Nepali interlocutors that allows for the capacity to become receptive to others' dukkha, the kind of emotionally laden ethical experiences and contexts usually designated by the English words *pain, grief, suffering*, and *hardship*. Although multiple moral actions and experiences play a significant role in the everyday practice of suffering among the Nepalis I met and worked with, I focus primarily on dukkha, as it is important as a site for cultural (re)production as well as a critique of the asylum-seeking process. More important perhaps, from the point of view of Nepalis, the question about who is or is not suffering is not even relevant or urgent as to the degree one has suffered or who is asked to reveal his/her suffering to whom and under what circumstances. The question for many Nepalis is whether it is even possible *not* to be identified as a suffering asylum seeker, notwithstanding the actual circumstances of one's legal status, because they are part of the emergent migrant community in the United States.

TWO / Language of Suffering, Language for Survival

LANGUAGE OF SUFFERING

In 2007, Obama's presidential campaign promised a path to legalization for the "12 million undocumented workers who are already here."[1] This promise added to the general euphoria about the possibility of legalization for undocumented, working-class migrant families across the country, among them my ESL student-participants and others in Nepali Queens. Addressing the issue of immigration reform, Obama stated how "many of them [undocumented migrants are] living their lives alongside other Americans. . . . Many of the kids [of undocumented migrants] . . . are citizens," and furthermore, the government needed to "bring those families out of the shadows" in order to put them on "a pathway to citizenship." At the same time, the Obama government supported deportation orders, citing that people who entered "illegally" would "have to pay a fine. They would have to learn English . . . [and] go to the back of the line so that they did not get citizenship before those persons who had come here legally." In the same campaign, he promised to "remove incentives to enter the country illegally by cracking down on employers who hire undocumented migrants." For example, the expedited requirement for potential employers to use government databases, such as E-Verify, to ensure the legal work permits of their employees discouraged hiring of undocumented migrants.[2] By the time Obama took office, the "Homeland Security State" was at the height of managing, policing, and disciplining migrant workers, thus outsourcing immigration enforcement to private citizens and businesses. The campaign's promised "path to citizenship" depended upon ongoing identification of "good undocumented immigrants" and, in turn, bringing them into existence.

Obama's presidency and the pro-immigrant rhetoric, coinciding with the financial crisis of 2008, however, led to nativism on the right as well as nativism on the left, creating polarized political debates and positions on immigration enforcement.[3] Given the socioeconomic downturn and the growing unemployment in the country, restrictive immigration legislation was favored. As expedited deportation materialized once Obama took office, it not so much halted but extended the promise of a "path to legalization" and resumed interior immigration enforcement in a new setting.[4] This setting was private and intimate, involving outsourcing of interior immigration enforcement to employers and other third parties, effectively, into the very spaces in which migrant suffering manifested. At the same time, immigrant rights groups and nongovernmental organizations that supported mobilization protests a few years prior gained prominence and received generous federal funding. As they recruited and worked among members of racialized, working-class migrants, like the Nepali-speaking communities, immigrant rights groups became powerful intermediaries, allies, and lobbyists for "good" (un)documented migrant families and communities. Yet the visibility of these communities, including that of the Nepali community in Queens, increasingly depended on the intermediary roles of private and nongovernmental institutions.

Not surprisingly, Adhikaar too had built an extensive support network by the time I was conducting fieldwork. Besides coalition building with other immigrant groups and migrant-activist communities, it also collaborated with nonprofit organizations, pro bono legal services, and human rights agencies in the tristate area and nationally. Its visibility and stability as a grassroots migrant-workers' rights organization, mobilizing, advocating, and providing direct services to people in the Nepali-speaking communities enabled and, in turn, depended on its continued collaboration with a range of individuals and institutions. This marked the significance of community organizers' roles as more than volunteer intermediaries and made the community center more than a language facilitation and workers' rights discussion space. It was also a space that facilitated the rise of a "visible" Nepali migrant community as early as 2007 in the city and, more than a decade later, reiterated their suffering invisibility elsewhere.[5] As a result, the more deliberate efforts toward addressing long-term issues affecting its members in the greater migrant community consisted of Adhikaar's advocacy, outreach, and direct service. One of these was the "English for Empowerment" course Adhikaar offered to the community members a year after its inception in 2006.[6]

A SUNDAY AT ADHIKAAR:
FIRST DAY AS AN ESL FACILITATOR

Since Adhikaar had limited resources, I joined a pool of volunteers who had been teaching English on weekends for almost a year. The class I was instructed to facilitate was one that an ESL volunteer had left in the middle of the nine-week ESL session. I was there as a substitute. As soon as I entered the classroom, I was taken aback by the welcome—the mixture of curious looks and genuine suspicion—that I received from the ESL participants. I politely took the empty seat by the door in that crowded room.

There was another volunteer already facilitating the class. The topic they were discussing that day involved placing calls, answering, and taking messages in English. They were doing role-plays, and participants were going around practicing making calls and answering. The volunteer was playing the role of a caller, and each participant took a turn responding to whatever question they were asked by the caller. The participants were asked to practice and simultaneously memorize the following phrases and questions related to telephone conversation:

"Could you please speak very slowly? I cannot understand what you are saying."
"Could you please spell your name and number for me?"
"Could you please repeat what you said?"

As I sat in the classroom and observed them, I was both fascinated and perplexed by this exercise. The ESL participants were receiving instruction and information not only on what to say but also on *how* to indicate their "limited" English-speaking ability to the caller on the other end. As I was trying to make sense of this exercise, I was asked to take over the class by the executive director of the organization. Having had no previous experience facilitating an English class and in that particular context of instructing adult Nepalis, I approached the class with trepidation.

As I continued the telephone conversation exercise, I introduced ways for them to remember details from a telephone conversation. I found myself lecturing on the usefulness of taking notes when answering calls and taking messages for someone else. I went as far as to instruct the participants to make a list, in order of importance, every time they had to answer calls and take messages. I wrote the following words on a blackboard behind me:

Name:
Number:
Message:
Day/time of the call:

When I turned around, there were blank stares on people's faces, accompanied with an uncomfortable silence. The perplexed faces and half smiles intimidated me at first. Trying not to be overcome by my nervousness, I quickly changed the topic to what I thought was simply a rhetorical question to generate conversation: Why do you want to learn English?

I noticed guarded looks being replaced by bright eyes, tensed faces gradually loosening up and transforming into communicative expressions, and hands flying everywhere. In a flurry of Nepali, the classroom became alive.

"We *need to* talk on the phone and take messages for our *sahu-jis* [bosses]!" one of them exclaimed.

"We *have to* tell their kids to eat, to do homework, and to go to sleep on time," another added.

"We *cannot do* grocery if we do not know the names of the vegetables and fruits that our bosses want us to buy from organic stores," someone from the back shouted.

"We *have to* learn all the names of the cleaning supplies to do our work every day."

"We *need to* take the train and change buses to go to work in Long Island, New Jersey, Connecticut. . . ."

I was struck by these answers. Not a single response had to do with reasons, as I had naively presumed, associated with pursuing higher education or obtaining an advanced degree. English for its own sake was not an issue raised by my eager participants. Rather, they collectively voiced the necessity to learn English to make their work—everyday lives—somewhat manageable. On a basic level, their responses revealed to me my own presumption, one based on a somewhat limited outlook (often arising out of a privileged social position occupied by "native" and/or near-native English speakers), about the very framing of the question.

In an attempt to continue the conversation, I mentioned that I understood everything they had just said. I asked them to clarify and expand on what they specifically meant by talking on the phone and taking messages for their bosses.

The ESL participants then went on to relate to me that although they spoke "some" English, they did not speak "good" English and, as a consequence, were hesitant and even anxious to answer calls at work, take messages, and relay them to their employers. Take, for example, the following anecdote shared by Sanju didi, who at the time had been working as a live-in domestic in Long Island for the last nine years: Once a person, who identified herself as Vera, had called for her employer. Because *Vera* sounded like *bheda* (sheep in Nepali) Sanju didi thought it would not be difficult for her to remember the name. When the employer came home that night, she could not recall the name of the caller. She knew it sounded like an animal in Nepali but could not remember the animal that the name reminded her of. She ended up telling her employer that *bakhra* (goat in Nepali) had called while she was out! All of us broke into laughter when she finished her story. But Sanju didi suddenly became silent, and everyone joined her in her silence. It was a comfortable silence—one with which my participants seemed familiar—that made me feel uncomfortable and, at once, a complete outsider. Although I could have interrupted it as an awkward silence by asking a follow-up question, I decided not to. The silence was awkward for me but not for my ESL participants.

In moments like this, I learned not only to observe the power of collective voice but also to acknowledge the significance of a shared silence. Sanju didi's anecdote about the difficulty of answering phone calls at work and the silence that followed it were emblematic of the stories that the ESL participants recounted to me. The difficulty, they emphasized, had to do with their limited understanding of English words and phrases and their need to speak "good" English. Once I was able to follow the logic of their answers, I became acutely aware that the question was not why (or why not) people *wanted to* learn English but why they felt that they *needed to* speak "good" English.

In that first session, I learned that the question of silence was just as important as, and even contradictory to, their collective claim about needing to speak "good" English. Indeed, silences, which sometimes entered the ESL classroom unannounced and oftentimes deliberately, ended up transforming both the classroom space and the direction of our conversation. In the following pages, I unravel such moments to better illuminate the intricate relationship between the individualized and collective articulation of suffering practices and the labor activities in which people regularly participated. In so doing, I also trace the gradual transformation of the ESL classroom into a productive space for the emergence of suffering narratives and rationales among student-interlocutors not only through continuous dialogue but also through momentary, abrupt silences. ESL participants' silences eventually helped me follow their rationale for learning English—one of the many problems facing them, inseparable from the experiences of racialization and low-wage labor incorporation.

In this chapter, I argue that the seemingly mundane commentaries about workplace grievances and proclivity toward learning English are key to understanding the pervasive and ordinary forms of suffering that working-class migrants and asylum claimants disproportionately experience. Drawing on and expanding the linguistic anthropological concept of *language use* (i.e., deployment of language as a resource by users to attain a meaningful social action in practice), I demonstrate how an analysis of my interlocutors' meaning-making practices reveal a complicated, and a deeply contradictory, reality: Nepali migrants' declared "need" to learn English specifically in relation to not speaking Hindi, despite readily accessible employment in the South Asian domestic labor industry upon migration.[7] In doing so, I position my analysis within the relational perspectives on migrant language, labor, and racialization (De Genova 2005; Urciuoli 2008; Shankar 2008; Reynolds and Orellano 2009). I argue further that my student-interlocutors' coarticulation of English-language constraint and *excess* Hindi in the process of being incorporated into the low-wage labor sector can add to a new understanding of *habitual suffering* (De León 2013), which posits routinized and widespread embodied and material suffering, an excess of which, over time, goes unexpressed even by those experiencing it. The interpretations of my interlocutors' experience run counter to the prevailing assumptions regarding the effects of English-language "skill" and labor incorporation on migrants' attitudes and behaviors.[8] In highlighting the experience of labor and racialization, Nepalis' responses emanate from a collective awareness of their marginalization not as "unskilled" but as silent as well as *silenced* workers in the domestic, often intimate, workspaces. Particularly, Nepali workers' declared *need* to speak "good" English, often articulated in relation to their *desire* not to speak Hindi, runs counter to the actual conditions of obtaining and securing employment as live-in or live-out maids, nannies, and housekeepers in the city.

LABOR, RACIALIZATION, AND *USES* OF MIGRANT LANGUAGE(S)

More than a decade of research on the interconnection between language ideologies, migrant labor, and racialization has shown that learning or speaking English guarantees neither greater integration nor upward social mobility for working-class, non-English-speaking migrant communities in US society.[9] Scholars after Silverstein (2005) have shown how racialization processes facilitate migrant integration into social and linguistic hierarchies negatively affecting people's life chances (Bonilla-Silva 2006), employment possibilities (Menjívar 2006), and internalization of their own oppression (Massey 2007; Maldanado 2009). Analysis of racialization and migrant-labor incorporation, in particular, has provided insight on the historical causes and consequences of producing and sustaining an endless supply of cheap and flexible work for capitalist development (see De Genova 2002; Ngai 2003). It is clear from this work that the interconnection between language, racialization, and low-wage migrant labor is neither straightforward nor somehow accidental but rather reflects the socio-structural conditions integrating people who must navigate to variable degrees their labor activities for livelihood.

In his study of migrant survival techniques in the context of cross-border migration in the Sonoran Desert, Jason De León argues that the specific material and physical injuries people endure are part of a broader *habitual suffering* that exposes people to the harsh environmental conditions (i.e., desert in this case) exacerbated by border enforcement technology and limitations of their own bodies and "use wear" (2013, 329).[10] People adopt, modify, and adjust bodily techniques and material use in confrontation with and circumvention of a wide range of physical, psychological, and emotional pain and injuries during the crossing process. De León notes the subtle and intimate connection between suffering and migrant materiality, in particular, use of objects and their modifications for survival, providing "phenomenological insight on types of suffering specifically linked to the migration process" (342). Building on this conceptual move, I show that such *habitual suffering* also exists in the lives of migrants and their communities within the US boundaries, disciplining and orienting much of their social lives and economic activities. Here suffering emerges and, in turn, is internalized by migrants through coarticulation of speech and silence, ultimately directing attention to the dual process of their labor participation and racialization.

Nepali migrants attending Adhikaar's English classes and workers' rights programs, in particular, rely on their social networks, hometown ethnic associations, and knowledge of longtime US residents (with or without citizenship) for employment-related information, including scales of wages, types of documentation, and ways to obtain them (figures 10, 11, and 12). Other equally important information entails searching for and finding affordable housing and accessing health care, banking, and education for their children. These activities often connect people to a wider migrant network, offering social and economic support, especially to those without familial support to draw upon or legal documentation during the early months, even years, after arrival; they also bind people into labor and moral economies that help them sustain a livelihood and remain in the country for the foreseeable future—a pattern prevalent among socioeconomically marginalized migrant communities across time and space in the United States.[11] Though seemingly fitting into this broadly generalizable migrant experience, from learning about document requirements and social networking to English-language acquisition and labor integration, Nepalis (arriving and settling in the United States between the late 1990s and the mid-2000s) specifically acquire knowledge about employability and the limits and opportunities presented by their multilingual aptitudes. As a workplace-based ESL instructor engaging with Mexican migrant workers in Chicago, De Genova (2005) has shown that to understand the effects of migrant racialization, one must understand its intricate connection to a highly exploitative, precarious,

FIGURE 10 Workers' rights informational meeting at Adhikaar. Photograph courtesy of Sonam Ukyab.

FIGURE 11 First Nepali-speaking Domestic Workers Forum, organized by Adhikaar in 2012. Photograph courtesy of Sonam Ukyab.

FIGURE 12 Dashain celebration at Adhikaar. Photograph courtesy of Sonam Ukyab.

and grueling manual labor that non-English-speaking, predominantly undoc-umented migrants are exposed to on a daily basis. In the Nepali case, their collective articulation of the "need" to learn English, in relation to not speaking Hindi, as they participate in a racialized labor sector follows a specific pattern of language use tied to suffering and survival strategies.

Sociolinguistic anthropologists have recognized that socialization into non-English language encompasses elaborate linguistic processes of marginal-ized identity formation and construction of social boundaries among its speakers (e.g., Zentella 1997; Urciuoli 1996; Bailey 2001; Mendoza-Denton 2008; Alarcón and Heyman 2014), and it can expose structural processes, including class prej-udices and racial formations (Urciuoli 1996), and resistance practices that can move beyond the US racial formation as indexical order for investigating into social difference (Dick 2010). Although sociolinguistics have contributed to our understanding of migrant language use, racialization, and intergenerational difference over the last two decades, this body of work has not given full at-tention to the English-language use among newly arrived migrants. Indeed, ethnographic research on newly arrived migrants' language use and racialization has focused on the heritage language performances that influence identity con-struction and facilitate either racialization or ethnicization processes.[12] Seldom have ethnographers employed migrants' English-language usage in the process of labor subordination and racialization, although several underscore structures of migrant racialization through English-language policy.[13] Below, I highlight a few key works that have informed my study of Nepali migrants' use of English language, racialization, and workplace negotiations within the low-wage and exploitative labor industry.

In his work on migrant-labor subordination and language use, De Genova (2005) discusses the particularities of Mexican migrant workers' experience of racialization that unfold in their interactions with workplace managers who consistently regard their labor as "ineffective" and attribute it to their "inability" to communicate in English. Yet the requirement for workers to speak English contributes, he writes, to the "generally dehumanizing [experience], displac[ing] the full extent of communication and creative expression possible in the workers' first language [Spanish]" (35). While De Genova highlights migrants' predicament of learning English as providing the conditions of possibility for "racialization of their own language as a palpable feature of the discrimination against them" (45), Jennifer Reynolds and Marjorie Orellano's work (2009) among Latino/a and Mexican immigrant child interpreters demonstrates how linguistically mediated racialization experiences and unequal subject positions help us understand the broader processes of "ethnolinguistic profiling that take place when 'language' is variously ethnicized and racialized" (212). Drawing our attention to interpreter-mediated interactions, Reynolds and Orellano argue that racialization can take "the form of misrecognition of language as autonomous code, rather than register in translation" (213). Their nuanced study of various social and institutional contexts of English-Spanish interpretation provides insight into both overt and covert ways of migrant racialization even in the most banal situations. Together, De Genova's and Reynolds and Orellano's works help us realize the significance of linguistically mediated discursive practices arising out of social encounters and labor integration informing the newly arrived migrants' (English) language use and experience of racialization.

In his argument against viewing migrant "artifacts as simplistic metonyms for generic and de-personalized suffering," De León remarks that these artifacts (e.g., worn shoes, dark clothing, empty water bottles, etc.) repeatedly chosen, used, modified, and discarded by people delineate a "dialectical relationship where objects . . . influence the physical techniques of border crossing" and, in turn, techniques becoming a part of learned behaviors through practice (2013, 331). He is critical of the ways in which migrant materials, often dismissed as garbage, have been appropriated by environmental degradation discourse to bolster border enforcement policies and have been separated from discussions of sociopolitical processes, global economic inequalities, and structural violence embedded in the use and logic of crossing activities and artifacts. Notwithstanding the starkly different context of migrants' border-crossing techniques and collective experience that inform De León's analysis of the materiality of habitual suffering, the particular ways in which internalization of suffering takes on linguistic forms and processes can sharpen our analysis of migrant labor and racialization occurring within the boundaries of the US state.

Hence, my expansion of the sociolinguistic debate on migrant language use will trace the experience of my ESL student-interlocutors. This approach allows me to (1) follow specific rationales of their declared *need* to learn English in relation to not speaking Hindi, (2) incorporate complex coarticulation of individualized workplace grievance and language need into a broader framework for understanding shared silence as linguistic and survival techniques, and (3) argue beyond migrant suffering imaginaries accounting for cross-border migration and focus on the more mundane social interactions, domestic chores, and workplace socializations.

LEARNING ENGLISH, SPEAKING HINDI

A few weeks into facilitating an ESL session on workplace negotiations and ways to confront employers about wages and benefits, the conversation suddenly transformed into a serious discussion on everyday survival strategies and suffering. I had asked the class whether they needed to speak "good" English or know English at all to keep working as live-in/live-out maids and housekeepers. Many of the student-participants responded with blank stares. I could not tell if they were confused by my inquiry or annoyed that I should ask such a question after having facilitated English-language class for nearly two months. I elaborated on the question and explained that, while I had the language *skill* to communicate and facilitate the class, they were the ones with the everyday work experience and skills to make the class useful. Then I added a contradictory remark without putting much thought into it: "You know, if you practice English every day, it will get better over time."

They simply nodded, and some even put on a forced smile. Nobody responded for a long time.

"Tapainko kaam ta sajilo cha ni, English padaune ho. Tara hamro ta dherai gahro cha ghaar ko kaam!" (You have an easy job of teaching us English. Ours is domestic work!) Mina didi, one of the ESL student-participants, had broken the silence. A thirty-eight-year-old single mother from Thongche, Manang, in the northwest region, Mina didi used to be a teacher in her village. She came to the United States three years ago and had been working as a live-in nanny in a South Asian household in Hoboken.

Still no one responded. I was taken aback by this pointed, but quite accurate, remark. The comment made me extremely self-conscious, and I continued our conversation in Nepali in hopes of shifting the tone of the discussion.

As I was speaking, Tenzin, who had worked in India before coming to New York four years ago, interrupted me. "Can you please not speak Nepali? I do not understand what you are saying!" she said. She looked serious.

I was utterly lost. I thought the participants were all "Nepalis" since the organization provided services to Nepalis and Nepali-speaking communities in New York City.

"What language do you speak at work then?" I asked.

"I am from Tibet. I only speak Tibetan and Hindi," Tenzin responded.

Meanwhile, I caught students from my previous English-language sessions exchanging silent glances. Then Sanju didi came to my rescue: "Bahini, haami ta Sherpa ho ni, tapain po Nepali. Haamilai Nepali ramro aundaina." (Sister, we are Hyolmo Sherpas and not Nepali like you. We cannot even speak Nepali properly. We did not go to school at home.)

I was even more confused by Sanju didi's comment about not being "Nepali." But before I could ask for an explanation, she redirected our conversation to my original question: "You are right. Even though we do not speak good English, we have experience, and what you just said [about] skills . . . yes, we have that. We know how to cook for them, clean their bathrooms, and take care of their kids" ("their" meaning the employers). There was a hint of uncertainty in her voice. "They [employers] know all this [our skills] already," she continued. "You know my boss always tells me that I will not be able to leave her family. She tells me that even if I find another family, I will not be happy. I just don't talk afterward."

All of us asked Sanju didi if her boss's prediction was correct.

She laughed sarcastically. "Of course, it's not true," she said. "It will not be difficult to leave that job. . . . If I get paid more money somewhere else, why will I stay?" In an elevated voice she added, "Does she think I am stupid?!" Suddenly, her tone became solemn. "That's why I am taking English class every weekend. I have a live-in job now. Before I get fired, I want to find a live-out job for the same money or more." She said it in one breath and became quiet. In a split second, her smile vanished. The enthusiasm and lightheartedness with which she began her story was now causing her discomfort.

Just when I thought I was starting to regain control over the direction of classroom discussion, four of Sanju didi's relatives—also Hyolmo Sherpas—said something to her in Hyolmo. This time, the other students, including Mina didi, Tenzin, and the three new participants from Mustang, and I were completely lost. It appeared from Sanju didi's tone and facial expression that they were trying to console her, but console her about what? I was no longer steering our classroom conversation.

"Could you all please speak English, because some of us do not understand your language, and this is English class," I requested, trying to lighten up the classroom environment, and once again, to redirect our conversation to the topic for the day.

No one responded to me. The Hyolmo participants were busy talking to Sanju didi. The classroom was transforming into a space for the participants to share their stories and grievances from work.

Then one of the Hyolmo participants, Pelki didi, Sanju didi's sister-in-law, offered us an interpretation, only to follow up with a rhetorical question: "We are telling Sanju didi that at least she is not asked by her American boss to speak Hindi to the kids she looks after. Now you tell us, Tina Miss, how can we practice English when our sahu-jis always tells us to speak Hindi at home . . . I mean, at work?"

I responded to her question rather clumsily: "So you do not understand Hindi?" By now I had stopped being obsessively self-conscious of what I was asking. I simply wanted to join the conversation and find out what was causing distress among the Hyolmo participants. "Oh! You have a very good job then, why you getting sad and complaining?" one of the participants from Mustang told Sanju didi, completely ignoring my question.

"Maybe your boss is right then! You will not be happy if you leave that job," Tenzin added, almost dismissive of Sanju didi's emotional state.

I was shocked by Tenzin's insensitive response to Sanju didi. At the same time, I was getting frustrated, being the only one left outside of what seemed to be an intense and engaging conversation. At that moment, my job as an English facilitator seemed both insufficient and less useful to advancing our conversation, let alone meaningful exchanges. I became more interested in learning about the connection between domestic work and speaking Hindi.

Again, Pelki didi offered to interpret, although everyone was already speaking English. "You see, Tina *bahini*," she took a deep breath and thought for a minute. Then continued, "So even with all the work experience we have, our bosses do not trust us. We go to an interview, and they always ask if we speak English. And we just tell them we speak Hindi. That is why we work for Indian sahu-jis."

Sanju didi, after composing herself, corrected Pelki didi, "Yes, but if you don't say you speak Hindi, then you will not get any work. How will you make paper then?"

"That is why I want to speak English. I do not want to speak Hindi anymore," Pelki didi interjected. Everyone in the room nodded in agreement.

Mina didi, who was quietly observing everyone's reaction, including mine, offered to further enlighten me. Perhaps it was evident from my facial expression that although I was following the various explanations and reasons given for learning English, I was finding it difficult to make the connection between learning English, not speaking Hindi, getting a job, and making paper. She kindly elaborated for me: "We all understand Hindi. That is why we come here . . . to speak English. Our Indian sahu-jis in the US don't want their children to forget their language, so they want their children to speak Hindi at home. And that is why we speak Hindi at work. Where is the time to practice English, Miss?"

"You see, after living in the US and working for all these years, we speak Hindi very well!" Tenzin said sarcastically. Her comment generated laughter from everyone.

"You know, Tina *bahini*, we tell our families back home that their Hindi will improve after they come to the US," Pelki didi teasingly added.

"We tell them 'Just learn Hindi, you will get jobs in the US!'" Mina didi exclaimed. "And we also warn them." She paused, read my expression first, and added, "'But there is no guarantee you will make paper!'"

LANGUAGE FOR SURVIVAL AND SILENCED ENCOUNTERS

At the outset, my student-interlocutors' grievances about being stuck in a Hindi-language domestic labor market, and their preference to work for white, English-speaking "American" families, whom they associated with better job opportunities, reveal seemingly straightforward logic underlying reasons for learning English. To employ this reading as an interpretive end, however, is to miss the analytic potential of a complicated rationale used by my interlocutors as well as the subtle forms of contemporary migrant racialization and labor mediated through paradoxical language-integration processes. Sociolinguistics studying the role of bilingualism among first- and second-generation migrant youths (Rampton 1995; Zentella 1997; Shankar 2008; Mendoza-Denton 2008), for instance, have called into question studies that conclude that English-language proficiency and variable degrees of "heritage" language abilities are evidence of migrant integration and "selective acculturation" (see, for instance, Portes and Rumbaut 2001). These studies have been critical in highlighting, instead, the intricate links between linguistic performances of ethnicities and racial formations—from use of stylized English in utterances to code-switching in their interactions at various social and institutional settings.

Concerning the logic of speaking Hindi as live-in and live-out domestic workers, then, my interlocutors pointed out to me the inverse relationship between speaking "good" English and not wanting to speak Hindi. The inherent contradiction surrounding their desire not to speak Hindi and the palpable fear of unemployment affirmed just the contrary of Mina didi's cynical pronouncement: while they advise their family members living in Nepal or India to learn Hindi, the workers themselves disliked having to speak Hindi, despite the likelihood of obtaining and retaining employment, and looked forward to learning English. Indeed, many of them had even come to see certain grievances and frustrations as business as usual, if not unreasonable, so long as they were not asked to speak Hindi by their employers. The participant's dismissive comment to Sanju didi—"Oh! You have a very good job then, why you getting sad and complaining?"—is indicative of such cynicism. Sanju didi also implicitly confirmed this reality when she added to Pelki didi's explanation of how they often admit to their potential bosses that they speak Hindi during job interviews: "Yes, but if you don't say you speak Hindi, then you will not get any work."

Participants' ambivalence toward speaking Hindi is inseparable from their declared need to speak "good" English; it is also evidence of their utter dependence on Indian employers in finding a foothold in the labor market in New York City. A larger question, one beyond the scope of my argument here but implicated throughout, concerns expectations of Nepali migrants to speak Hindi, not unconnected to the designation and reification of "South Asians" in the United States that invokes a static, homogenous, and Indian-centric social formation despite the prevalence of people with multiple homelands in the South Asian subcontinent, distinct migration trajectories, settlement patterns, and sociopolitical histories.[14]

In the view of Sanju didi and others who either had previously worked for or were currently employed at South Asian households, declaring one's knowledge of Hindi offered a realistic and readily accessible way to obtain employment. In this sense, my interlocutors' workplace grievances of not being able to speak "good" English while having to speak Hindi perhaps most closely resonate with and expand upon the idea of language "crossing" (Rampton 1995).[15] Ben Rampton discusses how such crossings, besides being stigmatized or a sign of potential resistance, are ultimately about navigating and negotiating structurally disadvantageous situations available to language users. Compared to conventional sociolinguistic anthropological approaches that delineate migrant language use and racialized identity formation into the broader "politics of difference," my interlocutors' shared predicament of working in a South Asian household and having to speak Hindi arise out of their linguistic ability as a critical feature of their socioeconomic marginalization. Tenzin's, Mina didi's, and Pelki didi's remarks that their Hindi "improved" after living in the United States, thus, reflect this convoluted reality.

According to Nepalis, working for Americans (understood as white families, where speaking "good" English would be required of domestic workers) was a better alternative to working for South Asian families, for they would no longer have to speak Hindi. Sanju didi's articulation of this blatant irony elicited

Tenzin's equally poignant and sarcastic remark, made with both annoyance and apprehension: "Maybe your boss is right then! You will not be happy if you leave that job." Tenzin's admonition signals a recognition of, and not a difference in opinion about, a bleak possibility arising out of a shared socioeconomic reality and awareness of their work situations. Her pointed remark paradoxically gave coherence to Sanju didi's assertion that employers are often aware of the workers' perpetual anxiety surrounding unstable employment, despite their skills and experience from which employers, invariably, benefit: "but they know this already." In pointing out this fact, Sanju didi was actually engaging with others and me in the classroom and simply (re)affirming the silence surrounding the common knowledge: the unequal power relationship that exists between employers, South Asians or white Americans, and domestic workers. Her pronouncement, which others in the classroom also attested, merely restated a well-known fact: it is seldom the knowledge that employers do or do not possess that makes them unable to relate to workers' experiences. Rather, it is another form of silence around the pervasive complicity among employers in this labor sector that my interlocutors were verbalizing. In this way, my interlocutors not only acknowledged but also expressed how they anticipated their continued labor integration in a racialized social formation, whether in speaking English or continuing to resist speaking Hindi.

Moreover, speaking "good" English has very little to do with resolving immediate employment problems, presumably with a South Asian family in the first place, as the participants' conversation illuminates. It provides neither job security nor an escape from humiliating experiences at the workplace. Quite the contrary. Workers are periodically silenced and, in turn, remain silent by learning and speaking English at work. Take, for instance, Sanju didi's account of her silent response to her employer's rather obtuse comment. Still Sanju didi's poignant retelling of the incident and her question—"Does she think I am stupid?!"— exemplify the dilemma of having obtained what other workers considered to be a "better" job with an English-speaking family. In posing that question and revealing her employer's absurd logic, Sanju didi was implicitly avowing what Narbada didi said to me, on more than one occasion, in passing: "Bahini, in this country, people think you are stupid if you do not speak good English. Sometimes it is better to remain silent."

One of the real reasons for discomfort, as exemplified by Sanju didi's emotional outburst and Tenzin's seemingly tactless response, was facing constant humiliation at work. Participants' limited English-language ability, as they insisted, constantly exposed them to being misunderstood at work, or worse, being *understood* as stupid. In light of this serious matter that workers explained to me, Sanju didi's exclamation—"Does she think I am stupid?!"—takes on a new meaning, a life of its own. Embedded in her question, which other participants attested by silently witnessing and later sharing in her silence, is the possibility of a two-sided interpretation: people are always looking for better options (i.e., better pay, work hours, etc.) no matter the constraints of what "better" may translate to as far as obtaining employment in the same industry goes, and employers who verbalize that workers would continue to stay in their homes if they had better options and improved socioeconomic conditions must be stupid.

As such, it is particularly revealing to consider an alternative reading of Sanju didi's statement, juxtaposed with the everyday shared silence among participants, beyond participants' acknowledgment of their similarly situated conditions of marginality. Implicit in her sarcastic laughter and silence is a response to her own rhetorical question—"I am not stupid"—and, further, the inverse of her proclamation—"Is she [her boss] stupid to think that I would stay if I was offered a better job?" This is a probable interpretation, one that is hopeful. Still another equally plausible and important interpretation of her response as silence is simply that—silence. No word could have possibly transcended the gulf that already existed between her *silenced* encounter with her employer. Hence, Sanju didi's decisive statement: "I just don't talk afterward." De Genova's engagement with Mexican migrant workers in Chicago leads him to conclude that people needed "to speak English in their confrontations with power—in the United States, English is the language of power" (2005, 52). In the context of my student-participants' language use in navigating the domestic labor industry, English is the language that silences them and Hindi is the language of survival. If in speaking Hindi, workers become a visible mass of labor supply to South Asian households, then in speaking English, they become a silent and desirable mass of migrants.

Still, silenced experiences at work, like that of Sanju didi, which other participants could immediately relate to even if not everyone agreed, are not outside but within the condition of possibility of becoming silent migrants. Her reenactment of the grave silence provided an important ground for other participants to share their work experiences and grievances. In expressing disappointment in her employer, followed by cynical laughter and silence, there was no need to speak further. Read as such, silence is a rule, and not an exception, in situations like the one Sanju didi described and other workers heeded in agreement. In narrating the episode of her abrupt interaction at work, Sanju didi was reenacting her *everyday* silenced experience for other workers and me. It is within this context of silence that I want to reread Sanju didi's *chosen* silent response: there is nothing left to say to someone whose absurd rationale prevents him/her from even considering the possibility of another's point of view. Interpreted this way, silence then becomes a deliberate *choice* of disengagement. It is not being unable but refusing to engage in a conversation. This silence as refusal of engagement further makes not knowing or speaking English—whether to defend one's position or to simply participate in a verbal battle—completely irrelevant.

The irony is that the language in which workers considered themselves "unskilled" was also the basis to relate their complaints about work in the context of the ESL classroom. The initial anxiety that the workers voiced regarding their need to speak English to obtain better jobs did not disappear with the renewed classroom discussion of their working conditions. Rather, it allowed participants to articulate the point that their grievances and complaints from work were seldom about the actual *work* they performed, or even about having to speak Hindi, but were more often about wanting to avoid confrontations and humiliations at work.

I left Adhikaar that Sunday afternoon energized, mildly amused, but mostly restless. I had yet to learn about the possible encounters my participants had with the English language in and outside their workplaces. My student-participants' keen awareness of the incessant problem with English revealed a still greater irony: speaking "good" English should become the medium through which they express, and not necessarily overcome, the limitations provided by language use at work. And this language-related work, as I would soon learn, was far from the only problem confronting many working-class, undocumented Nepalis in the city. There existed a parallel, equally precarious, situation for my interlocutors outside the context of Adhikaar: language racialization and labor subordination jointly manifested in one's situated experience of temporary and permanent legalization.

A DAY IN NEPALI QUEENS OR "LITTLE NEPAL"

I caught up with Mina didi and Tenzin after class one Sunday. As soon as we stepped outside, Mina didi asked me what I did on days I did not teach English or volunteer at Adhikaar. While I had learned to offer a generic response to satisfy people's curiosities—researching Nepalis' experiences migrating to and working in New York City—I knew from my interactions with her that she *really* wanted to know. I also thought she might be able to help me think through my asylum-interpretation work given her self-designated role as my interpreter in our ESL classroom. I told her that I volunteered as an interpreter for asylum seekers.

"Do you also write *their* stories?" Tenzin interrupted.

I was taken aback, literally. I was suddenly several steps behind them. They turned around, paused, and waited for me to catch up.

"*Whose* stories?" I started walking fast, as though I was worried I would lose them.

Tenzin looked at Mina didi and waited for her to clarify. Although she did not, I felt like my other "work" of asylum interpretation had somehow made Tenzin uncomfortable.

As we passed Woodside and approached the busy Seventy-Third Street and Roosevelt Avenue, Tenzin bade us goodbye. She had to catch the New Jersey transit from Penn Station to go to her employer's house in the suburbs of New Jersey, where she lived from Sunday through Saturday morning. On Saturdays, Tenzin and Mina didi shared a room in an apartment in Woodside rented to them by Mina didi's relatives from Manang.

"Would you like to have a cup of tea in Rato Bhale?" I asked Mina didi.

"I do have to do grocery near Rato Bhale restaurant . . . maybe we can go there," she agreed, to my pleasant surprise.

Sunday in Jackson Heights is one of the busiest days. You often find yourself pushing through the crowd as you walk, as queues spill out into the pavement from grocery stores, sari stalls, cafés, restaurants, and banks. Walking from one corner of the street to another can take double the time it normally takes. When we arrived at Rato Bhale, there was already a long queue of people at the order counter. A small hole-in-the-wall with only three long benches, it was one of the few restaurants that serve both Nepali and Tibetan style momos and, like several Nepali-owned restaurant businesses, it no longer needed to advertise itself as an "Indian" restaurant and attract customers by primarily serving North Indian cuisine. This was not the case when I first moved to New York, back in 2003; there were only two Nepali-owned restaurants in Queens and a total of five in the entire city. In the span of less than a decade, there were already two or three Nepali-owned restaurants on every street in Jackson Heights.

For the Nepali-speaking customers, Rato Bhale was a meeting place where relatives, friends, and peers exchanged information of all sorts, from sharing and obtaining contacts for housing and employment possibilities to "talking politics" about home and the United States, from exchanging local gossip to selling tickets for various Nepali social events, musical functions, cultural shows, and festivities all year long. Quite naturally, it became one of my favorite hangout spots after ESL classes.

After ordering *chiya* (milk tea) at the counter, Mina didi and I took the only available seat in the middle of a street-facing bench. We both watched passersby and cars stuck in traffic. As we sat sipping chiya, we talked about our families and lives in Nepal before moving to the United States. Mina didi said she returned to her home village in Manang before completing twelfth grade because her grandfather was becoming politically active in the United Marxist-Lenin-Communist party and was running for a local office. The family needed her help with the election-related activities at home. She got involved in politics and never returned to Kathmandu to finish secondary school. After a few years of working and assisting her grandfather in his political activities, she started teaching in a school in her hometown. She taught for ten years there. I also learned Mina didi had a seventeen-year-old son in Pokhara, living with her older sister's family. She and her husband were separated a long time ago. Her mother, father, and younger sister all lived in Manang but not her younger brother, who was in Kathmandu running a small business.

Taking another sip of chiya, she said, "Aba ta kaam matra garne, paisa pathaune gharma; tehi ho mero kaam" (Now I just work, send money home to family; that is my work). She added, abruptly changing the topic, "Tapain le aruko asylum garnu huncha bannu bhayeko hoina, aghi haami hindai garda?" (Did you say you did asylum for others, earlier while we were walking?)

I clarified that I only *interpreted* for Nepali-speaking claimants whose asylum cases had already been filed or who were receiving assistance through a human rights agency that worked with Adhikaar.

"Maile garda yesto kehi thaha thiyen ta. Mero mama ko chora le Chinatown ko lawyer ma lagidiyeko thiyo. Tyo din haru ta samjhina pani man chaina. Kaagaz nabanai farkaun bhanne dherai socheko pani thiyen. . . . Ahile ta Nepali ma bolnu pani huncha kaagaz banauna?" (When I *did* mine, I knew nothing. My cousin brought me to a lawyer in Chinatown. I do not even want to think about those difficult days. Many times I had thought of just returning without making paper. . . . So now you can *speak* Nepali and make paper?)

Before I responded to her question, she abruptly got up and gathered her belongings. "Oh ho, dhilo bhaisake cha. Arko hafta betunla hai, Miss." (Oh wow, it is already late. Will meet you next week, Miss.)

Mina didi's rhetorical question—Now you can *speak* Nepali and make paper?—would only make sense to me a year later when she shared with me her experience of "making paper" (discussed in a later chapter).

With a gentle smile, she said, "Bhaihalcha ni. Bhetdai garunla ni. Tapain yehin basnu huncha?" (Sure. We will meet again. Do you live nearby?)

I told her my apartment in Sunnyside was about a twenty-minute walk from the restaurant and an even shorter walk to Woodside. We exchanged our numbers that day and agreed to resume our conversation another weekend when she is back in the neighborhood. Though brief, my conversation with Mina didi that day was a turning point, a minor breakthrough, during fieldwork, where a pattern emerged redirecting my observation, engagement, and participation in the greater Nepali community thereafter.

As I watched her disappear into the crowd outside of Rato Bhale, my mind started wandering. Mina didi's remark—"You can *speak* Nepali and make paper"—left me both perplexed and curious about her particular asylum claim. It also made me think about the perspectives and experiences of asylum claimants for whom I was providing Nepali-English interpretation assistance. Kumar dai, a claimant-interlocutor employed at an Indian restaurant in the city, told me that everything he earned working at the restaurant for seven years was mostly spent on rent and "making paper." As a source of anxiety and risk, legalization was similar to remaining undocumented:

When I started my asylum application with the help of a lawyer back in 2003, I knew it would take at least two years. My lawyers were helping me during that time and charging me a lot of money, but I could still work.[16] The case got rejected because I could not present some documents. Like other Nepalis, I knew about the *free* service from a friend but my sahu never asked about my paper after the first time my case was rejected. So I thought why bother. . . . Now he is saying to me that if I do not have paper, I might have to look for another job. Even restaurants do not want to hire if you do not have paper these days because of the fear of immigration raid. I can understand their situation too. My sahu has been kind to me. Working here [in the restaurant] all these years is how my children are going to boarding school in Kathmandu. How can I just stop sending money to my family? I did not have a choice but to try my luck again. . . . What to do, bahini?!

People increasingly understood their circumstances of employment in the low-wage labor sector through a naturalized division of legalization practices: although those without legal documentation were often at the mercy of their employers' goodwill, not everyone blamed their employers. Some, like Kumar dai, were even willing to empathize with their employers' quandaries. Both Mina didi and Kumar dai were correct, however, in pointing out that "making paper" through pro bono legal assistance was not a readily available option for many people. My interactions with them outside Adhikaar and asylum-interpretation contexts made me aware of the potentially double-bind situations of people who had been living and working in the country for almost a decade. First, one of the most common reasons people contemplated embarking upon asylum legalization was somehow closely related to their temporary and precarious working circumstances. Kumar dai's consideration of seeking pro bono legal assistance, for instance, was inseparable from material consequences in terms of becoming unemployed and possibly remaining unemployable and undocumented for a foreseeable future. Second, it was often through close associates in their networks who had regularized their status or were themselves immersed in the process that they learned about asylum. Locating resourceful individuals and institutions, as I learned then, was an important preliminary step to begin the process of "making paper." For individuals like Mina didi, who relied on her kinship network as she had done to locate a lawyer, hinted at a difficult and long-term investment in finding legal assistance and representation.

Broaching the topic of "making paper" often involved engaging a listener in one's dire situation back "home," including economic instability and prolonged political and civil unrest at the time, often by comparing and contrasting with US immigration politics. In the absence of the more intimate setting of Adhikaar's ESL classroom and workers' rights information session, gatherings of people at local restaurants and in the privacy of their homes inevitably would end up in debate and critiques of the changing immigration enforcement and its impact on their working lives and legality. Some of my interlocutors openly admitted that educating and convincing people of the situation of Nepal required them to constantly speak of suffering and that inability to do so could risk losing a potential opportunity for seeking information and advice, from housing to employment possibilities, asking for financial assistance and favors from long-term residents and citizens. The most common type of suffering talks during my fieldwork days involved debating indefinitely whether and how the Maobadi (Maoist) situation in Nepal aided people to "make paper" in the United States. Newly arrived migrants justified this practice as necessary because the US officials expected documentation and therefore would reject the ones without social and economic contacts of relatively privileged and powerful community members in Nepali Queens, no matter how convincing and "real" their suffering. The asylum filing deadline and periods of unemployment placed additional pressure on people to make the most of every possible social interaction, community gathering, and function.

Suffering talks could also involve discussions about the ongoing trials and tribulations of Nepalis employing different avenues for "making paper." A person might be skeptical about those seeking asylum and claim to know the difference between "truth tellers" and the lies they *must* tell to survive in the country. Others offered the explanation that suffering asylum seekers, in reality, are different from the official story that wins in the courtrooms or asylum offices. They would add that when confronted by an insensitive civil servant or an impatient official, people might hasten to withdraw from the deeply discomforting and anxiety-producing situation in which they find themselves by unintentionally exaggerating information or forgetting details relevant to their claims during asylum interviews. Still, one seldom admitted without some hesitation to having "made paper," for that person is seen not to have fully integrated and socialized into the mainstream US society and not to realize (or care, in the case of having acquired legal status) that discussing one's story to strangers could put his/her integrity in line. Although it was surprising that Mina didi had casually shared with me that she had "done" asylum, it was not unusual. I was not, after all, a legal expert or state official interrogating but a volunteer at Adhikaar and interpreter explicitly researching community members' migratory trajectories, sociality, work, and dilemmas of legalization.

THREE / The Logic of "Claimant Credibility"

ASYLUM OFFICE, ROSEDALE, APRIL 2010

"Sending me back [to Nepal] is equivalent to giving me a death sentence! I want to live freely in this country [the United States]." My focus was on keeping the index and middle fingers of my right hand tightly crossed under the table as I uttered these words.

"Cut! That was great," I was waiting for someone to announce through a bullhorn, as though we were on the set of a theatrical production.

Instead, my concentration was broken by Priya's muffled shriek and the attorney's sigh of relief. I looked over my shoulder and received an approving glance from Lisa and Annie, the lawyers representing Priya's asylum claims. However, the asylum officer, a young woman in her midtwenties, had a blank look on her face. She seemed either confused or completely unmoved. Perhaps it was business as usual for her; I could not say for certain. I am not sure if I was more surprised or disappointed that the officer did not burst into tears, but it did not seem to matter either way. What mattered at the time was Lisa's assurance. Her approving nod to both Priya and me assured us that we had given our best performance.

Lisa's sympathetic glance, however, made me feel both relieved and uncomfortable. On one hand, I was grateful that Priya and I would no longer be summoned to the law firm for tedious question-and-answer sessions, which we had been doing for the last six months, twice or more a week, for between two and six hours at a time. On the other hand, it was as though Priya and I went from being treated as two adults—the asylum seeker and the interpreter—to being one person in that half-hour interview at the asylum office.

Earlier that morning at 5:00 a.m., while waiting in the lobby at a café, Lisa had told me not to be stiff and stoic when I interpreted for Priya, especially the part where she would become emotional. "You know you should also let yourself cry," Lisa had politely, but firmly, instructed me as she continued drinking her coffee. I simply looked at her in awe, unable to take another sip of coffee. Priya and I stole silent glances. Lisa's well-meaning comment had made me extremely nervous. All that instruction of displaying Priya's suffering the right way for a less-than-half-hour interview with an asylum officer, who seemed completely unimpressed by our grand performance, left me dazed.

Lisa added a closing statement, and I completely zoned out. Ensuring consistency and enacting the correct emotions for each possible question that the asylum officer might ask had made me anxious and completely numb. And now that my part had ended, I could not concentrate on what was being said.

The asylum officer asked us to return in two weeks to pick up the decision letter. All I remember was getting in a cab that was called for us.

SUFFERING DOCUMENTATION AND THE FORM I-589
(SIX MONTHS PRIOR TO THE ASYLUM INTERVIEW)

While all legal documents related to asylum claims are important, Form I-589 and the client's affidavit, among other witness affidavits and expert reports, are perhaps most critical for the asylum case to be read closely and considered by the immigration judge. After being repeatedly asked by every pro bono lawyer to *communicate* to the asylum claimant the highly sensitive and significant nature of the two documents, I assumed my role as a participant-interpreter seriously: obtaining both general and specific facts, ensuring utmost accuracy and "objectivity" at all times, as I was asked to interpret and explain to the client was the single most important task in producing these documents. The data entered in the I-589 application form, after many hours (four to six) of interpretation for several meetings (up to three or four), would be supplemented by the client's affidavit, which required many meetings and interviews lasting anywhere from six to eight months to up to a year. Documenting and producing an affidavit, in other words, was highly sensitive, time consuming, and indispensable, as I gradually came to learn, to the asylum-seeking process. If Form I-589 is an abridged version of the asylum claims highlighting experience of (primarily, but not exclusively, political) violence and past persecution, the affidavit is a detailed, extensive, and individualized account or suffering documentation of said violence and persecution.

The topic of our asylum interpretation session on a Friday evening in October 2009 (in the conference room of a private law firm, located in Midtown

Manhattan) was the Form I-589, Application for Asylum and for Withholding of Removal.[1] Page 5 of the Form I-589, as any lawyer working on an asylum application will tell you, is the most critical, yet most difficult section of the written application. Page 5 lists reasons for filing asylum based on specific grounds of "race, religion, nationality, political opinion, membership in a particular social group, and torture convention." Upon reaching page 5 of Form I-589, lawyers repeatedly ask claimants to narrate in vivid, emotive, and meticulous detail their specific experiences of persecution. These documentation sessions can last anywhere from six months to two years and extract detailed information and descriptive images of a claimant's past experience of violence, culminating in a witness statement that is two to three hundred pages long.

"To answer the most important questions in the I-589 Application Form, we have to know the exact dates and detailed description of Priya's experience of harm," Lisa explained. She asked me to interpret, in particular, the importance of communicating the utter terror Priya experienced in the past. Her memories needed to be verbalized in Nepali and recorded in the Form I-589 as a clear, coherent, and chronological narrative.

After three long hours of going over the first question on page 5, which asked the claimant about her past experiences of "harm" or "mistreatment," the interpretation session came to a halt. Lisa and her cocounselors debated which, if any, of Priya's experiences counted as appropriate accounts of "harm," "mistreatment," or "threat."

"People not wanting to sit next to her, give her any work, or associate with her is sad, unfair, and an experience of discrimination, but certainly not torture," Lisa said during the documentation session.

"But it is a type of mistreatment, no?" I asked for clarification, before interpreting Lisa's concern to Priya.

"Yes, but you see, cases that are usually granted asylum involve severe torture, like capital punishment or FGM [female genital mutilation]," Lisa replied.

Priya kept adding to the list of "harmful" experiences she encountered in Nepal. Upon repeated emphasis to recall an incident of physical attack, Priya started recounting one particular event that Lisa agreed to be a perfect fit for the asylum testimony. However, Priya was hesitant to speak about the incident, let alone explain particularities of her experience. I spent another two hours interpreting back and forth between them, with little success.

Finally, Lisa said, "I understand how difficult it must be to recall and share something that you have been trying to forget for the last eight years, but now you have to remember it for us to document it. . . . You see, the asylum officer may not know where Nepal is or if it is a country," she added.

"Perhaps Priya can start writing journals every day about her painful past and traumatic experiences, and we can reschedule our meeting in two weeks, and she can just read it to us?" Jessica, Lisa's cocounselor, who had been seated quietly, jotting down notes, suddenly chimed in enthusiastically.

Lisa brightened up, utterly pleased with her colleague's suggestion. "It is an excellent idea. So, we can all meet next time and just go through each incident in detail."

As I interpreted their proposal and excitement to Priya, she said softly, "Tara malai English ma lekhna ta garho huncha ni." (But it is difficult for me to write in English.)

"You can just bring the Nepali version, and Tina can read it to us in English, right?" Lisa suggested.

The interpretation meeting ended that day with an understanding to come together in two weeks, same time and same place. Priya was instructed to reflect on the incident with the specific date, place, and time, and her reaction to the harm done to her. I, however, was alerted about my additional role—as a document translator—in the next interpretation meeting.

When we met two weeks later, Lisa, Jessica, Priya, and I sat down to continue with our asylum documentation from where we had left off. Priya pulled out a sheet of paper in which she had documented the incident she started to discuss with us in the last meeting. She handed the piece of paper to me and said apologetically, "Maile eitnai lekhna payen. Aru lekhna garho bhayo. Harek hafta cha dinai kaam thiyo. Pheri yesari kahan lekheko thiyen ra kahile? Sorry." (I could only write this much. To write more was difficult. I had to work six days a week. Besides, when did I have to write like this ever? Sorry.)

I did not have to interpret much this time. Lisa and Jessica stared at the piece of paper and checked both front and back of the paper. Although it was written in a language they could not read, they seemed disappointed by the length of the paper. I was then instructed to translate it into English for them. I finished translating Priya's writing in less than a half hour.

Lisa cleared her throat, leaned forward, picked up her pen, and started scribbling in a notepad. After some time, she looked up at Priya, and without taking her eyes off her, she started talking to me. "You know how long it has taken for us to understand Priya's experience. At the asylum interview, she will not be given time to explain herself. She will simply have to respond to specific questions asked by the asylum officer. Besides, the officer may not be patient with Priya. She has to know the exact dates and in chronological order and be consistent, as we have been emphasizing."

There was a brief silence after I finished interpreting their concerns to Priya.

Lisa and Jessica then thought of trying something different. They recommended the following: "Perhaps it would be easy for Priya to simply write everything she needed to as though she was not sharing it with anyone. She can give it to you every week, and before we meet, and you can just email the English versions to us before every interview."

I agreed without asking further questions. I volunteered to translate Priya's journal entries into English and bring them to the law firm for our subsequent meetings for the next several weeks. I was, after all, as much caught up in the moment of sheer frustration and disappointment shared by the pro bono lawyers as I was in the moment of vulnerability and anxiety shown by Priya.

CREDIBILITY IN ASYLUM RECONSIDERED

After months of document translation and interpretation, the I-589 form was finally ready for submission. Put together in a language that shifted between a highly individualized account of fear and legal prose on persecution, Form I-589 was meant to present a legally compelling introduction of Priya's case to the asylum officer.

One late evening, Lisa reflected on the question of credibility in asylum: "Credibility is not so much established as it is undermined during merit hearings. So far as the claimant credibility goes, we get asylum cases through referral from human rights organizations, where the cases already go through a rigorous screening and eligibility process. What we are thinking when we take asylum assignments is not 'whether this asylum claimant is credible' but 'how do we do everything' so that the judge or the asylum officer does not question credibility. The asylum officer needs to witness the claimant's suffering and imagine what Priya went through to find her credible." Lisa had represented a dozen asylum claimants and had a 100 percent success rate in winning asylum cases. When asked what factors contributed to or determined success rates of the credible asylum cases, she mentioned the importance of providing detailed, vivid, and descriptive images of specific violent incidents from the past that will ultimately facilitate writing a moving affidavit. "Two things matter most once the case is in front of the judge or the asylum officer: one is luck—some judges are compassionate and known to grant asylum, and others are not—and the other is consistency—it is OK to forget specific dates and details due to stress or pressure in front of the judge, but one should not provide conflicting information," Lisa explained.

Lisa's somewhat abstract and intertwining logic of assisting claimants already marked "credible" and "*do[ing] everything*" to prevent credibility from being undermined during a hearing was intriguing. For there was no phrase I heard more often than "claimant credibility and consistency" during my asylum interpretation work. Whether I was assisting attorneys with interpretations or interviewing them about specific cases, this concept permeated almost every conversation I had with people assisting asylum claimants.

This logic surrounding claimant credibility, however, is not an end of the asylum suffering documentation. Rather, it is as an invitation to investigate the practices and paradoxes that permeate the professional lives of asylum lawyers and make them highly influential actors in the asylum system.[2] Here, my argument builds on anthropological studies of credibility in asylum systems in Western liberal democracies while also broadening the field of inquiry.[3] Scholars have studied asylum credibility through legal accounts given and performed by claimants during asylum-eligibility determination interviews, during corroboration by country condition experts and medical report writers used in the assessment of claims during courtroom hearings, and as a tool for "moral" judgments.[4] The process of establishing or undermining credibility animates much of the asylum trial hearings, although credibility-determining criteria have been generally recognized as highly ambiguous: prosecutors and immigration judges assess credibility on the basis of limited "oral evidence against a range of written evidence, looking behind both, to make an assessment of the motivations of those who produced the evidence" (Kelly 2012, 64–65). At trial hearings in the United Kingdom, Tobias Kelly contends, judges and immigration officials tend not to believe claimants but view them instead as "active agents who are always capable of manipulation" (47). The scenario for asylum cases denied on the basis of credibility that make recourse to the immigration court, for instance, corresponds to just a fraction of cases, which are perceived as wasting the court's time.

These methodological approaches share a tendency to construe the meaning and significance of credibility in asylum primarily as a legal terminology employed by asylum experts, lawyers, and judges to either critique or support an asylum decision. *Credibility*'s meaning is primarily assumed rather than described.

Kelly, for instance, citing one of the plausibility clauses used in an asylum decision in the United Kingdom, writes, "'A story may be plausible and yet may properly be taken as credible; it may be plausible and yet properly not believed'" (2012, 64). Didier Fassin, in his work on contemporary French immigration politics, has highlighted that the question concerning legalization of undocumented migrants is "less about who is *legally* present than who can *legitimately* claim legal status" (2001, 4). Similarly, but with a reverse logic, I propose that contemporary US asylum and interior immigration enforcements are animated less by who can legitimately establish credibility than by who is already assumed not to be credible unless proven otherwise.

The question of credibility meets yet another challenge: not everyone in the asylum industry providing legal representation to claimants is driven by a desire to protect the "genuine refugee." Rather, as Miriam Ticktin has written with respect to French medical teams and humanitarian-aid workers writing medical reports for sans-papiers, some people saw themselves as professionals engaged in simply doing their work and were often "overwhelmed by their [undocumented migrants'] need rather than inspired by it" (2011, 104). Credibility logics employed by pro bono lawyers, as US civilians and private citizens, pose a number of analytic problems. First, how might we develop theories that account for these social actors making decisions for asylum claimants and participating in the contemporary politics of the asylum process, in a variety of ways, employing their decision-making power, without either overemphasizing their actions as forms of (political) consciousness that may not have been part of their reasoning or rationalizing their concerns as genuine, nonpolitical, and misplaced? Second, how might we acknowledge that their professional opinions and job responsibilities—as judges, lawyers, asylum officers, or human rights workers—play a decisive role in the everyday making of "desirable" migrants and management of "credible" claimants?

This involves looking afresh at how credibility in asylum is brought about, forming part of the shared worldview, actions, and liberal politics. For what is understood to be "credibility" and "consistency"—the fundamental basis of the asylum law, which both citizens and noncitizens consent to—is a sociopolitical construction, one that is recognized only through the frame of asylum institutional authority. In this case, credibility and consistency are produced through the discretionary power of the US state–authorized representative—the judge—and nonstate institutional partners and individuals—lawyers and human rights advocates.

While this chapter also stresses the limitations and ambiguities of practices and discourses centered on credibility in asylum, it does not focus on what remains inaccessible or invisible. Rather, I suggest looking at what is made *accessible* in the process and subsequently made meaningful to those advocating for its significance, for emphasis on the ideal of credibility puts legal procedural detail in the spotlight, concealing the ideological agendas supporting it. This resonates with a rarely discussed paradox inherent in the term *credibility* itself. In common speech, *credibility* refers to a situation or a person that is reliable, trustworthy, plausible, and free from inconsistency, much like Lisa's explanation (above). But this increased believability is gained only upon allowing one's credibility to be put to the test, so to speak. In other words, questions of credibility arise out of doubt or suspicion, outright or anticipated, that is seldom acknowledged. In a literal reading, it is paradoxical in the sense that when someone is put to the credibility test, it is already assumed that he/she is untrustworthy. Applied to the case at hand, credibility directs our gaze on details of the here and now, resulting in two parallel outcomes: it obscures larger political agendas and simultaneously takes for granted the ideological positions occupied by social actors (i.e., legal professionals, experts, and practitioners, in this case). In addition to acknowledging the dominant ideologies and power relations that condition abilities to define performances of claimants as credible, I propose conceptualizing credibility that considers actions of and explanations provided by lawyers and human rights advocates, who are not only entrenched within the asylum institutional culture but are also shaping its meaning, operationalizing it, and reinforcing its importance for their clients and interpreters like myself.

In what follows, I do not engage directly with the questions of how the credibility of claimants and their accounts are assessed through rigorous interviews to determine eligibility (Cabot 2013) or what constitutes credibility assessment during courtroom hearings (Good 2011b; Kelly 2012). The concept of "claimant credibility" constitutes a set of ad hoc rules and regulations that confronted my interlocutors. Therefore, I ask what rationales underpin my legal interlocutors' use of the concept of (asylum) credibility in everyday practice and how it reinforces their work and suffering imaginaries in assisting with and representing asylum claimants. How does putting claimant credibility to work enhance my advocates' own credibility and that of the asylum system they are operating under? Thus, this chapter follows how lawyers constructed credibility and imbued it with meaning during the pretrial asylum assistance. Before following their legal rationale, I provide a brief overview of why and how suffering documentation became critical to the logic of claimant credibility in asylum.

ASYLUM AS INTERIOR IMMIGRATION ENFORCEMENT

Crucially, between 1980 and the early 2000s, a new kind of asylum legalization emerged, staggering both in its departure from preceding legislative efforts and in the stark similarities with which it categorized and disciplined the lives of diverse, working-class, racialized migrants. By the beginning of the century, this new kind of asylum became thoroughly naturalized and entrenched in the over-lapping discourse on migrant illegality and deportability, for the asylum process today fits into "the border enforcement strategies that preemptively illegalize mobile people" (De Genova and Tazzioli 2016, 5). How asylum was interpreted and incorporated into US constitutional law and administrative procedure had its own impact on the bureaucratization of asylum in two crucial ways: first, the overlap of legislative and moral discourse staged in the 1980s, involving various actors and institutions, generated a linguistic repertoire—"well-founded fear," "possibility of persecution," "clear probability"—associated with asylum; second, and subsequently, suffering recognition, appropriation, and representation be-came grounds for beginning the legal counsel and advocacy for an individual's "right to asylum." While it may seem commonsensical to assume suffering based on "past persecution" as the legitimate ground to claim refugee status or seek asylum, what this study points out is precisely the naturalization of such legit-imacy and the near impossibility of locating suffering articulation, imaginary, and interpretation outside the asylum institutional frames and development.

Where the asylum debate and advocacy surrounding suffering claimants are concerned, the (old) sanctuary movement of the 1980s led to a politicized and sensationalized controversy. Scholars have explored the possibilities and the limitations of the sanctuary movement's activism because of the centrality of the liberal framework informing the movement's history, politics, and activist vision.[5] My aim is not to expound on the possible merits or potential threats of the liberal politics orienting the sanctuary movements' organizing and mobi-lizing strategies. Rather, it is to highlight the material effect of the construction of US asylum and the consequence for asylum legalization in the post-2001 decade, especially following the 2006 pro-immigrant mass mobilization and the visibility of a *new* (undocumented) migrant workforce. More important perhaps, the asylum advocacy brought together a wide range of legal, political, social, and institutional actors—their collaborative work since has been central to the asylum process.[6]

Asylum institutions, including legal-juridical procedure and documentation, which were generated amid deportation proceedings and criminal prosecutions against religious activists and civilians who had assisted undocumented Central American migrants in filing their asylum claims, not only led to the implementation of asylum into the US constitutional law. They also laid the groundwork for the bolstering of key defenses of reasoning, validity, and ruling surrounding asylum suffering documentation. The logics of asylum within the interior immigration enforcement and legal discursive field of the time mapped the critical terrain and terminologies available to experts and state authorities, including immigration judges and asylum officers, legal experts, and civilian advocates during asylum encounters. This chapter illuminates how these conditions continue to unfold on the ground today—following the logic and explanation related to the concept of "claimant credibility" offered by lawyers and human rights advocates—and the way institutionalized knowledge and legal-juridical procedures are poised to handle what were once disputed, charged for, and rejected based on internal bias, inconsistency, abuse of power, and arbitrariness in asylum.

For asylum seekers and their advocates, legal encounters present a mixture of opportunity and limitation, given the indeterminate scope and interpretive possibilities of the written legal rules, whose experts—from asylum officers and state authorities to lawyers and immigration judges, from human rights activists to religious leaders and private citizens—keep multiplying as their expertise becomes increasingly specific and highly contingent. A rather different understanding of asylum legalization, institutional development, and asylum-seeking mechanisms emerge from the vantage point of these sites as part of the evolving interior immigration enforcement. For asylum constitutes a field of interior immigration enforcement, a field orienting administrative practices, bureaucratic requirements, and institutional parameters aligning with and, in turn, producing legal subjectivities alongside attempts to produce, incorporate, and discipline the low-wage migrant workforce.

Migrant (il)legality, labor, and asylum institutions became so thoroughly entwined in the evolving immigration bureaucracy that legalization in the decades following the sanctuary movement of the 1980s came to be understood as part of suffering narrations, witnessing, and documenting in ways it had not before (Mayo 2012, 1485). The challenge of embedding asylum within wider immigration enforcement involved balancing migration control through deportation and asylum legality, including logistics and reconfiguration of institutions, actors, objects, terminologies, and corresponding systems of governance. One of the asylum eligibility-determination functions, for instance, became the articulation and maintenance of institutional codes, asylum expertise, and civilian advocates assisting claimants with the documentation prior to asylum interviews and courtroom hearings—all acting, one way or another, under the state-promulgated immigration enforcement rules applicable to the then newly incorporated asylum process. The form and content of asylum itself underwent changes: its interpretive possibility expanded, including the frames and parameters for claiming asylum listed in the I-589 form; evocation of seemingly unrelated episodes and events from claimants' working lives becoming critical to credibility-establishing criteria; inconclusive and inconsistent asylum decisions, though recognized as juridical authority and discretionary power of asylum officers or immigration judges, went largely unchallenged and naturalized as legal-juridical arbitrariness, or "refugee roulette" (Ramji-Nogales, Schoenholtz, and Schrag 2007). The superimposition of newly reconfigured asylum requirements occurred in parallel to changes in what specific ways "refugees and asylum seekers" were characterized, by the state, in wider public imagination, as viable political identities. As institutional codification and legislative decisions pertaining to asylum decisions gained prominence, so did the interpretive power and involvement of legal experts, judges, and lawyers, revitalizing and reorganizing the terms of asylum assistance itself.

MAKING A CREDIBLE CLAIM

If, on one end of the spectrum, there are lawyers who strictly adhere to the asylum law as per the UN Convention against Torture's definition of required eligibility of claimants demonstrating "past persecution" and "well-founded fear of future persecution" (UNHCR 1992), then on the other end there are lawyers committed to progressive combinations of interpretive law and liberal politics. These lawyers advocate a broader understanding of immigration law and feel obligated to assist the asylum claimants that they regard as credible and "vulnerable." Indeed, many pro bono lawyers working on Nepali cases that I encountered espoused this liberal political stance. Equally important, why should certain lawyers, many of whom are litigators and have neither expertise nor interest in immigration law, take up the pro bono work of assisting and representing asylum claimants from six months to up to eighteen months or longer, depending on the individual case hearing date, application submission deadlines, and legal bureaucratic responsibilities?

In my initial discussions with asylum lawyers, I followed their rationale about the link between their acute preoccupation with credibility and the massive back-log of asylum cases awaiting legal representation and the all-time high rejections despite proper representation. Mary, a litigator who had previously worked as a clerk in the Ninth Circuit and was then assisting a Nepali claimant, Purnima, admitted that credibility-establishing work was often demanding:

> As a public counsel, I saw many asylum cases—potentially credible ones—that were rejected simply based on the I-589 application forms and without being heard. There was this period of backlog in the asylum system; my colleagues and I would often discuss cases that we had to reject. Private law firms have stepped in and solved the problem of backlog. Providing legal counsel and establishing credibility is making the entire process manageable and efficient. The cases that would have otherwise been overlooked or slipped out of the system are getting legal representation. I value credibility-establishing asylum work, although it is unpaid time and underappreciated investment you are putting in. But it is rewarding work.

Nearly every advocate I encountered took it for granted that claimant credibility is the most critical aspect in asylum assistance and legal representation. This is what Elizabeth, the pro bono lawyer representing Tshering's (whom we will meet in the next chapter) case had to say: "What asylum legal representation does is try to improve the credibility of our clients. When you have so little time to work on asylum cases, given that it is not our area of primary business, I do think about credible claimants whose claims are denied. . . . It is not fair because sometimes it is not even the claimants' fault. It is up to lawyers to extract information carefully from claimants and prepare them thoroughly. As you have seen with Tshering's case the last one and half years."

Still, a claimant's own words, as Lisa elaborated, establish his/her credibility: "The story has to be told in the claimant's own words in whatever language they speak. You see, I can write their stories, but the words and the voices have to be theirs [claimants']. Their native language will be very different from legal terminology or phrases and sentences we write. And it is not easy for claimants to discuss their violent past with strangers like myself. But we have to obtain detailed descriptions before we can make the story coherent and put it together in the affidavit and file the I-589 form." Crafting a credible claim, according to Lisa, depended on making claimants' words visible and legible in the I-589 form. Or, as will be discussed extensively in Tshering's case in the next chapter, it depended on imaginable suffering. Having attended a workshop on asylum law and legal representation and conducted follow-up conversations with human rights and legal experts, I had learned that all pro bono lawyers were trained to empathize with claimants, as they invoked messy and inconsistent accounts of past persecution—especially those they considered "culturally specific" and untranslatable—for the purposes of the asylum documentation and coconstruction of a suffering testimony. That credibility can never be completely unambiguous—it merely manages to push the limits of the corroborative evidence provided by the claimants or his/her legal representative a bit further during hearings without necessarily overturning denied asylum claims (Good 2011b, 4). However, this assumes subscription to a standard narrative surrounding credibility, which is different from what advocates and pro bono lawyers called claimant credibility.

What struck me initially was that many lawyers articulated claimant credibility as the primary goal of all asylum legal counsel and representation, but no single rationale was to be found. They adhered to different practices of what it entailed and how it materialized optimally in asylum. Still, their inability to describe credibility (except as having a "consistent narrative," as Lisa indicated) continued to intrigue me. Elise, a pro bono lawyer in another private law firm, for instance, expressed that even in the extreme and extraordinary case of torture, interpretation of *imaginable* suffering was required to establish credibility. Drawing on the case she had successfully represented, Elise admitted that it is often "difficult to know exactly what part of the claimant's life would ultimately be considered significant at the asylum hearing. In Radha's case, as you saw, everything we did was to go around explaining the nine-year lapse in filing the asylum application." The deadline to file the I-589 form is one year, and the case Elise represented and I provided interpretation for during prep sessions prior to the hearing involved a Nepali female claimant seeking asylum on the basis of political violence she suffered prior to her arrival to the United States.

Elise continued, "Can you believe that it has a one-year deadline, and we were stuck having to make up for nine years of . . . Radha's stay in the US without filing for asylum. I mean, even her marriage to the white American guy was kind of suspicious, since it lasted less than a year. We explained and provided evidence of how she was traumatized by her marriage and was taken advantage of by so many people for the last nine years in the US!" Elise did not find any contradiction in the fact that her claimant was deemed credible and ultimately granted asylum on the basis of her miserable life in the United States and not Nepal. When asked how details of Radha's bad marriage in the United States were considered relevant to her asylum claim, Elise mentioned that it was a combination of Radha's "extraordinary personal circumstances," including mental health problems and depression, and the political changes occurring in Nepal that prevented credibility from being undermined. Since I had attended Radha's case hearing, I asked Elise if the fact that the judge mentioned she had retired American friends living in Nepal had made a difference in her decision. Elise agreed, "Yes, of course. We were extremely fortunate to have had a judge who knew about Nepal and had friends living there. Her cultural knowledge played a key role in going forward with Radha's case and reinforcing her credibility." To Elise then, the fact that Radha's credibility and the judge's decision depended on so-called "cultural knowledge" about Nepal and its ongoing political situation did not seem contradictory or legally irrelevant. Indeed, Radha's was an *extraordinary* case.

More important, the asylum documentation and pretrial sessions provided a platform for producing credibility. Lisa, for instance, had laid out two ground rules at our first meeting. She told both Priya and I that "cases that are usually granted asylum involve severe torture, like capital punishment or FGM." This was meant not only to educate us about what qualified as credible claims but also to encourage and instruct Priya to describe experiences of "harm" and "mistreatment" that involved physical violence that would count under the asylum legal framework of torture. Another important aspect of this process has to do with how lawyers attempt to solicit descriptions of torture and persecution from their clients that fit the needs of the I-589 form. For Lisa's own understanding of what counted as severe "mistreatment" was drawn from her previous experience of successful asylum legal counsel and representation. Her familiarity with asylum representation ultimately convinced Priya (and me) to participate and follow her instruction throughout the asylum interpretation. The overt introduction given to the two questions, especially the emphasis on three to four particular incidents of "harm" to be described in detail with vivid images, gradually led to active involvement on the part of the claimant throughout asylum documentation. Priya was encouraged, even instructed, to consider, among other things, the difficulty of recalling her past.

The asylum documentation sessions were then seen as a set of preliminary work to producing credibility by asylum lawyers. The case of Priya, in particular, illuminates how credibility is managed through structured and careful guidance by Lisa and Jessica to file the I-589 form. Although the dialogical encounter constantly interjected, even suspended, the act of documenting, exposing what Heath Cabot has called "indeterminate effects and potentialities of encounters," it was short-lived (2013, 453). The asylum assistance served a key purpose: the materialization (and transformation) of the I-589 form and the claimant's repeated performance into suffering artifacts to prevent credibility from being, in Lisa's words, "undermined."

Lawyers' rationalization of claimant credibility in the asylum pretrial proceedings and their interactions with claimants further revealed a fixed faith in credibility and its actual manifestations in their enactments. On the one hand, I learned of constant adherence to credibility that existed prior to taking up asylum cases. On the other, I witnessed instances where advocates explained "failed" asylum claims despite being credible. Whether or not claimant credibility was questioned or completely undermined was neither uniform nor unambiguous. Despite the lack of clarity as to what credibility was, lawyers implicitly agreed that in addition to suffering documentation in the I-589 form and affidavit that accompanied it, the claimants' performance of their testimony was an important part of reestablishing the credibility of their claim. The next two subsections examine the ambiguity within and varied explanations offered by lawyers on claimants' performances and their sustained involvement in "credibility-establishing work" and efficiency.

CREDIBILITY PERFORMANCES AND LIMITS

The credibility-establishing or credibility-undermining work animating much of the asylum documentation in the human rights offices and law firms, unanimously recognized by asylum advocates and pro bono lawyers as highly ambiguous and arbitrary, raises urgent questions. For one, these arbitrary practices lay bare the "interpellating function of power" (Gribaldo 2014, 751), where deviations in testimony reveal not so much a claimant's inappropriate performance, corresponding to differential expectations and institutional constraints imposed on him/her. Rather, as we see in Lisa's disciplining of Priya, the possibility of and the limit to (un)imaginable suffering exist throughout the legal-juridical proceeding. Lisa, upon winning Priya's case, responded in the following way:

> LISA: If you are an asylum claimant, you will not know the US asylum law. Most probably, you will not even know English. I do not mean to sound disrespectful toward my clients, but their native language and authentic voice will be very different from legal terminology or phrases and sentences I write as a lawyer. When I take a case, my job is to make sure that

claimant credibility is not simply unquestioned during the hearing, but it is also apparent to the asylum officer or the judge. While it is not easy for clients to discuss their experiences of past persecution in vivid detail, it is equally time-consuming and difficult work for us to obtain that information before we can make their claims coherent, put it all together in the affidavit, fill out the I-589 form, and prep claimants during the witness preparation.

TINA: So, establishing claimant credibility is essential throughout the asylum process, yet the way it works is ultimately how an individual claimant performs at the hearing?

LISA: Yes and no. To establish credibility and make it visible you just have to be a good actor. Take Priya's case, for example. Remember how we all worked hard. How I instructed you not to interpret stoically and Priya to not hold back if she felt like crying? You saw how the officer was moved by her story during the interview? The claimant's performance has to match the demonstrated credibility in the I-589. I knew that Priya would be granted asylum as soon as we exited the asylum office that day.

Lisa described successful asylum cases as those that not only established credibility through consistency but also made it conspicuous through performance during the asylum interview—*you just have to be a good actor.* By explaining asylum outcomes in terms of successfully making credibility visible through performance, Lisa offered a general critique, if unintentionally: asylum judicial procedure might subvert the professed reasons for granting asylum. Lisa indicated that claimant credibility went unquestioned in Priya's case because her compelling performance "moved" the asylum officer. While credible performance resulted in a favorable outcome, it depended on the credibility-establishing work that had been done previously. Indeed, Lisa's offhanded comment about having instructed Priya to perform at the hearing is quite telling: performance, interpreted as credible, cannot influence an asylum decision, but it can potentially counteract an asylum officer's skepticism.

Elizabeth has an understanding of credibility similar to Lisa's in terms of guiding claimants during documentation and witness preparation but is skeptical of overemphasizing claimants' performances. When I asked her about the relationship between credibility and performance, she mentioned that credibility is driven by "more than one aspect of the claim and the affidavit that accompanies it, clearly . . .":

ELIZABETH: I feel that claimants end up teaching us so much about their countries, political situations, and their circumstances. In addition, the field of asylum law is under immigration laws, which keep changing, and if we are not on top of it, the claimants may not receive good legal advice. If you miss something seemingly minor in their narratives during witness preparation and the public prosecutor picks up on that . . . well, you are screwed.

TINA: What about the claimant's performance during the hearing? Does it increase the chances of credibility not being undermined?

ELIZABETH: It is difficult to say. I have seen a case being rejected on plausible performance: this woman was bawling throughout the hearing, and the judge rejected her case, saying it was a bogus claim based on her performance. Yet I still think some lawyers emphasize the importance of witness preparation and spend more time with claimants, so they know exact dates, major episodes related to their claims like the back of their hand. You have to *prepare* them to be questioned about anything and in any order of events in their lives. It is OK to forget dates, but you cannot provide conflicting information . . . the testimony has to match the affidavit. But if you overdo it and their responses become too rehearsed, mechanical, or simply over-the-top and dramatic, then it does not appear authentic; claims may be rejected based on credibility like in the case that I just mentioned.

Elizabeth spoke of claimant credibility without directly referring to the asylum assistance work. She measured credibility in terms of maintaining a balance between the asylum documentation and the witness-testimony preparation: the claimant is not inconsistent or ill prepared but at the same time does not appear "too rehearsed, mechanical . . . over-the-top and dramatic." Excessively dramatic and "over-the-top" performance has the potential to be dismissed as a bogus testimony and can be used against the claimant. In order for the claimant to pass the "credible fear" test, they argued, testimonial content and performance should have the capacity to be interpreted as having "emotional sincerity" without being dismissed as disinterested. At the same time, the prolonged encounter with claimants was one of the critical elements to producing credibility despite not influencing an asylum decision one way or another.

EFFICIENCY AND UNCERTAINTY

Mary, for instance, acknowledged that pro bono lawyers like herself working in private law firms have made the asylum process efficient. Yet the efficiency talk she discussed (above) was a basis to deflect attention to the credibility-establishing work she performed, which encompassed, in her words, "essentially unpaid time and . . . underappreciated investment." This enabled me to make further inquiries:

TINA: What in your opinion consists of credibility-establishing work?

MARY: Are you referring to witness-preparation meetings or external research and collecting of documents for filing asylum claims?

TINA: Everything that you consider credibility work.

MARY: Well, the external research that consists of finding country-condition experts, medical practitioners to corroborate on the cases requires a lot of time, but I would not quite call it hard work. As for asylum documentation, you know how much time we have devoted with each claimant. Just filing the I-589 form and answering the questions on pages 5 and 6 require a minimum of three months. And that is just two pages of the form we are talking about. . . . You have seen the affidavit for Purnima we submitted. To be able to capture vivid details of persecution that claimants suffered so long ago, extract the information carefully that fills holes in their stories for a holistic picture to emerge that can then be translated coherently in a legal statement of two hundred to three hundred pages is a lot of work, wouldn't you say?

TINA: Yes. Absolutely. But is it the time invested during asylum documentation and claimants you represent(ed) that you consider work of establishing credibility?

MARY: Look, although putting time into something that is unpaid is not the same as work, you become well acquainted with your claimant's circumstances. The sad stories they have to repeatedly talk about during asylum interpretation are sometimes difficult to *imagine*. Most lawyers who have worked on asylum realize that claimants have to retell their stories multiple times for the purposes of asylum documentation, and once they are granted asylum, they will never have to talk about it. In that sense, it is difficult as you get to know them personally, and in many cases, you have to establish a relationship until they get asylum.

As my exchange with Mary illustrates, credibility is not necessarily naturalized, or exclusively spoken in relation to advocates' encounters with claimants; it is seen as something inseparable from accounting for, structuring even, claimants' participation in the asylum suffering narration and documentation process. Claimant credibility is further interpreted as a thing in concrete, a sign of careful and interactive preparation, as in the documentation of the I-589 form, accompanied by the claimant's performance. At the same time, the extensive face-to-face engagement and building of relationships with individual clients was recognized as consequential in shaping claimant credibility beyond efficiency. Mary spoke of credibility as something concrete in relation to her experience working on asylum cases in general as "underappreciated work" and "unpaid time." She further emphasized credibility in terms of case variances, individual accounts, and management of it during the merit hearings or asylum interviews.

> TINA: So would you consider this asylum documentation as the only basis
> for establishing credibility? What about the relationship with claimants?
> For instance, in the case of Purnima . . .
>
> [Mary interrupted before I could finish formulating my question.]
>
> MARY: I know what you are getting at. I mean, it is all about ensuring that
> credibility is not questioned during the hearing. Yes, you wonder about
> the arduous process of getting to know your client, their past and current
> experiences, and whether the relationship you have built with them has
> any role to play . . . of course.
>
> TINA: Do you think it affects your work and ways that credibility is then
> established in general, or does it not?
>
> MARY: I think the fact that cases are referred to us by human rights agencies
> means that we are dealing with credible claims already. I mean, the ones
> we represent have credible claims, and the background research about
> their home countries and locating experts pretty much takes care of the
> rest. And, yes, in terms of building a relationship and ensuring claimant
> credibility, a face-to-face interaction has an advantage over a random
> person with a client number.
>
> TINA: So how does close interaction with claimants detract from or rein-
> force credibility?
>
> MARY: That is difficult to answer. You have to be cautious in this line of
> work. Each case is different . . . but the amount of work you put in is the

same. The long hours of gathering information for the I-589 form and interviewing claimants are unpaid. . . . This can go on for several months, and when they are not granted asylum it is disappointing. It is like not being compensated for your work . . .

TINA: And why is it that credible claims get rejected despite having gone through a rigorous screening process at a human rights agency?

MARY: Well, you do not always get a patient judge or a sympathetic asylum officer. The public prosecutor's job, for instance, is to find holes and inconsistencies in the I-589 form and affidavit and ask questions during cross-examination that recast doubt on a claimant's credibility. That is why many credible claims are rejected and hearings are unpredictable. You can never know what part of the claim would be considered significant and relevant in winning the case. So you prepare and advise your clients of uncertainties throughout the asylum process and still work around establishing credibility . . .

TINA: And claims that are denied based on credibility are often irreversible, correct?

[I had, after all, learned to speak like asylum lawyers given my own long-term engagement in the field.]

MARY: Exactly! See, you can be a lawyer too.

TINA: Is that the reason you shifted focus on Purnima's unsuccessful first marriage in Nepal and domestic violence episode, followed by divorce, rather than her initial claim of persecution based on political activism?

MARY: Yes, one of the reasons, for sure. In my experience, claims based on domestic violence are less likely to be rejected outright on the basis of credibility. You were there [immigration court]. You saw how the judge granted Purnima asylum within fifteen minutes of her merit hearing.

Whether the lawyers expressed claimant credibility as work efficiency, as Mary had done, or striking a balance between documentation and performances, as Lisa, Elise, and Elizabeth indicated, they acknowledged that face-to-face encounters with claimants over time formed the basis of a trusting relationship with them, laying bare an important, often unacknowledged, aspect of credibility in asylum. While they explained claimant credibility as something that existed prior to asylum documentation and interpretation sessions in private law firms, they still rationalized credibility in relation to their specific work, including long-drawn-out and intimate engagements with claimants, gauging and correcting their performances to establish and continually reinforce it. Yet none of them readily expressed (or even hinted) their skepticism about either the claimants with whom they worked or the asylum bureaucracy and documentation, even as they witnessed cases being "unfairly" rejected based on credibility. In this sense, pro bono lawyers are critical facilitators, not only translating the legal process to claimants or assisting them but also influencing the asylum institutional structure (and practices therein) of producing and representing credible claimants and shaping what counts as credibility. They are resourceful actors, working within their legal conventions and convictions and shared rationales, sometimes contradictory and oppositional to and, other times, drawing on their knowledge practices regarding credibility while gauging their own credibility.

First, credibility is becoming a key liberal political arena through which asylum claims are being made, assessed, rejected, or approved in Western democracies.[7] A problem arises, however, when scholarly critiques of asylum credibility cannot move beyond liberal politics and inquire how changing dynamics between legalization and temporary migrant subjectivities might have conditioned both "the culture of suspicion" in general and anxiety around asylum expressed through spectacular performances of suffering (Bohmer and Shuman 2018). Rather, as this chapter has shown, credibility in asylum allows powerful social actors to impose their decisions unopposed if not completely unseen. In other words, credibility becomes an indispensable tool employed by private citizens and social actors not only in defining who is or is not a "credible" claimant but also discursively producing, policing, and universalizing the concept of credibility.

Second, credibility is the primary incentive apart from the job responsibility in the broadest sense; its advocates and practitioners benefit from it. Credibility-establishing work, in particular, pertains to experiences and responsibilities described by legal actors in the asylum institution—human rights workers, pro bono lawyers, asylum officers, and judges, as state and nonstate institutional actors connected by the asylum process. Practicing credibility is not the raison d'être for assisting asylum claimants, as my legal interlocutors admitted. Yet it was something repeatedly offered as an explanation of a valuable resource. In professional conversations, public speeches, and asylum interviews, credibility appears at times to be a driving factor, whereas—upon requesting a concrete example or a more detailed experience—most, although not all, of those who have extensively worked with asylum claimants admitted to doing their jobs as efficiently as possible. As a result, the type of investment and work pertaining to asylum is simultaneously emphasized as claimant credibility and job responsibility, constituting an interesting paradox, in which producing credibility toward an object—Form I-589—encompassed adherence to asylum organizational orientation and indeterminate logics.

Yet my Nepali migrant and claimant interlocutors seldom understood or used the legal term *claimant credibility* in the way their legal advocates did. Instead, they explained dimensions of their encounters with asylum documentation, self-reflexively critiqued their own active involvement in the witness preparation in law firms, and commented about ongoing suffering prior to, during, and after asylum interviews at the immigration courtrooms or asylum offices. Interweaving these aspects through ethnographic descriptions presents a more complete picture of Nepali claimants' reflection of their own understanding of asylum legalization. For these cases are neither isolated nor individually specific; rather, they present a glimpse, a dimension, of how asylum seeking is experienced in the everyday, illustrating an observable pattern that has emerged over the last decade.

FOUR / Testimonial Coconstruction in the Asylum Backstage

SUFFERING INTERPRETATIONS

Tshering had applied for asylum in the spring of 2009 within four months of his arrival to New York City on a religious, or R1, visa. Describing himself as a Buddhist monk who had been a target of Maoist violence in Nepal, Tshering filed for asylum on the grounds that he was persecuted for his religious opinions, political activities, and refusal to financially support the Maoist party. Two weeks after his interview with the United States Citizenship and Immigration Services (USCIS) in New York, he received a letter—his asylum application was denied. The asylum officer reviewing his claim was suspicious of his monkhood because he was married and had a child, whereas Buddhist monks are supposed to be celibates. This denial of his asylum application was only the beginning of his protracted entanglement in what I call "the asylum backstage."

By the asylum backstage, I refer to human rights offices and private law firms where claimants and their advocates, interpreters, and lawyers are all interlocked in a face-to-face encounter through multiple, prolonged, and sustained dialogical engagements prior to an asylum interview or a court hearing. The role of coconstructing a suffering testimony in the asylum backstage cannot be emphasized enough: initial screening and eligibility determination of a claimant at a human rights agency for possible access to pro bono legal representation; credibility-establishing meetings in law firms, where lawyers attempt to identify, appraise, and encourage appropriate composure and demeanor from claimants that can correspond to their verbal account and affidavit; and documentation and the witness-preparation sessions, where lawyers prepare claimants as they rehearse and repeatedly deliver testimonies for their hearings and asylum interviews. Here, I take readers into the midst of the asylum institutional spaces to reconsider the relations between *imaginable* suffering and the figure of the claimant-victim orienting much of the asylum backstage work, including advocacy, pro bono legal counsel, and representation. I highlight the subject positioning and imaginative work around suffering that individuals like Tshering, who are constituted by the US state, must do to reconstitute themselves in order to self-present in a particular way within the asylum institutional spaces. If asylum is a type of "construction work" (see Dahlvik 2017), then coconstruction of suffering testimony, as the chapter shows, is its unfinished product.

In tracing this asylum backstage, my argument in this chapter unfolds in two steps. First, I demonstrate that the coconstruction of a claimant's testimony is achieved through a series of overlapping institutional, interpretive, and documentary practices whereby imaginable suffering gradually comes into focus and orients much of the asylum interpretation and the witness preparation. The frames of victimhood, upon which the claimant's account initially depend at the human rights agency, gradually expand as other institutional actors, namely pro bono lawyers, engage in the protracted process. During the asylum interpretation and the witness preparation, the lawyers' effort to frame a singular notion of victimhood either based on past persecution or the likelihood of future persecution becomes difficult, absurd even, as their own frames shift and claimants introduce new ambiguities into their performances of suffering. And yet, despite the work of coconstructing an imaginable suffering testimony and mutually established frame of victimhood in the asylum backstage, the asylum interview or courtroom hearings can reintroduce, as Tshering's courtroom testimony will show, new interpretive frames—the one that is based on credibility sidestepping every question of imaginable suffering.

Second, and subsequently, such a testimonial coconstruction in the backstage depends on and permeates into the claimant's continuous switching between a paradoxical agent and victim throughout the process. In particular, my interpretation of Tshering's case will show how asylum performance, though contingent on multiple subjectivities imposed on him, is ultimately about balancing the dual positioning of oneself as an agent of his suffering claim and as a victim of his circumstances, or "paradoxical victim."[1] Much like Virginia Signorini's (2015) observation about the production of a claimant's memory in asylum narrations, asylum advocates, interpreters, and lawyers all participate in "a coral work" of constructing a suffering testimony in the asylum backstage. The asylum backstage also renders visible a profound inconsistency in crafting a witness testimony, managing politically viable claimant categories, and eliciting imaginable suffering that far exceeds "existing templates of victimhood" (see, for instance, Cabot 2013; Kobelinsky 2015; see also Beneduce 2015). More important, I argue that the type of testimony delivered during asylum trials cannot be seen as an end of investigation into either the category of victimhood or suffering. Rather, during the asylum witness preparation, the overlapping conceptions, interpretations, and imaginations of suffering emerge, displace, and interject all at the same time. Such articulations of suffering testimony in the asylum backstage also necessitate contextualization of how and why certain categories became politically viable and were employed by advocates—human rights experts and lawyers included—in disciplining and preparing claimants for asylum trials in the post-9/11 asylum-seeking process.

An entirely new asylum infrastructure was introduced to the sociopolitical landscape of the United States after the post-9/11 institutionalization of the Department of Homeland Security (DHS). The state violence and the production of migrant criminality were the newest and most significant manifestation of the then newly reestablished "Homeland Security State" power and authority in post-9/11 immigration politics. The effects ranged from restrictive immigration laws and policing of undocumented migrants to the general increase in anti-immigrant sentiments and a heightened sense of "national security" in the public sphere, separating "citizens" from "noncitizens" (Maira 2010; Coutin 2010; Talavera, Nunez-Mchiri, and Heyman 2010). In 2002, the US Department of Justice (DOJ) issued a statement declaring "that local police have an 'inherent authority' to enforce all aspects of immigration law," which had not been the case prior to the government initiatives following the 9/11 events.[2] Capitalizing on this volatile political moment, namely the rhetoric and initiatives introduced by "the war on terror," federal immigration enforcement lobbied to enable local-level enforcement, policing, and criminalization of migrants, which had already begun by the passage of 1986 Immigration Reform and Control Act (IRCA) and the 1996 Illegal Immigration Reform and Immigration Responsibility Act (IIRAIRA).[3] While the adoption of the Refugee Act of 1980 made possible the asylum application provision through the "defensive asylum frame," the passing of the 1996 IIRAIRA enabled the "affirmative asylum frame," including direct filing and submission of the Form I-589 with the USCIS.[4] The IIRAIRA, however, reconfigured the time frame under which a person could apply for asylum: it introduced an application deadline of one year following entry into the country, after which potential claimants were ineligible for asylum legalization unless they proved the existence of "exceptional circumstances" for the delay.[5] Tshering's case exemplifies how affirmative and defensive frames exacerbate claimants' entanglement in the asylum bureaucracy.

The United States spent the post-9/11 decade (2001–10) disbanding the Immigration and Naturalization Services (INS), introducing the Homeland Security Act of 2002, and placing Immigration and Customs Enforcement (ICE) and Customs and Border Protection directly in charge of asylum decisions. In practice, this widened the category of "noncitizens" into types and temporalization of legally documented, noncriminal, and surveilled workers, including refugees and asylum seekers. As a result, protracted asylum legality and prolonged vulnerability developed alongside interior immigration enforcement. Yet the arbitrary granting of asylum at the time appeared a positive relief of liberal governmentality during indiscriminate migrant detention, deportation, and criminalization. Likewise, legal intermediation offered through counsel, advocacy, and representation during asylum documentation, interpretation, and witness preparation has become routinized, with interpreters, lawyers, and claimants each inhabiting their respective roles: as engaging storytellers, active participants, and performers, claimants are expected to provide individualized, if disjointed and incoherent, accounts of suffering; multilingual interpreters, like myself, are invited to do cultural interpretation work while remaining "invisible" for the most part; as aspiring or experienced litigators with general interest in immigration law, pro bono lawyers and human rights workers also perform the multifaceted and layered work of interpretation—deciphering asylum law to successful applicants, transforming applicants into asylum claimants, evoking and directing appropriate responses from claimants to make them legible to immigration judges and asylum officers, crafting lengthy and coherent affidavits from the fragmented life stories of their clients, and coproducing superior suffering testimonies to be delivered by claimants in asylum offices and courtrooms.

VICTIMHOOD BEYOND ASYLUM POLITICS

Scholars have particularly identified the production of suffering in asylum as a politicized process central to understanding the relationship between trauma, testimony, and victimhood (see, for instance, Malkki 1995b; see also Fassin and d'Halluin 2007). Recently, constructivist accounts of suffering among asylum seekers have highlighted the analysis of forms of asylum testimony as a critical issue.[6] Consideration of the production and the uses of written testimony has made it possible to take into account how testimony comes to replace and stand in for asylum seekers' scars, "psychological traces," and victimhood (see Fassin and d'Halluin 2005; see also Ticktin 2006). The production of victimhood works through the process of subjectification, whereby power not only formulates the subject but is also, paradoxically, what "one depend[s] on for existence" (see Butler 1997; see also Foucault 1982). The asylum institutional space is such an instance of power and domination that, during witness preparation particularly, it prescribes a certain framework for victimhood intricately embedded in the process of subjectification.

In his critique of the contemporary institutional management of asylum seekers in Western Europe and North America, Didier Fassin has argued that the ways in which asylum seekers' accounts are recognized to be "true" are inseparable from the restrictive "logics of immigration control" (2013, 39, 47). If the regime governing asylum laws in the United States and Europe in the mid-twentieth century was about distinguishing "asylum seekers" from "refugees," he further insists, the asylum system since the latter half of the twentieth century has been determining, or rather questioning, the legitimacy of claims of asylum from immigrants. Indeed, if, as Fassin argues, these institutions increasingly assess the truth of an asylum claimant's suffering testimony based on its narrative coherence and verifiability, the question then arises: How can we as ethnographers go beyond analyzing asylum testimonials as "suffering narratives" produced by claimants within the constraints of truth regimes? How do fundamentally different conceptions of suffering emerge throughout and beyond the asylum process? Thus, rather than assuming a priori that suffering in asylum necessarily stands in relationship to truth and therein claimants' performances, Fassin's work encourages the following question: What type(s) of suffering need to be consistently overlooked, even dismissed, to ensure the recognition and the validity of suffering in asylum?

While Fassin argues that the increased scrutiny has led asylum seekers to present new evidence of the alleged suffering and "past persecutions"—corroborated by expert professionals, reports of medical practitioners, and country-condition witnesses—my examination of a claimant's articulation of suffering and employment of politically viable categories—"asylum seeker" and "migrant worker"—interchangeably during the asylum backstage enables us to understand that such proliferation of new types of suffering testimonies is not simply occurring within but also outside the asylum sociopolitical context and in an important way.

The institutional norms and asylum documentation, such as the filing of the Form I-589, or testimonies delivered in courtrooms, often makes one overlook practices in the asylum backstage or pretrial proceedings whereby claimants, human rights advocates, pro bono lawyers, and interpreters all participate in the coconstruction of a suffering testimony. In showing how the claimant's testimony is coconstructed prior to reaching the courtrooms or asylum offices, this chapter illuminates the spaces where the victimhood frames are expanded and (re)formatted, ultimately appropriating (un)imaginable suffering. Still, the articulations of suffering and victimhood cannot be seen in terms of a simple opposition to agency during the intermittent moments when claimants "assert existence" in courtrooms through the legible subtleties of resistance marked by silence or speech.[7] Rather, victimhood, in all its complexity, exceeding available institutionalized templates within and outside of the construction of asylum witness testimony, might best be understood in a continuum of learned dispositions, practices, and performances, legal-juridical or otherwise. Approaching suffering as I do in this chapter—as an analytical starting point rather than an end—illuminates specific ways how and in what particular ways "practices not only follow a priori reasoning but justify it in retrospect" (see, for instance, Fassin and Rechtman 2010, 276). The sustained inconsistent frames of victimhood in asylum—the realm of the unimaginable, even of excess imagination, as part of coconstructing suffering testimonies—open up possibilities for tracking its regenerative capacity. These inconsistent frames also allow anthropological questioning of what *else* might be at play when concepts like suffering, without distinct social and institutionalized histories, are reworked in the everyday through specialized (legal-juridical or otherwise) practice and parlance.

When it comes to asylum, the victimhood of the claimant is prefigured by the logics and practices of global interconnections, which by now have become commonsense. Not unlike the asylum eligibility determination, where "the picture of a case" is coproduced, yielding new ways of knowing, reconfiguring, and transforming "dominant images of deservingness, victimhood and vulnerability" (Cabot 2013, 453–54) from within the testimonial frame, human rights advocates and lawyers draw on their own expertise of representing asylum cases to construct suffering testimonies. However, claimants' own suffering accounts are employed as necessary blueprints by their advocates and lawyers for gauging not only the truth about their victimhood but also one that is reproduceable multiple times, albeit with finer modification. This suffering account or blueprint further becomes the core for a particular cultural imagination—a distant, dangerous, and disenchanted situation of people, objects, and events. Through invoking a violent past, the frame of victimhood is given concreteness by freezing time and space. Yet this is not without a purpose: it can conveniently occlude everyday (and equally) *imaginable* suffering intrinsic to the production of the legal field, where the asylum system is one such process, and the kind of symbolic and material violence that the process itself can inflict upon claimants.[8] For instance, the shifting and inconsistent frame(s) of victimhood emerge from seemingly different approaches to and understandings of suffering: a prerequisite to claimants' ability to adequately categorize themselves as suffering victims of their past in Nepal and simultaneously as hardworking migrant-agents able to overcome the hardship of their circumstances. As a result, this self-identification of victimhood entails occupying paradoxical subject positions for claimants, as Tshering's case below will illuminate.

THE ASYLUM BACKSTAGE I: ELIGIBILITY DETERMINATION AT A HUMAN RIGHTS AGENCY

I first met Tshering in the fall of 2009 at a nonprofit human rights agency in Lower Manhattan, where I provided interpretation assistance for many Nepali claimants and their human rights advocates. The human rights agency, through their "Refugee Protection Program," provides asylum-eligibility interviews and screenings of prospective refugees and asylum seekers. Since the political events following September 11, 2001, the program saw a significant increase in the number of asylum applications. As a result, the organization expanded and branched out into various subsidiary programs, including the Asylum Legal Representation Program, placing claimants regarded by the agency to be credible on the path toward institutional and in-depth legal consultation, offering access to pro bono legal representation in private law firms.

Cynthia, a human rights advocate, asked Tshering a rapid series of questions related to his journey to the United States: his home addresses in Nepal, his reasons for seeking asylum, and the specific dates of his encounters with the Maoists in his village in Solukhumbu. She also asked about the details of the events that led Tshering to fear for his life: the repeated death threats and phone calls from the Maoists, his abduction, and his narrow escape to the United States via Kathmandu. Although his initial asylum request was denied based upon the government's determination that he was not a "real" monk, Cynthia did not ask questions related to Tshering's life as a monk in Nepal. Instead, she asked questions that were very specific. Her questions eventually managed to elicit the following account, which I paraphrase based upon my fieldnotes here:

> Tshering is a thirty-eight-year-old male, monastic painter, citizen of Nepal. He should be granted asylum in the United States because the Nepali Maoists persecuted him on account of the following: a) his anti-Maoist political opinions; and b) his membership in the particular group of Buddhist monastic artists. Before his escape to the United States, Mr. Tshering endured repeated persecution and intimidation from the Young Communist League (YCL), the subsidiary political group under the Maoist political party. Mr. Tshering is entitled to asylum in the United States because he has a well-founded fear of further persecution, in the form of physical violence, brutal assault, abduction, and extortion, if returned to Nepal. The Nepali state authorities were and remain unwilling to protect Mr. Tshering, as the Maoists play a significant role in Nepali government and the police turn a blind eye to the Maoists' violence and continued use of torture, extortion, and murder. Since his escape from Kathmandu, Nepal, Mr. Tshering has been living in New York City and holds a steady job at a local grocery store.

Together, Cynthia, Tshering, and I coproduced an account of suffering, and this narrative enabled Tshering to continue with further documentation, interpretation, and witness preparation. Through this coproduced narrative, Cynthia had interpreted Tshering as a claimant with a "credible asylum claim," granting him access to pro bono legal counsel and representation in a private law firm.

Along with Tshering, I, too, was transferred to a law firm for the next two years. For claimants like Tshering, all too often inscribed as credible victims, their victimhood is a critical entry point for receiving further institutional assistance. In this case, securing access to pro bono legal representation and integration in the asylum institutional framework can affect how a claimant's testimony and frame(s) of victimhood would be reworked and the multiple ways his/her suffering account may be reinterpreted, modified, and reimagined. Nonetheless, pro bono legal assistance plays a significant role in increasing the claimant's chance of being on the pathway for potentially obtaining asylum.

THE ASYLUM BACKSTAGE II: CREDIBILITY-ESTABLISHING MEETINGS AT THE PRIVATE LAW FIRM

At this stage of the asylum-seeking process, the claimant who can position himself/herself into categories of credible victim and migrant-agent interchangeably directs much of the asylum interpretation and witness preparation. If the asylum backstage I, in a human rights agency, is where the drama begins, this is where the plot thickens. The claimant is instructed to narrate his account of suffering repeatedly—where fragmentary narrations of decontextualized images convert into a coherent narrative, silences transform into speech acts and soliloquies, disengagement slips into momentary outbursts, past runs parallel to the present, and (mis)interpretive possibilities of what counts as persecution enter and exit.

In the early afternoon of cold December 2009, I met Tshering outside the private law firm, where his case had been transferred. As we made our way into the lobby of the law firm, two lawyers received us and introduced themselves as Tshering's lawyers. The four of us took an elevator, and Tshering and I were taken to a spacious, nicely lit conference room on the thirty-third floor. Immediately after we took our seats, the lawyers began speaking about why they had decided to take Tshering's case.

"We believe that the fear Mr. Lama has is based on the well-founded fear of being persecuted if returned to Nepal," Elizabeth, who introduced herself as the primary counselor, assured Tshering. Her colleague and cocounselor, Michelle, nodded in agreement. By now, I had become somewhat familiar with the official declaration that every lawyer working on asylum cases must reiterate, almost in the precise tone delivered by Elizabeth—the "'well-founded fear of being persecuted.'" The lawyers then explained the lengthy process that would involve putting together Tshering's asylum file—the I-589 form, client affidavit, expert-witness affidavits, country condition reports, and corroborating documents, including letters he received from his wife describing the dangerous situation for his family in Nepal. Michelle mentioned that they had started searching for expert witnesses right away, especially an expert on Buddhism, even an anthropologist, who can attest to Tshering's monkhood, and a medical practitioner/psychologist to interview him and take photographs of his bodily injuries that he sustained as a result of the Maoist attack.

Elizabeth interrupted, "However, it may be difficult for Tshering to speak up and express his experience to a psychologist." She continued, "The fact is that Tshering is stoic like my Tibetan clients seeking asylum on the basis of religious persecution; it is generally difficult to express emotions or share traumatic pasts with others for them. They are Tibetan monks and tend not to be transparent and expressive if and when they speak of their feelings."

Having done their homework on Buddhist religious practices, the lawyers began their interrogation enthusiastically. "What specific sect of Buddhism do you belong to in Kathmandu?" asked Elizabeth. I interpreted for Tshering, who seemed both confused and lost, as I was. Then Michelle explained that the Dalai Lama belonged to a particular sect of Buddhism, which is different from the one Tshering belonged to. After Michelle clarified her question, Tshering spoke for almost half an hour, giving a detailed explanation of one of the four sects of Buddhism he belonged to—Nyngma-pa.

"Did neighbors in your village in Nepal recognize your family—your father and grandfather—as lamas?" Elizabeth continued with her investigation.

"We are all lamas. But they call us monks," Tshering kept insisting, as I kept interpreting on his behalf, word for word, without offering my interpretation of his words and phrases, and looking for cohesiveness in his sentences.

"Actually, my father used to tell me about his estranged sister—my aunt—who became a nun at a very young age. She did not eat meat and actually left the house to go live in the forest for many years. She became a hermit and was never married or interested in the material world." Tshering's eyes brightened with excitement. "She was not quite like the rest of the family members. I heard this story many times from my grandfather and father. She was the *real* lama, you know." He paused and appeared to be miles away, entangled in his own thought.

These initial suffering interpretation and documentation sessions at the law firm were centered on reestablishing the credibility of Tshering's case through his monkhood. Tshering painstakingly explained that the sect he belonged to often encouraged Buddhist monks to have families. While his father and grandfather were both monks in his natal village in northeast Nepal, who taught Buddhist scriptures and performed various religious ceremonies and death rites for people, Tshering was a monastic painter and earned his living by making *thangka* paintings and working at a monastery in Kathmandu. The same monastery helped him apply for a religious visa to travel to the United States. Moreover, Tshering's last name, Lama—*lama* in colloquial Nepali also means monk—added to further confusion, which, according to the lawyers, made his claims of "past persecution" implausible and undermined his credibility.

Elizabeth explained that one of the expert witnesses on Buddhism that they had in mind for the case would provide an expert-witness report on the "actual" difference between *lama* and *monk*, but she wanted to learn what Tshering knew, if anything, about the difference from a layman's perspective. The two lawyers then assured Tshering that they would rectify the error made in his initial asylum interview: Tshering's inability to explain this difference in English, in the absence of an expert-witness report and testimony, had put him at a disadvantage. They emphasized, however, that Tshering's own words and lay understanding of the difference still needed to be included in his asylum application and during witness preparation for possible cross-examination questions prior his merit hearing, which was not scheduled for another two years. It is important to note that this "lay understanding," while still being considered critical background to Tshering's suffering testimony, would eventually be dropped during the subsequent interpretation meetings in the private law firm.

During this early stage of the interpretation session, Tshering recounted a general story about the Maoists' attack. As a religious and monastic artist, Tshering said that he and his family supported the monarchy in Nepal and not the Maoist party, politically and ideologically. He would explain that during the "people's war in Nepal" in the 1990s, his village was attacked by the Maoists, resulting in the death of over two thousand people in 2004. This, he reminded the lawyers, was a widely acknowledged and known fact in Nepali history. Taking out the newspaper from his bag and pointing to a picture, Tshering would start talking about the magnitude of the attack in his village. While he and I would be talking, lawyers often redirected him through me to provide a specific background of his earlier days in the village. They asked him, again and again, to stick to his *own* subjective experience of persecution and not resort to the "generally known facts" about the attack published in the media.

Within six months into the asylum documentation and interpretation, Tshering was disciplined by his pro bono lawyers into a different type of claimant subject: the one that aligned with his lawyers' understanding of a credible claimant with an ability to overturn his misfortunate past and redirect his new life as an industrious and potentially valuable, if temporary, legal migrant in the United States. Likewise, steps to achieving an agreeable template for victimhood were prolonged as multiple interpretations of suffering intervened during those stages. The reconstruction of Tshering's testimony was different from the time we had met at the human rights agency.

Indeed, when interpreting for claimants like Tshering and their lawyers, I was often struck by the peculiarity of inhabiting the same space as people with starkly different, even competing, worldviews and imaginations. In the midst of my translations, I noticed lawyers' fascination with the details of violence experienced by claimants, and I observed lawyers' discomfort when claimants settled into abrupt silences as they recounted traumatic events. Although claimants and I would be the ones speaking and interpreting, taking turns quite naturally, the lawyers' rhythmic scribbling in their notepads directed our three-way conversations. The moment the scribbling stopped, the lawyer could no longer imagine the claimant's suffering, and our conversation would grind to a halt. It was often an out-of-body experience in more ways than I can accurately capture here.

Interpretable only through claimants' words was a world inaccessible to their lawyers and me. Yet, like Tshering, I would be guided by lawyers' imaginations of suffering, imperfectly accessible to me and the claimant. Sitting there before the asylum claimant and lawyers, the thing palpable was the active imagination, mediated by intense engagement during the coconstruction of a suffering testimony. A type of suffering evolving within these asylum spaces of encounter and intermediation was laden with parallel, uninterpretable, competing, and sometimes mutually incompatible opinions and social worlds inhabited by people with differently situated experience, stake, and urgency. The asylum interpretation and witness-preparation sessions resulting in testimonial coconstruction prior to asylum hearings—critical elements in the asylum-seeking process—were mediated by imaginable suffering, or rather *imaginability*, whether of physical violence or of emotional trauma experienced in a distant past and place that can establish the frame of victimhood, ensuring, in turn, the active and agentive participation of the claimant in the process of his own subjectification. Moreover, this frame relies on arbitrariness, ambiguities, and continued misinterpretation within, and not necessarily outside, the legal institutional terms of engagements, namely "facts," "evidence," and "truths."

Recorded below is one of the many interpretation sessions in which I participated with/for Tshering at the law firm.

THE ASYLUM BACKSTAGE III: RECONSTRUCTING A SUFFERING TESTIMONY, MARCH 2010

As we entered through the large tinted glass doors in the law office, one of the three pro bono lawyers working on Tshering's asylum greeted us. "How are you doing, Tshering?" she inquired, as always, before beginning the asylum interview session.

"Bahini, dherai gaharo po hundo rahecha. Ghar chodeko jhandai teen barsa bhaisakyo. Budhi ra nani ko ta dherai samjhana aunchan." (Sister, things are quite difficult. It has been almost three years since I left home. I miss my wife and daughter a lot.) Tshering responded in a muffled voice to what was obviously a polite greeting indicating formality that is not intended to evoke a detailed, let alone emotional, response.

"I am doing fine," I interpreted rather plainly.

The lawyers exchanged silent glances; all of them turned toward me, indicating their apparent dissatisfaction with my short, abrupt, and inadequate interpretation of Tshering's rather lengthy response.

"What Tshering said has nothing to do with either his asylum claims or his well-being," I clarified. For the last two years I had been interpreting for Tshering, I was instructed (by the lawyers) not to let Tshering wander off and discuss what would be considered *irrelevant* to his asylum claim. Naturally, I had come to assume the role of an interpretation police officer. I had also become a professional interpreter: I was now trained to do what I couldn't do two years ago—to remove the so-called *irrelevant*, and unnecessary, descriptions from the asylum claim.

The lawyers seemed quite content with my (added) explanation, which still had *nothing* to do with Tshering's actual response. Yet somehow it did not seem to matter. The lawyers went on to explain to me, to be interpreted to Tshering, the status of his case and their continued effort in contacting and ultimately gathering supporting documents, including reports by medical experts and country experts.

Sitting next to me, Tshering had a vacant look on his face. Both he and I had been sitting in the law office on the thirty-third floor of a Midtown Manhattan office building for almost an hour. While waiting in the lobby earlier, Tshering had shared with me his long and difficult work schedule that started every morning at 3:00 a.m. and ended around noon. He worked as a deliveryman, driving a truck and delivering baked goods for grocery stores in the Upper West Side and Midtown, not far from the law office where we were having our meeting.

He had described to me how the buildings and the neighborhood looked starkly different during his work hours. He worked in a restaurant nearby in the evenings and had mentioned to me, on several occasions, how difficult it was to take days off on short notice to attend these meetings. He was worried that he would be fired any day.

I wondered if the lawyers noticed the vacuous look that Tshering had the entire time, but I also feared that his expressionless face could be interpreted as him not taking the interview seriously.

"OK, let's just move on to our asylum topic for today," one of the lawyers announced. "Now tell us again what happened to you, Tshering, in the fall of 1999." Trying my best to imitate the lawyer's solemn voice, I interpreted for Tshering. He looked at me and paused for few seconds before responding. "I think I started painting for the Gumba [Buddhist monastery] in Boudha, Kathmandu," he said cheerfully, reclining back in his chair.

The lawyer seemed surprised by Tshering's response. She looked at her senior colleagues, seated adjacent to her, who exchanged silent glances. Judging from their predictable facial expressions, I elaborated the question in Nepali for Tshering: "Hoina dai, 1999 ma Maobadi tapain ko buwa-aama ko ghar ma pahilo choti aayeko hoina ra?" (No, older brother, didn't the Maoists visit your parents' house for the first time in 1999?) Obviously, I was way too familiar with his story. All of us were. The latest version of the testimony was circulated a few weeks before the meeting.

"Ohh tyo . . . ho ta ni! Maobadi gharma aye ani aama-buwa lai dhamki diye" (Oh that . . . yes that's true! Maoists came to my parents' house and threatened them), Tshering admitted, as though it was some kind of trick question, when all along it was his story from which the lawyers had been asking questions for half a year. The lawyers were trying to fill in the gaps in Tshering's testimony with detailed descriptions and vivid images and ensure the consistency and flow of his suffering narrative before filing the final version of the affidavit to the immigration court. His hearing was scheduled to take place in a couple of weeks.

I looked at Tshering, indicating that the lawyers were expecting him to say more in response to that question.

"Aama-buwa ko man ma dar pasyo ni tyas pachi ta. . . ." (Literally: Fear entered into my mom and dad's hearts after that. . . .) As he spoke these words, his face turned red, as though he was somehow being transported back into Solukhumbu village in Nepal. I was, however, relieved to see that Tshering had finally caught up with (the game of) invoking the right kind of sentiment demanded by that specific question at the interview. Yet his eyes failed to express the mixture of moderate shock and excitement that his voice seemed to be communicating; they simply remained dazed, refusing to collaborate.

Such seemingly disengaged demeanor shown by Tshering at this early stage of the asylum interpretation would eventually get straightened out in the later round of the witness-preparation procedure. Still Tshering's nonverbal cues during his asylum interpretation sessions would often manage to create what could be interpreted as an emotionally detached ambiance in the conference room. It was as if all of us—Tshering and his engaged listeners and active participants—had been confronted with the absolute boundary of our own suffering imaginaries and interpretive frames of victimhood. The severity of the subject—the Maoists' first visit to Tshering's parents' house—seemed to be undermined, if temporarily, by the way he was (and was not) communicating.

Noticing that Tshering and I, his interpreter, appeared disengaged from the serious matter under discussion, the senior counselor in charge of the case, Elizabeth, leaned forward. Clearing her throat, she interjected: "OK, perhaps we should move on to the part where you suffered violence in the hands of Maoists in Kathmandu then."

I interpreted for Tshering, trying to translate the perceived urgency of the matter at hand. Tshering suddenly fixed his composure, sat upright, and tried to stay alert.

"Can you please describe in detail the pain you suffered and continue to suffer as a result of the Maoist attack in November 2004?" Elizabeth asked.

This time I interpreted for Tshering, without adding my own explanation. For he and I both knew it was the most important part of his asylum claim—the part with which he was most familiar. He had not only learned to describe the violence and pain he suffered in vivid detail but had also mastered the art of successfully framing his experience within the larger context of his asylum narrative.

Tshering began (re)telling his story, starting with the Maoists' initial visit to his parents' house in Solukhumbu in 1999, followed by his first encounter with the Maoists in 2001, leading to the attack in Kathmandu in 2004. He provided background with vivid images and description and offered a nice chronological order to every incident: starting with the Maoist visit to the parents' home, the repeated threats he received over the phone and in letters, and the final warning from the Young Communist League, followed by their visit to his place in Boudha. He painstakingly described the beatings he received: the pain he suffered in his back, chest, arms, and right hand as a result of this life-threatening attack. He unbuttoned his shirt and started pointing to all the scars and injuries on his chest and leg, where Maoists stomped on him and hit him with a gun.

While buttoning his shirt, he started talking, or rather complaining, about a severe, ongoing pain in his knee and the left foot. "Maile katti doctor lai dekhai saken yahan, tara ghooda dukne ta kaam hoina jhan badhto po rahecha. Maile pain killer haru pani liyen, bengay lagaayen dukheko thaaunma, ra ani aru dherai aushadi haru pani liyen doctor le diyeko. Khoi kehi asar bhayena tara. . . ." He talked for almost twenty minutes about his suffering and fell silent in the middle of the sentence.

I interpreted for the lawyers, word for word, and in the same manner Tshering described his intense pain: "I have gone to doctors many times, but instead of diminishing, the pain in my knee keeps intensifying. I have taken painkillers, applied ointment to the sore parts, and taken medications prescribed by the doctor. Well, nothing seems to have any effect. . . ." As I uttered these sentences, I realized this was new suffering information he was giving us.

The lawyers were as surprised by this unsolicited information as I was. One of them asked for clarification. "So all this pain is from the Maoist attack in November 2004 in Kathmandu?"

I had barely finished interpreting the question into Nepali when Tshering started to laugh. "Oh no, not the severe knee pain that I have had for so long. It is from working at the restaurant here for the last two years, having to stand on my feet every day," he and I both nonchalantly responded. I joined Tshering in his laughter until we both realized that our laughter was out of place; the lawyers started sifting through their notes, looking concerned and utterly confused.

Tshering, however, seemed wistful, lost in his own thought. Instead of talking about his past persecution and the Maoist attack—the subject matter of his asylum interview—he started telling me how he was suffering in America. "Khai ke garne bahini, ma ta America aayera laato bhayen. Yeti dherai barsa America basi saken, English ta birsen jastai lagcha. Baru Kathmandu mai English bolin thiyo school maa padaaun da. Yahan ta English ko naam ma bolne nai 'Sir, would you like chicken tikka masala or chicken korma?' Khai kaahan ko English bolnu ho America ma? Yahan arkai dukkha paincha. . . ." (It is really strange, but I feel like I have become dumber now that I have lived in America. I used to understand some English back home when I taught in a school in Kathmandu. I speak less and less English here. All I have to say now is "Sir, would you like chicken tikka masala or chicken korma?" How (or when) do I get to speak English in America? Here, there is a different kind of suffering. . . .)

By this point, I had stopped interpreting altogether. I just let him talk. In a way, I failed to redirect Tshering from wandering off and prevent him from volunteering *irrelevant* information. In retrospect, I wonder if I could have possibly done anything. He had decided to change the subject abruptly and for no particular reason. Perhaps, for Tshering, his past experiences in Nepal and current circumstances were not disconnected. Or perhaps he deliberately decided to stop talking about his past and focus on the present. Or perhaps he was simply exhausted.

As soon as he stopped talking about his asylum suffering story, I stopped being an interpreter. The interview ended early that day. The lawyers instructed Tshering to study the Nepali version of his affidavit for the upcoming interview, particularly the sections that discussed the Maoist attack and his suffering related to those incidents. The lawyers mentioned that the interview did not go as well as they had hoped for and that we would revisit the questions that Tshering did not adequately answer.

I communicated the lawyers' dissatisfaction to Tshering, who looked relieved that the meeting had come to an end for the day. We were given a new date and time for the next interview.

Tshering and I left the law office to get coffee and continued talking about things *irrelevant* to his asylum claims.

THE ASYLUM BACKSTAGE IV:
WITNESS-TESTIMONY PREPARATION, MAY 2011

Nearly two years into the witness preparation and two months prior to his merit hearing, lawyers still referenced Tshering's religious background as a Buddhist monastic artist in Nepal, but only to inquire about his involvement with religious and political teachings in the Nepali migrant community in New York City. The question of whether he was or was not a monk had somehow faded into the background of his testimony for reasons not known to me. Specific questions about his religious past ("What specific sect of Buddhism did you belong to in Nepal?") were replaced by generic questions about his life and work in New York ("How have you been supporting yourself in the US since your arrival? Have you been filing taxes the last two years you have been in the country and working?"). The lawyers' inquiry into Tshering's present life and employment in relation to his profession in Nepal expanded the parameters of the testimony to be delivered in court. As a claimant waiting for his asylum decision for two years, his current life and work were increasingly disrupting the narration of his life and experience related to "past persecution" in Nepal. However, I judged from my interviews with the lawyers that they had expected Tshering's description of his current work life to project a temporal argument onto his asylum claim: he would continue to be an economically productive member of society, an example of overcoming hardship and "extraordinary circumstance." The emphasis on Tshering's life in the United States meant that the lawyers somehow expected this to intervene in the new testimony and to be reproduced with sufficient detail.

During the witness preparation, Tshering, overall, *did* conform to the lawyers' expectation of a credible claimant's disposition: He was alert and became visibly sad, showing "emotional sincerity," when asked about his home and family in Nepal. His eyes lit up while speaking of his youthful days working as a monastic painter in Kathmandu. However, he seemed disengaged while recounting his encounter with Maoist rebels. His expressionless face, uncommunicative eyes, and stoic demeanor while demonstrating bodily scars and injuries from "past persecution"—the most critical element of his testimony—delivered in Nepali, nonetheless, managed to communicate distant yet adequate shock. The vivid description of the persecution and the sustained back injury were delivered in a nonchalant manner. Yet he would go into greater detail about his pain in the leg and work in the United States, driving a truck and working in the grocery store—information previously deemed peripheral to his original claim. It became evidence of how Tshering brought his previous, raw account of suffering in line with the lawyers' newly emphasized criteria of the claimant's capacity to overcome "extraordinary circumstances." Thus, despite visibly distant mannerisms during a portion of his responses, Tshering, according to his lawyers, could still be identified as a credible claimant.

Ironically, the reason for his asylum denial—the failure to establish his religious identity as a Buddhist monk in a way that linked to the mainstream characterization in the American imagination—was no longer considered central to the newly reconstructed suffering testimony. One of the reasons, I would later learn, was Michelle's increasing skepticism regarding foregrounding Tshering's monkhood, given the limited religious activities he was able to conduct since coming to the United States, and she instead proposed to pursue a different line of credibility-establishing criteria—the hardworking migrant-agent. More important, the last two years of the asylum interpretation and the witness preparation was akin to a training ground that disciplined him—through the testimony constructed in collaboration with his lawyers—on how to properly present himself to the court as a claimant capable of overcoming extraordinary past circumstances. He had shown signs of discomfort in having to undress in front of people previously. Two years into the witness preparation, he had trained himself to become familiar with not only referring to the prepared testimony but also corroborating it by showing bodily scars, or, in the words of his lawyers, "evidence of past persecution."

Consequently, the testimony to be given in court now emphasized two kinds of evidence concurrently: evidence of "past persecution" and potential for future productivity, allowing Tshering to be interpreted as a credible, nonreligious, and nonpolitical claimant. If the credibility of Tshering's testimony depended on proper self-presentation as a Buddhist monk previously, it now depended on appropriate yet malleable embodiment and enactment of victimhood that required him staging himself as a claimant-agent with "well-founded fear of future persecution" and simultaneously as one capable of overcoming "extraordinary circumstances."

The witness testimony takes center stage in courtroom hearings. During asylum trials, prosecutors routinely seek to undermine claimants' testimony during cross-examination. The method applied often undermines evidence, as happens with the necessity to balance the testimony with "fact-finding" criteria to weigh evidence provided from both parties in the juridical field. Here, the claimant is asked to provide evidence that can sufficiently meet the public prosecutor's and judge's imaginations of suffering, victimhood, and expectation of what counts as logical prevention of the said persecution being repeated in the future. Tshering's asylum trial below elucidates this intertwining logic.

TESTIMONY DELIVERY, THE COURTROOM HEARING, AUGUST 2011

Tshering sits to the judge's left on a raised platform, behind a long wooden table that is turned at an angle so the audience can see him. Seated to his left are the court-appointed interpreter and the lawyers representing him. They each have a microphone attached to the table. Seated across from him at the opposite end of the platform (and turned halfway toward the audience) is the public prosecutor, also seated behind a microphone. Rising between these two tables, at the front wall of the platform, is the judge's table on a raised stage.

Tshering has known about his merit hearing for at least eight months now. His lawyers impressed upon him the absolute importance of this day. He was made aware that the past two years of documentation and witness preparations would all culminate in establishing his credibility in court through his oral testimony today. He was repeatedly told that consistency and coherence needed to be reflected in his testimony and that his performance must contribute to the judge's imagination of his past persecution.

One of the lawyers turns to the claimant and proceeds with background questions. Where was he born and where did he grow up in Nepal? What did he do for a living and how did he support his family? How would he describe his life in Nepal before the Maoists waged the people's war against the Nepali state? Having been thoroughly prepared, going over these questions and answers during the witness preparation, he responds with confidence. He had been properly instructed not to divert from the subject of his asylum claim and to answer questions coherently. The lawyers had repeatedly emphasized that he should appear natural yet confident, and his courtroom testimony should appear not "too rehearsed" despite having rehearsed the last two weeks.

When asked about his family, he is not to discuss his father's occupation or siblings' lives but only his immediate family left in Nepal—wife and child—regardless of the fact that he sends money home and supports them. Similarly, when asked to describe his life before the Maoist conflict in Nepal, he should start out giving the general atmosphere in his neighborhood, community, and town and elaborate on his personal experience. He was to reveal only those activities of his past leading up to his first encounter with Maoists.

The direct examination takes longer than a regular inquiry mainly because of the four-way mediation: the counselor asks the question, the interpreter translates from English into Nepali, the claimant responds in Nepali, and the interpreter translates back into English to the judge. Half an hour into the direct examination, the judge grows impatient. He interrupts and tells the counselor he can jump to the part about why his claimant is seeking asylum so as not to waste the court's time. As per the judge's instruction, the lawyer shifts to the topic of his client's asylum claim: experience of his past persecution, repeated death threats from Maoists that culminated into a life-threatening physical attack from which he narrowly escaped.

The lawyer starts asking open-ended questions, jumping ten years later into his client's past—the initial encounter with Maoists. Could he describe what happened to him the fateful night of November 2004 when he was home with his family? He closes his eyes and nods his head. There is a complete silence except for the court clerk, seated to the judge's right, typing away on her laptop. The audience waits. The claimant starts telling his story of the encounter with Maoists, who, after forcefully entering his house, hit him in his legs and head and dragged him outside his house at gunpoint. They made him walk two hours through the back alleys of his neighborhood and on a mountainous road, finally arriving at a desolate area in a forest. He could see only a small teahouse from afar. For the next twenty minutes, the claimant narrates the physical violence in a chronological order: the Maoists brought him to a desolate place, kept hitting him, and when he resisted they stomped on his leg and hit him with a gun in the back of his head—a blow that made him lose consciousness for two hours. The Maoists left him that day with a warning. He spends another ten minutes speaking of the back and head injuries he sustains as a result of the particular attack.

He finishes the story, and the judge asks the prosecutor to begin cross-examination. The prosecutor is interested not in Tshering's account of persecution, but in finding holes in his oral testimony. He begins by asking the claimant whether, if he could see a teahouse from where the Maoists allegedly took him, the area was not completely desolate after all? If he could see the teahouse, then that meant people in that teahouse could have also seen him being attacked. Why did he not shout for help? Why did he say that there was nobody around that could have seen him or rescued him?

The lawyer objects to the prosecutor's method of cross-examination, which progressively becomes aggressive toward his client. He interjects that his claimant already mentioned the teahouse was visible only from afar. The judge, who had seemed somewhat disengaged, leans forward and overrules the objection and allows the prosecutor to continue. The prosecutor, in turn, continues finding problems with the order in which Tshering recounted his story. He asks him whether the Maoists physically attacked him before or after he refused to follow their instructions. Tshering hesitates but confirms that it was, indeed, after he refused to obey that the Maoists started hitting him. The prosecutor turns to his notes in front of him and points out that there is no mention of struggle or physical attack until after the claimant was taken to the desolate area, according to the affidavit, and that Tshering hesitated in his oral testimony. Another forty minutes is spent in the cross-examination.

By this time, the judge expresses his annoyance. He announces that the hearing has unexpectedly taken half a day and he has to attend to two other hearings, one of which was supposed to have taken place an hour ago. He calls the counselors to approach his desk and asks them if they could reach a settlement. The prosecutor refuses to settle the case with the granting of the "withholding of removal" status and not asylum. The judge reschedules the rest of the hearing for another date and time.

The lawyers appear flustered. Tshering, however, seems calm with utter disbelief and confusion about what just happened. How, after two years of (re)narrating the same story over and over, could it be that the only fact that got the prosecutor and the judge excited was the description of a teahouse (and the scenario that ensued: Could he see the teahouse from where he was taken by Maoists? Could he not see people there and have shouted for help? Surely someone in the teahouse would have come to his rescue). The seemingly tangential detail became a turning point in the trial—it managed to become larger than, and the crux of, either his claim or victimhood. Or, rather, the teahouse was the only *imaginable* string on which his asylum decision hung.

At this point, my own imaginations turn a bit more toward the fantastic, and I wait and wonder if the judge would demand either the Maoists in Nepal to verify said location of Tshering's abduction or the owner of said teahouse to testify in the court. I also imagine Tshering's lawyers seeking an additional psychiatrist's report confirming the likelihood of hallucination that their client suffered as a result of the blow to his head during abduction. My imagination, however, is interrupted by a sigh of relief let out by the DA on the other end of the courtroom. I notice the performance lapse between his straight face and contented eyes. Perhaps content that he might have prevented an imposter—a migrant—from remaining in the United States, doing his job, and securing the "homeland." The judge, however, looked neither relieved nor content. Grumbling on his way out, he directed the court clerk to deliver the new hearing date and time to Tshering's lawyers.

UNIMAGINABLE SUFFERING

The courtroom scene and Tshering's inconclusive testimony bring us back to the initial encounters with which I began this chapter—the asylum-credibility determination interview at the human rights agency and the transfer of Tshering to the private law firm shortly thereafter, where Tshering and his lawyers reconstructed his account of suffering to fit into an imaginable and credible suffering testimony to be delivered in the courtroom. While the initial interpretation routine seemed critical in organizing and managing the structure of legal intermediation and the subsequent witness-preparation sessions, Tshering's lawyers had not shown disappointment in nor disapproval of his suffering performance throughout the testimonial reconstruction in the law firm. One possible explanation for their own stoic demeanor is that imaginable suffering, above other things, was always factored in to anticipate judicial arbitrariness. While Tshering's participation in cultivating certain norms, behaviors, and performances was significant throughout the interpretation meetings, the asylum backstage produced and, in turn, was sustained by lawyers' inconsistent victimhood frames. The witness preparation in the asylum backstage provided a necessary groundwork, where Tshering's lawyers invested in reconfiguring victimhood that they deemed *imaginable* yet malleable enough for Tshering to align his performance with the reconstructed testimony to be ultimately delivered in the courtroom.

Yet the bizarre reception and outcome of Tshering's courtroom testimony was a result of neither narrative incoherence nor variation in the style of his speech and performance. Rather, the indeterminate outcome of the trial shows how insertion and normalization, authorization even, of asylum victimhood can go outside the realm of any particular, *imaginable*, suffering and its testimonial coconstruction. Tshering's case is not simply about the issue of "decontextualized" testimony due to narrative inequality in courtroom hearings and the subsequent authoritative "recontextualization" of suffering accounts (see, for instance, Jacquemet 2009; Blommaert 2001). It is also about interpretive, inconsistent, and multiple frames of victimhood disrupting and disabling a singular notion of suffering in asylum, despite the socio-legally and institutionally prescribed form or content. What is at stake in asylum then is not simply the problem of institutional transformation and translating of a migrant or claimant's subjective experience.[9] Rather, the stakes are how these contradictory logics unfold counterintuitively: the claim- ant testimony is coconstructed during the documentation, interpretation, and witness preparation, whereby the testimony is formatted to be credibility-proof as a claimant learns to self-identify himself/herself as a credible victim and an agent, simultaneously. As Tshering's case shows, reliance on a particular verbal or performative measure of victimhood or agency became increasingly unsustainable, ironically, with the progression of his own entanglement in the asylum interpretation and the witness-preparation sessions. Furthermore, his recognition as a credible claimant—and, above all, his suffering testimony—was open to multiple reinterpretations and imaginations, yet it ultimately remained *unimaginable* in the court. The emphasis on the "teahouse," as a concrete effect of juridical arbitrariness, altogether displaced questions of his testimony's legit- imacy or any meaning attached to a particular understanding of victimhood.

Moreover, the credibility of Tshering's case initially based on monkhood, which the human rights advocate and lawyers had pointed out to be the strongest basis of his asylum claim, was dropped by his lawyers as part of the legal strategy. In replacing the question of monkhood with Tshering's everyday life and work in the city, his identity as a monastic artist and painter was also dislocated, though it never disappeared completely. The witness testimony delivered in the court in no way highlighted Tshering's monkhood identity. Instead, it emphasized Tshering's industriousness and active membership in his adopted homeland despite past hardship and persecution, which his lawyers insisted would be more relevant but became intangible, even irrelevant, in the court. Furthermore, both the testament to his diligence and the alleged persecution not only were overlooked but also completely receded in the background, bringing into focus the previously unimagined elements in his testimony. In other words, the same inconsistent victimhood frames that had allowed Tshering's suffering to be interpretable and somewhat imaginable throughout his immersion into the interpretation and the witness preparation resurfaced, enabling the legibility and imaginability of his courtroom testimony.

In arguing that claimant testimony is coconstructed, and the asylum frame of victimhood is inconsistent and multiple, my purpose has been to question the distinction made between a claimant's *own* account of suffering and the courtroom delivery of a witness testimony. Whereas lawyers insist that claimants' "own words" and "voice" must be audible in courtroom testimony, supplementing the claim documentation with speech cannot guarantee asylum. As illuminated by Tshering's inconclusive courtroom testimony, the witness preparation did not assist in overturning the initial verdict; rather, it allowed judicial arbitrariness to be inserted into, and as part of, the multiple, interpretive, and *imaginable* suffering. Put another not so far-fetched way, Tshering's testimony did not so much fit into as expand the victimhood frames and suffering in asylum.

This chapter has approached the asylum institutional encounters, interpretation, and witness preparation as backstage phenomena enabling multiple, overlapping, and often inconsistent frames of victimhood. Tshering's trial revealed an extreme example of this inconsistency and foregrounded the effects of asylum and the condition of the impossibility for US courtrooms and asylum institutions to consistently imagine suffering or victimhood in one particular way or another. Yet the interpretation and witness-preparation sessions render visible that suffering in asylum was not, if ever, meant to be construed in opposition to the agency or victimhood of those claiming asylum nor was it to be represented as a neatly categorized identity for a specific suffering account to be legible or have a defined purpose. Indeed, the actual individualized, or collective, suffering testimony seemed to matter less in the human rights agency, the law firm, and the immigration court. Neither the newly coconstructed suffering testimony nor the accompanying victimhood frame merged to make a broader historical or political representation validating the claim of past persecution or served as a resolution of some sort on a particular judgment about injustices or violence taking place outside the United States. It was neither consistency necessary to justify truth about suffering in asylum nor concern with establishing a single undeniable truth about recognizing, interpreting, and legitimizing a credible claim or claimant in these legal and juridical spaces. Instead, the institutionalized mode of asylum documentation, interpretation, and witness preparation, authorizing contextual specificity and narrow imagination of suffering, aided in upholding an arbitrary asylum decision in the immigration court. The recognition of Tshering as a claimant-victim with the capacity to overcome "extraordinary circumstance" reveals not so much (or not only) his legal visibility through testimony but, rather, the political viability of inconsistent frame(s) of victimhood linked to dispositions that can establish and undermine credibility, concurrently.[10]

FIVE

The Production
of Claimant-Workers

"TRUTH IS SIMPLE"

"*Truth*?" Mina didi said in a measured tone. "No one wants to hear the truth, but everyone *knows* it already," she continued. "Everyone wants to hear a good story in this country." After a long pause, she said, "We work hard in people's houses, cleaning bathrooms, cooking, and taking care of others' children. That is the truth. It is very simple. If you do not have papers or know English in this country, you continue doing the work because you need the money. Even if you make paper and learn some English, you still do the same work. Maybe you get lucky and find a good boss who treats you well, but you will not get good money. If you get lucky and get more money, the boss will not be nice."

As a teacher herself in her hometown in Manang, western Nepal, she had taught different subjects to young and old people in her village for ten years. "This English teaching you do," she would often tell me, "is like what I used to do in my village. Teaching Nepali to elderly people in our village who only spoke Manange or Tibetan. At least in our village the old people did not have to work. It was only to kill time in their old age. Here, we work like donkeys for six days and take English classes to feel dumber."

At the time of the interview, Mina didi had been granted asylum. She was recounting to me her asylum experience: narrating multiple asylum stories as well as multiple ways of narrating a given suffering story. She seemed still visibly disturbed by the asylum-seeking experience despite having received a favorable outcome. By sharing with me how and in what specific ways she narrated her asylum suffering story, Mina didi broke several of the unwritten codes associated with "making paper": "I had to work so hard. I spent so much money to make Nepali passport and obtain Nepali citizenship in Kathmandu before coming to the US. I am still sending money home to my brother to pay the middleman. I thought the days of hardship and difficulty were over and I had bought happiness when I came to the US."

She took a deep breath and looked outside the café window. After few seconds, she continued, "Kahan ko sukkha paunu ni ho hamiharu jasta lai ta?" (Is happiness ever possible for people like us?) Her sharp and biting remark held me hostage, unable to respond in time. She continued without waiting for my response:

> I was already homesick and working hard as a live-in domestic worker with an Indian family in Connecticut. It had not even been a year when I was asked to get my Tibetan citizenship card and papers from Chinese government to make another paper to stay here. For that my brother (in Nepal) and I had to go through so much trouble and hard work to keep paying so many people to get all the right papers. And the most difficult part here is that you have to say your story in front of the immigration officer. I went to Jamaica office first with the lawyer that the Chinatown people got me. After working so hard and memorizing everything for almost a year, I did not get asylum! I had to tell my asylum story twice . . . can you believe that?

In Nepali Queens, people adopted and expanded the sociocultural category of kaagaz banaune ("making paper") through a retrospective logic and described their subjective entanglement with asylum, protracted and often derailed legality, and impending labor subordination into the US society. People's grievances about the asylum-seeking experience intersected with, interrupted, and above all informed their everyday labor activities outside the asylum legalization experience. Specifically, asylum seeking and/as *work* and suffering were about subjective transformation and becoming claimant-*workers*, providing the condition of possibility for labor precariousness. For my ESL student-participants and claimant-interlocutors, asylum documentation, interpretation, and witness preparation encompass material objects produced through suffering, work, and daily struggle, an aspect of legality critical to their social position and relationship to the US state. The fact that obtaining asylum is a beginning of the arduous ways in which people were integrated to becoming perpetual workers—with or without paperwork—was all too obvious for Nepalis.

It is perhaps an apt description of the process itself, indicated by the Nepali phrase *kaagaz banaune*, which makes sense, empirically and conceptually, as an ongoing process of be(com)ing subjugated indefinitely to the "document" one makes. Asylum seeking, from their perspective, is a system for abstracting testimonies from the suffering work coproduced in the legal spaces of human rights agencies and private law firms and transferring them onto affidavits and I-589 forms, which, ironically, silences them. However, such an understanding of suffering is not limited to testimonies produced, performed, and delivered in courtrooms or asylum offices; it extended to other aspects of claimants' lives, as they saw the entire asylum bureaucracy and immigrant-integration system as a series of protracted entanglements inseparable from suffering and paperwork. The central issue this chapter is concerned with is not *whether* "the work of making paper" is a socially constructed phenomenon but *how* and, more important, what are its uses, types of demands, and risks.

At the same time, the reason for emphasizing the time interlocutors spend on participating into or, rather, producing everyday labor precariousness through this "work of making paper" is that this is time that could also be used in any other way. It is not a mere coincidence that people choose to use their time to develop capacities and subjective transformations for (potential) employment and asylum work since the latter is embedded within and arises out of their precarious working lives. Asylum seeking came to be interpreted on the same continuum as other work that takes up people's time. The difference is that claimants have little resource to calculate, in advance, the worth of asylum-seeking work, not because they do not know what ought to be a fair return. Quite the contrary: it is obtaining asylum that should be the end of their work. What is important is not just that in relating asylum-seeking experiences people expressed frustrations and anxiety similar to typical work grievances. Even more disturbing, as this chapter shows, different modes of work become qualitatively blurred—virtually interchangeable as alternate forms of precarious labor and lives.

In this way, exploration of implications of precariousness and labor precarity in relation to asylum seeking makes visible not only the new anticipatory logic structuring precarious labor but also the legalization temporalities that overlap with, intervene into, and exacerbate "inhabiting precarization" (Jokinen 2016). Learning to narrate one's story of persecution in a compelling way is central to asylum-seeking work. Yet finding resourceful individuals in one's network and learning to deliver coherently "the asylum story" is not enough. Rather, the gradual transformation of one's interiority and the ability to prove one's capacity to inhabit a contradictory subject position—a hardworking migrant-claimant—must align with the kind of precarious worker demanded by the US economy.

"MY STORY IS NOT"

The more Mina didi shared the details of her story, the more confused I became. Mina didi had applied for asylum as a Tibetan refugee. When asked if she knew what she had to do to apply for asylum, she responded:

> No, I was just told by my cousin that I will have to work hard for the next couple of months to learn the story to make papers to live here. But I did not know what kind of story was needed from me. I did not know the system here. My cousin took me to the woman in Chinatown, and she recommended that I could make papers because I am Buddhist like Tibetans. But the woman asked me if I could read and write Tibetan. I was worried because I could only speak Tibetan language. All those years of studying and learning Nepali in the government school and passing SLC was useless here. I was sad at first. Then the Chinatown woman told me that she would make me a tape of my story in Tibetan that I needed to listen to every day at work.

When I asked what kind of story she ended up telling, she said, "The same story that everyone knows. I was born in Tibet, and all my family members had to leave and come to Nepal because of the Chinese government. We lived in Nepal as refugees and suffered a lot in the hands of the Nepali government. You know they want all the proofs of us being Tibetan, and the upper Manang is near Tibet. But it is not really Tibet. Manang language is similar to Tibetan language. I got all the photos of my Tibetan dress, my house, and the area we lived in Manang. I asked my brother to send me everything."

Our conversation takes place in a café located halfway between her apartment in Woodside and mine in Sunnyside. It is interrupted every couple of minutes by the 7 subway line tracks running directly above the restaurant, as in every other Nepali neighborhood—Elmhurst, Northern Boulevard, and Jackson Heights. It is an interesting art that one picks up in this part of the city, as I eventually did, when the train interrupts your train of thought constantly. There is no point in trying to compete with the loud noise of the train; you simply cannot win. Rather than follow your train of thought, you learn to follow the train's schedule. You start a conversation and stop, quite naturally, every time you hear the train.

Then (try to) utter a sentence or two, while people are getting on and off the train. Once you hear the train doors shut or the announcement—"Please don't hold the doors. There is another train right behind us"—you wait a few seconds for it to leave the station. Then you continue your conversation from where you left off. The way one learns to discipline one's thoughts to follow the rhythm of the track is a particular skill that city dwellers can distinctly relate to. Not to mention, it gives conversation a unique character.

Doing interviews in the Nepali neighborhoods in Queens, I either appreciated the interruption or became increasingly impatient, depending on the context and the topic of conversation with my interlocutors. Noisy trains can be a welcome disruption to divert unwanted silences and awkward moments in the field, but at the same time, they can be a nuisance when you are deeply immersed in a conversation with someone and especially learning new information about your interlocutors, colleagues, and collaborators. This also means that the person sitting in front of you can change his/her mind in that split second—between the arrival and the departure of the train—whether or not to continue discussing what they were talking to you about right before the train arrived. Or worse, they can decide to simply cut off the conversation and not dwell on the subject matter further. Having conversations in local parks, cafés, and restaurants, in the Queens neighborhood, you always had to factor in this possibility. In sum, the unpredictability of both the content or the direction of my informants' stories often mirrored the ambivalence of the whole asylum-seeking process and suffering narration—the constant second-guessing, reevaluation of the interviewees' agenda or declared interest, and reciting of stories to different authorities and interested parties.

Luckily, Mina didi had come prepared to finally tell me *her* story, which she began almost a year ago but never completed. She showed me some photos of herself in a Tibetan outfit, of her house, and of a Loshar celebration with her family. While showing the photographs, Mina didi took a deep breath and continued, "You know all these photographs and papers of my Tibetan citizenship were not enough to make papers here?"

I nodded, not entirely sure what she meant.

"You see, my new story was that my cousin and I were carrying a Tibetan flag during a protest in Kathmandu. The woman in Chinatown said that Tibetan flag was not allowed to be carried in Nepal, so the Nepali officials arrested us after one of the protests we attended, and they put us in jail for a week." She went into details about where and when she was carrying the Tibetan flag—near a Buddhist monastery, she explained. "I spent days and nights listening to the Tibetan tape that Chinatown woman made for me. She said I will have to describe the prison life, how it looked from outside, inside, and how many people were arrested in that protest. I also had to remember how many people were put into our cell and what they did to us—all the beatings, scolding, and torture." She continued, "It was not enough that I had to ask my brother to get more papers from the prison. The date I was arrested, the name of the prison, the photo of the jail . . . everything. I kept calling my brother in Kathmandu to send me all the photos of the jail nearby and the papers from the Nepali government officials."

"And that is how you got asylum?" I asked.

"Asylum? Oh yes, that is how I made paper," she said. "I had no idea that I would also have to remember the images of the jail, the color of my cell, for example, and other detailed descriptions of the officers who arrested us in Kathmandu. The Chinatown woman recorded everything for me in a tape. I don't think I worked so hard my entire life. But it was still not enough. I was left with more suffering."

I thought the story was over; she had gotten asylum. I was mistaken.

Mina didi's voice got louder in the café, and people started staring at us. She did not seem to care. "After I studied and listened to the tape that the Chinatown woman gave me for almost three months, she told me that I would have to practice answering questions of my story on the tape. But you see, I had to learn again not to remember the story exactly the way I had listened and memorized. Can you imagine my surprise?"

I was beyond disbelief, but the initial shock and confusion was slowly giving in to my anticipation of more twists and turns in Mina didi's story—to a point where I could no longer imagine what would come next.

"Yes, I had to learn to forget that story after four months of practicing so hard," Mina didi said softly.

"Forget that story?" I asked, utterly confused.

"You see, the Chinatown woman said that I couldn't answer lawyers' questions directly because it would look like I had rehearsed my story. But that was the truth: I had rehearsed that story and quit my job for two months to memorize that tape. I did not have any money left with me. If only I knew English, I probably would have gotten asylum the first time." She fell silent.

"And that is how you got asylum," I tried to continue our conversation.

"I did exactly what the Chinatown woman told me. I worked hard to forget—not my story but how I had remembered it the first time. I finally learned another different way to tell the same story and answer different questions. The Tibetan interpreter at the courtroom translated my story well. She understood what I had said. She helped me," Mina didi said.

"What about the Chinatown woman?" I asked.

"She made me work hard. She was strict, but she helped me and other Nepalis make papers. I paid her money. Bahini, no one understands your dukkha [suffering] for free in this country. . . . You just have to work hard. That is why I am taking your English class at Adhikaar," she smiled sarcastically. "See, I told you the *truth* is simple. My story is not," she teasingly added.

Mina didi's convoluted account of asylum seeking reveals the connection between "making paper" and suffering, and between suffering and "working hard" as equivalent forms of labor. Indeed, work and suffering were central components of her experience. She told a story about an initial asylum interview gone wrong even after "working hard for a year": about learning a completely new story, about being able to recite the story in Tibetan, and about "learning to forget" so the story would appear believable. Throughout recounting her asylum-seeking experience, she understood learning and narrating the asylum story at different moments as "work" and suffering. In turn, her understanding of suffering was intricately connected to and informed by the asylum-seeking process.

Mina didi's asylum-seeking experience brought to the forefront two interconnected dilemmas about living in the United States: learning to narrate a given "suffering story" granted her asylum but did not substantially change her livelihood, and "the work of making paper" exacerbated her suffering in multiple ways. Mina didi's retelling of her story further challenges the linear logic of asylum "suffering narration" based on a singular, interpretive past event or one's lived experience. Rather, her experience of learning and reciting a believable asylum story in several languages, deliberate appropriation of cultural artifacts (i.e., photographs and her "Tibetan" dress), and showing knowledge about key historical and political events from the past composed her complicated asylum-seeking experience. This experience involved, for Mina didi, the "work of making paper" and dukkha while anticipating "more suffering" as long as she chose to live and work in the United States. Similar to her avowal—"No one understands your dukkha for free in this country"—many in the greater Nepali Queens community saw "making paper" as an event and "work" inseparable from an incomprehensible collective suffering.

ASYLUM MIGRANT LABOR AND (IL)LEGALITY GOVERNANCE SINCE 2006

Paradoxically, the 2006 immigrant rights mobilization protests had also set into motion entirely new terms and conditions for migrant deportability and criminality, disciplinary measures, and a renewed rationale for deservingness beyond economic utility and into the realm of legality, civic membership, and participation. Seeking employment, in particular, started "assum[ing] a central role in interior [immigration] enforcement initiatives at both the local and federal levels," expanding governance of "immigration through crime" (Horton 2016). At the same time, lawyers, legal experts, and asylum advocates, whose work had started gaining prominence in the preceding decade, became indispensable as intermediaries and facilitators of asylum law, and as service providers, producing knowledge about the asylum process, bureaucracy, and documentation. Their legal intermediation included the content of asylum screening, advocacy, and assistance to potential claimants in asylum offices and immigration courtrooms. In effect, the involvement of the institutions offering legal services not only generated asylum knowledge but also interpreted claimant *deservingness* in new ways.[1]

One might even say that bureaucratic categorization of "refugees and asylum seekers" expanded the criteria for deportable migrant individuals. People changing their status from undocumented to an "asylum claimant" could obtain a work permit. Although people could directly file for asylum with the USCIS, only applicants supported by "credible claim makers" like the human rights agencies would pass the initial round of screening and move to the next stage of the asylum filing and documentation, which was no secret among my claimant-interlocutors. While many knew that they would need to go through a series of institutional encounters and interviews before ever being considered for asylum eligibility, others had little knowledge of the actual steps involved in seeking asylum. Such a path to legalization did not so much change labor insecurity and the precarious lives of people; those issues simply came to the forefront with people's protracted legality.

Both the stability and the permanency of migrant (il)legality are sustained, De Genova argues, because "while deportation is obviously devastating for many people who are actually deported as well as for their loved ones and so many others directly connected to them, the most productive power of deportation operates for the great majority of people who are susceptible to deportation but who do *not* get deported" (De Genova 2018, 24). Deportation, according to De

Genova, "ever increasingly supplies capital with the ever-renewable resource of routinely disposable labor, in the exquisite form of illegalized (hence, deportable) migrant labor" (26). Certainly the critical scholarship on US immigration and migrant illegality, in particular, indicates some of the institutional developments of deportation from the nineteenth century on—racialization and normalized identification as "legal" versus "illegal" impacting vulnerability and labor subordination, legality, and socioeconomic (im)mobility; increasing reliance on and reinforcement of bureaucratized categories, including "undocumented," "unauthorized," "economic migrant," "refugees," "asylum seekers," during juridical procedures; documentation requirements as forms of social control within state borders; and expanding arenas of state domination and policing—and reflects the emergence and sustenance of the asylum process.[2]

The effect of deportation law, others contend, cannot be understood to account for all aspects of people's experiences of illegalization, especially life after being deported; nor can assumptions be made about historically specific ways the condition of deportability itself unfolds among affected individuals, groups, and societies (see, for example, De León 2013; see also Lecadet 2017; Golash-Boza 2015; Khosravi 2016). Likewise, this study claims no homogeneity in the lived experience of asylum legality across different times, spaces, and affected people. Emphasis on the particularities of asylum potential, subjectivity, and temporality affecting my interlocutors notwithstanding, institutional configurations that have occurred in the making of asylum as a *system* in the past decades inform how (and in what ways) asylum seeking has come to define people's relationships, labor incorporation, and survival strategies. In other words, if deportation is "a tactic of domination . . . [that] contributes to the precarization of migrants" (De Genova 2018, 24), asylum ensures the continuation of that precarious production by incorporating those who do "*not* get deported" through their own active volition.

Crucially, asylum legalization and the generation of liminal legalities are not only new and important features to sustaining migrant deportability or detainability but are also in themselves critical to disciplining and temporalizing precarious migrant workforce.[3] For the securitization tactic alongside indiscriminate practice of deportation meant governing migration through illegality would ultimately become unsustainable; asylum legality, already incorporated and transformed to fit into the US constitutional law over the last four decades, could now be reactivated, made functional, and expanded as a legitimate intermediary arm of the interior immigration enforcement. The ad hoc system of asylum materialized under the DOJ and DHS, managing and, in turn, producing temporary migrant workers who were neither "illegal" nor "legal" but inevitably deportable.

PRECARIOUS PRODUCTION OF CLAIMANT-WORKERS

Although the asylum-granting model underpinning liberal values of protection appealed to Nepalis, much as it did for El Salvadorans in the late 1980s and 1990s and continues to do for people seeking asylum worldwide, it presupposes rather than proves the actual alleviation of people's suffering, fear, and anxiety around labor and legalization. Moreover, it contradicts a central contention of the US immigration and migrant-integration scholarship: a pathway to legalization eliminates migrants' participation in all kinds of informal labor economies. For Nepalis in Queens, a range of temporary labor activities seemed defined by unclear and overlapping aspects of legalization. Asylum seeking, according to many, was not a resolute course of action to embark upon but an indeterminate positioning in relation to everyday precariousness.

At some point, people would typically seek status regularization through either employment or other means available to them. They often did so with caution and ambivalence about how starting the legalization process might negatively affect their earning capacity and ability to support families in the United States and back "home" in Nepal, India, or Tibet. Legalization often involved social and financial risks, for people were aware that attempting legalization might bring little to no change to their ongoing socioeconomic insecurities. Such was the case for Maya, whose experiences Reema related to me during one of our ESL breaks:

> REEMA: You see Maya here has suffered a lot. She has not been back home for almost ten years. She has not seen her husband and kids all this time. Her sahu-ji promised to make paper for her for last six years, but he never did. Then after her cousin came to the US, he made asylum paper and promised to help her make paper. She worked with the lawyer for two years and took another housekeeping job on weekends on top of her full-time restaurant job to pay her relatives and the lawyer. That is OK, we all have to suffer to get something. But you know what happened? They tried to help, but all her money is gone now, and she did not get paper. After two years, the lawyer just told her that she was already here for seven years and her case was not like her cousin's. Why promise her for

two years then? So, I am telling her to go to the lawyers in human rights office. They do it for *free*. She does not want to do it.

TINA: You do not want to make papers anymore? [I asked Maya.]

MAYA: You see, *bahini*, Reema didi is telling me that I have to quit my job to make paper. But what if I do not get paper after working hard like last time? If I quit my housekeeping job to work for paper and have to wait like last time? I keep promising my children in Nepal that I will see them soon. I left them when they were five and seven years old; now they are fifteen and seventeen. . . . Sometimes I think maybe this is my luck, but other times I do want to do something about it . . . for my children.

REEMA: That is why I am telling you to make paper again [addressing Maya]. You have nothing to lose if you do not get it [asylum], but if you do, then your kids can come here.

MAYA: I am no longer worried about not making paper but waiting without knowing. At least now I am making money and sending it to my family. My kids are both in good school in Kathmandu. I have heard that many people who tried making paper *that* way [through human rights agencies] are called in front of the judge. And if you do not speak good English in front of the judge, you are either sent back to Nepal, or worse, wait in this country forever. You cannot live here and work peacefully because you do not know when you will be required to leave.

REEMA: But you are waiting here without paper, without any hope. Better wait and hope that you will make paper. And for that you need to take risk, is it not true, *bahini*?

TINA: I don't know. What will you do, Maya? [I did not think I had any answer to Reema's question, so I tried redirecting our conversation to Maya's dilemma.]

MAYA: I don't know what to do either. I just know that I do not want to wait and suffer for another ten years.

This conversation suggests multiple layers of legalization and suffering explanations for Nepalis considering seeking asylum while also supporting their households in the United States and Nepal. Most people, like Maya, contemplating whether to refile their asylum claims viewed seeking pro bono legal assistance as a last resort. Many echoed Maya's dilemma about the type of indefinite investment one might have to make and the risk of not obtaining paper while exacerbating their already precarious circumstances.

While the notion of precarity is construed as a rather broad concept referring to debates on late capitalism and the condition of post-Fordism (Hardt and Negri 2000; Lazzarato 1996), I employ the concept here to discuss asylum seeking in relation to "precarious labor and precarious life" (Millar 2014, 35; Allison 2012; Stewart 2012; Mole 2010; see also Neilson and Rossiter 2005). In particular, the notion of "precarious worker" (Mole 2010)—occupying contradictory subject positions in anticipation to rather than a consequence of neoliberalism as a key to understanding "precarization" (Jokinen 2016) and an incomplete process—is relevant to understanding accounts of asylum-seeking work and the centrality of subjective transformation from within the context of the asylum process.

The concept of precarious worker emphasizes the lived experience, temporal knowledge practice, and moral claims made in anticipation to becoming certain types of working selves and collectives (Mole 2010; Jokinen 2016). Such anticipation produces and is productive of contradictory aspects of precarious labor and the consequence of these contradictions in the subject formation: everyday labor practice reflects a heightened sense of anxiety about the future yet necessarily depends on the "future-oriented temporality," resulting in the dual embodiment of worker-citizens as permanent and/or precarious subjects (Mole 2010, 42). Here, the present becomes critical, where "every moment" of inhabiting precarity, Eeva Jokinen notes, "activate[s] the possibilities of innovation and creative action (and floating)" (2016, 91)—mobilizing repetitive actions, norms, and behaviors.[4] According to this anticipatory and repetitive logic, people reorganize their working lives in ways manageable to anticipating precarization, which while an incomplete process, reinforces, normalizes even, "labor [itself] as naturally unstable" (Mole 2010, 43). Asylum seeking as a field of work would fall into this framing, where claimants' investment into the process is never apparent until their immersion into it, whereby people find themselves participating in undefined, work-like characteristics while negotiating their often-precarious labor situations. Moreover, the asylum process that structures claimants' engagement within and beyond the legal realm cements understanding of status regularization as an ongoing, incomplete process yet potentially within one's reach.

While the notion of precarious worker often refers to the "living labour" (Lazzarato 1996, 2) and the materialization of subjectivity as production in the context of precariousness (Allison 2012; Stewart 2012; Muehlebach 2012; White 2012; Millar 2014), practices that enable resistance against, while gradually conforming to, the contradictory formation of worker subjectivities (Millar 2014;

Mole 2012) is also central to accounts of asylum seeking. People's participation in precarious labor, while not directly related to asylum seeking, is, however, sustained by the demands of intangible labor and indefinite time invested into the process. Asylum seeking, in this sense, produces new life forms, where inhabiting transitory moments, anticipating subjective transformations, and the "feeling [of being] ontologically divided" (Mole 2012, 43) become all too normalized in managing and mobilizing one's permanently precarious situation.

A POLITICAL ACTIVIST OR A VICTIM OF APOLITICAL VIOLENCE?

"What do they know?" Nodding her head in the direction where the three lawyers, including Mary, were seated, impatiently waiting for me to interpret, Purnima looked at me with utter disbelief and said in Nepali, "It is so difficult to get a divorce in Nepal. Getting a divorce in Nepal is like asylum paperwork in America—not simply difficult but almost impossible. Do you understand?" (Eeniharu lai ke thaha ra, Nepal ma divorce lina kasto garho cha. Nepal ma divorce linu bhaneko ra Amerika ma kaagaz banaune jastai ho—dubai dherai jasto paindai paindaina. Bujhyau timile?) She laughed sarcastically.

"It is very difficult to get a divorce in Nepal," I interpreted for the lawyers, realizing the near impossibility of interpreting the specific cultural reference of Purnima's comment.

I begin here in the midst of one of the interpretation sessions for Mary and her team of pro bono lawyers representing Purnima, who was in her early forties, living in New York City with her second husband for five years and filing a political asylum claim. The interpretation session, running over six hours that particular day, was scheduled by the lawyers, who had worked on her case for the last ten months, primarily to verify all the legal documents, including Purnima's affidavit and affidavits from her parents, coworkers, neighbors, and landlord in Nepal attesting to the physical abuse and domestic violence she suffered in the hands of her first husband in Nepal. The deadline to submit the legal document, including the I-589 form and affidavit, was around the corner, and Purnima and I had been summoned to the law firm to go over the paperwork.

During the lengthy weekly asylum documentation in the law firm that followed, Purnima, upon receiving guided instruction from lawyers, was asked to (re)narrate her account of persecution chronologically, to provide detailed descriptions of her political activities, including campaigning against the Maoist party during the 2008 general election in Nepal. Six months into the asylum process, however, one of the lawyers had withdrawn from the case; in her place, Mary joined the team. Mary had pointed out a discrepancy in Purnima's background. It seemed absurd and questionable, said Mary, that it had taken eight years for Purnima to file for divorce from her ex-husband despite having experienced physical abuse within the first year of her marriage. The newly recruited associate's interest in grounding Purnima's intimate, rather than political, account of persecution had structured the subsequent asylum interpretation meetings.

During one of the witness-preparation sessions, they noticed that divorce papers were missing from Purnima's file. The lawyers were stressed and asked Purnima if it was possible for someone in Nepal to fax a copy of her divorce papers in the next two days. Purnima explained (through me, as her interpreter) that it was not an easy task to obtain documents from Nepal, but she would call her parents and try to obtain a copy of her divorce papers. However, it was to the inquiry about *why* it took so long to get a divorce from her former husband that Purnima was responding to.

I had started interpreting for Purnima almost a year ago, sometime after I had met Tshering and Priya and provided interpretation for their asylum claims. I first met Purnima at the nonprofit organization where she had submitted her claims for political asylum based on the alleged persecution she suffered in the hands of the Maoist political party. Purnima had dwelled exclusively on her days of active participation in an opposing political party and campaigning against the local branch of the Maoist political party—Janatantrik Terai Mukti Morcha (JTMMJ)—during the 2008 general election in her hometown in Barahi village, southern Nepal.[5] She had narrated what I thought to be a compelling story about the Maoist attack she suffered.

Purnima had previously filed for political asylum, claiming that the local Maoist party targeted her and threatened to kill her while in Nepal for three intercon-nected, if deeply convoluted, reasons: (1) personal enmity between her maternal uncle, a wealthy, landowning Brahman belonging to an upper-caste family and the leader of the local Maoist group, whose family had worked for two decades on Purnima's uncle's land until the mid-1990s, right after the end of the absolute monarchy and the rise of multiparty, parliamentary democracy; (2) her active in-volvement in the women's branch of one of the opposing political parties—Nepali Congress Party (NCP)—in her hometown and nearby villages between 2005 and 2008; and (3) her repeated resistance to supporting the Maoist political ideology and activities and, in particular, refusal to provide financial support to the local Maoist party (JTMMJ). Her family background—upper-caste, Brahman, and landowning Pahari (hill people)—was central to her narrative of navigating her personal and professional experience at a time of tremendous political transformation in Nepal.

She had filled out the I-589 form with the help of her husband, but her claims were denied at the asylum office even before the interview process began. When I interpreted for her at the human rights organization, she kept dwelling on the way the person in charge—an asylum officer—had completely dismissed her without even listening to her story. She was emotional while sharing the incident with the human rights lawyers and me. She emphasized that the encounter was one of the most humiliating experiences that had made her feel worthless. The human rights lawyers never inquired into the details of her experience at the asylum office, and I did not see her again until six months later. The summary of her case was circulated to private law firms, and one of them accepted to represent her. Purnima's lawyers then contacted me to provide Nepali-English interpretation.

After the first few interpretation sessions at the law firm, I inquired about her experience at the asylum office. Purnima said, "Malai bolna nai diyena. Mero naam ra ghar ko address sodhya sodhai garyo. Ani timile English bujhdaina bhanera thulo awaaz ma gaali po garyo. Ma darayen, harbaraayen, ani jhan bolnai sakina. Asylum ko kunai kurai sodhena." (I was not allowed to speak. They repeatedly asked my name and address. Then the person yelled at me and asked me if I did not understand English. I became scared, nervous, and could not speak at all. Nothing related to my asylum story was asked.) Purnima was distressed that she had been denied asylum without even being heard and that somehow her linguistic in/ability was emphasized during that brief encounter with the asylum officer. As a result, her asylum claim was rejected at the asylum office and had been given a hearing date a year after her initial rejection. She had then applied to the Refugee Protection Program through Human Rights First (HRF) for assistance two years ago, and the organization recommended Purnima to a private law firm in the city. The HRF also recommended me to the same law firm, where litigation lawyers, providing pro bono services, were now handling Purnima's case.

Purnima's lawyers were well aware of the rejection of her asylum claims by the US government, but it was the first time she had a chance to speak about that experience she found to be one of the most distressing times in her life. The lawyers unanimously agreed that the asylum officer who had interviewed

Purnima had been unfair in dismissing her case and had grossly overlooked the evidence. Further, they explained that the officer clearly had no idea of the particularities of Purnima's past experience with violence and the medical report that attested to her psychological state. The lawyers periodically asked me to explain to/interpret for Purnima that the merit hearing would be different because the lawyers would be accompanying and representing her in the immigration courtroom. The lawyers' consensus regarding the unfair rejection of Purnima's asylum claim was based on two interconnected issues that I was asked to interpret for her: (1) she did not have a legal representative at the asylum office who could have assisted her with the preparation prior to the interview, and (2) the asylum officers handle so many asylum cases on a regular basis that they do not have time to pay attention to details or be patient with claimants, especially ones who are not well versed in English. I relayed this information to Purnima in the measured tone with which her lawyers had articulated it.

While Purnima was grateful that the lawyers were now working on her case, she seemed somewhat surprised by the legal rationale offered to her concerning the initial rejection of her asylum claim. She kept insisting, "Hoina . . . tara tyo asylum ko manche le ma sanga tyasari hepera kura garnu pardaina thiyo bhaneyo ke. Tyo po bhaneko maile ta. Maile athawa mero kura biswas nagarne alagai cha, tara tyasari gaali garne arkai thuanma cha." (No . . . but that asylum officer did not have to speak to me in such a rude and humiliating manner. That is what I am talking about. Not believing my case or me has nothing to do with treating me like that.) She turned to me and demanded, "Yo uniharu lai bujhai deu na timile." (You explain that to them.)

I explained Purnima's grievances back to the lawyers, who simply nodded and responded to her, through me: "We understand your frustration, and that is why we are going to prepare you for the court hearing."

Before I could interpret back to Purnima, she grumbled under her breath, "Eeniharu lai kehi thaha chaina. Bole bolai garchan kehi sundainan." (They do not know/understand anything. They keep talking without listening.)

On more than one occasion, Purnima had been instructed to give her answers in clear and concise sentences without rambling on about issues unconnected to her asylum claims. Further, she was to pay close attention and respond to each lawyer's questions without looking at me. If she did not understand the lawyers' questions or needed clarification, she was to interrupt the lawyers in the middle of the conversation rather than depend on her interpreter's explanation because an interpreter was not an expert on asylum law.

While most lawyers working with Nepali claimants rarely instructed me to follow some kind of strict interpretation rules, the ones assisting Purnima were particular about my role as an interpreter from the very beginning. They were insistent on laying ground rules even before the asylum documentation began.

Nonetheless, Purnima had become increasingly doubtful, despite her lawyers' assurance that switching focus from her political activism to the domestic violence she suffered in Nepal would make her claim "more credible." Take, for instance, her outburst during a train ride after one of the interpretation sessions:

> When is this going to end? How many more people do I need to talk to before they finally believe me? It has been more than two years since I have been telling my asylum story . . . to asylum officers, interpreters, human rights lawyers, psychiatrists, and now these lawyers [pro bono lawyers representing Purnima]. All I talk to people—my family, friends, and neighbors—about is my case [asylum]. I had to quit my babysitting job because I needed to come prepared to lawyers to tell my story at least twice a week during the first few months of asylum interviews. You know it. I never told you, but that boss fired me last year. I was upset with her, but I now understand her problem. Who will want to hire a nanny who needs days off on short notice? Of course, people see you as unreliable. Now I work for another family, and I have already asked for so many days off. My current employer is nice, but this time I did not mention anything about my legal status. But it is only a matter of time. I am waiting for her to say something to me. It is difficult to do your job well, especially looking after small children, when your mind is somewhere else and all you are thinking about is your case. I cannot concentrate on anything. I don't even feel like calling my parents and kids in boarding school in Kathmandu. Before I worried about not having a job, and now I am complaining about this work. I am tired.
>
> [. . .]
>
> My life story has become a piece of amusement for people. I have become an amusement for everyone . . . for my own relatives and lawyers . . . and perhaps to you too, no?

Before I could say anything, she added with a forced and an awkward laugh, "I am an amusement even to myself these days."

When asked if her current employer knew about her ongoing asylum case, she looked at me with a mixture of shock and disbelief. "Are you crazy? If the employer knew about my case, I would not have had this job." Purnima explained how her frequent visits to doctors and lawyers are better kept a secret from her employer. She continued, "She will not want me to take care of her child anymore. She will think I am crazy if I say I am seeing a psychiatrist. And if she finds out that I am making paper through asylum she will definitely fire me. You know both my employer and her husband are lawyers. I am trapped in such a dilemma. I do not know what the real purpose of all this work is. Now you tell me, should I work or do this work of making paper?"

Purnima cast herself as a hardworking individual who is disgruntled about not being able to concentrate on her job and perform it well because of the "work of making paper" she needs to focus on. At the same time, Purnima's declaration of being "tired" should be contextualized beyond the realm of physical or mental exhaustion. For she self-reflexively draws on her current dilemma as that of being "an amusement" to people—to whom she has been narrating her asylum story—and to herself. Not being able to concentrate on work and being invested only in the work of making paper is then akin to futility and having excess suffering. That emotional investment in the presumably serious business of her asylum plea increasingly culminated in her not being taken seriously—leading to a perception that her whole life had become a kind of absurd joke. It is then a matter of practical concern that is not simply preventing her from be(com)ing a good worker but also creating anxiety about how she may be perceived as a fool or a person driven to distraction. This explicit self-deprecating commentary has a social significance; that is, asserting one's involvement in the asylum process as legitimate work and a valid justification for not being a diligent worker-subject is parallel to the neoliberal labor regimes that normalize precariousness by mobilizing people's fear around joblessness and work loss as a type of "social death" (Mole 2010, 44). Toward these ends, her question to me—"Now you tell me, should I work or do this work of making paper?"—is a form of self-affirmation, used in this particular context as a justification to herself and to me, her interpreter and interlocutor, about the actual work she has been engaged in for over a year.

First, the subjective complexity demonstrates the significance of interiority in the asylum process. The emphasis on claimants' intimate stories in asylum documentation has potential not only for structuring and subsequently transforming testimonies but also for providing a pedagogical scope for (re)inventing themselves into worker-subjects through "the work of making paper." This is because the notion of interiority refers to something that can be reworked in order for people to fit into the demands of precarious labor outside asylum work. Suffering here is expressed as a dilemma—one central to the discourse on moral questioning—over hardship more than it is a feeling of sadness or distress. Others are not holding Purnima's sharing of her suffering against her, but it is a type of self-imposed predicament with potential social consequences, requiring constant reasoning and reevaluation of one's actions. Purnima reflected on her subjective experience of "making paper" in relation to work and suffering simultaneously. She particularly spoke of suffering work while recounting and reinterpreting the repeated performances required of her throughout the asylum documentation and the witness preparation in the law firm.

Second, people enmeshed in different stages of asylum documentation inhabited protracted legality through what they described as "the work of making paper" intervening into and shaping their labor situations. Those in the midst of initiating asylum documentation, like Purnima or Tshering, described the process as a form of labor disrupting their lives, whereas those awaiting decisions reflected on the period of "making paper" as having replaced their working lives altogether: from locating resourceful individuals in their networks to learning their asylum story, from memorizing details to coherently recounting their stories, from practicing delivery of their testimonies in courtrooms to waiting after the hearing. While many expressed asylum seeking as work, prospective claimants are also enticed by its potential for securing better employment. The next two sections examine the development, familiarization, and internalization process by claimants using a retrospective logic to understand their active participation and subjective entanglement with asylum documentation and the impending labor subordination into US society through the sociocultural adoption of "making paper" and suffering.

SUBJECTIVITY AND POTENTIAL

People seldom describe asylum seeking in terms of legal integration or settlement per se. Rather, it is seen as a potential of obtaining employment with better working conditions, contributing to subjective transformation. The actual scope for such an employment is low, but because the potentiality is there, it is something not completely outside one's reach and, thus, realizable. The employment potentiality is often key for people adjusting, corresponding to, and reconfiguring their irregular status and precarious working lives. In this way, many explain asylum seeking as opening up the space between complete despair and certainty, where the potential payoff can be greater compared to the initial resources required of individuals. And potential, everyday asylum seeking merges with transformation and reinvention of people into individualized and flexible claimant-workers, thereby facilitating people's participation in labor precariousness.

Maneuvering potential in asylum-seeking work can be described as becoming open to and increasingly aware of one's participation in precarious working conditions. One of the ways in which the production of precarious collectives in asylum seeking connects to labor value is that the value is produced by a claimant-worker's labor and subjective investment in the process and precarious workforce, simultaneously. Here, the anticipatory logic functions to make claimants more apprehensive than hopeful, yet they must continue to fashion themselves into a particular kind of worker-subjects orienting toward a future that may or may not be.

The significance of people's anxiety upon immersing themselves in the asylum process and their continued entanglement into the work-like characteristics became clear to me while providing interpretation for claimants like Kumar dai.

"Bahini [sister], I passed finally." I could hear excitement in Kumar dai's voice when he called me on the phone after his asylum hearing. "I have spent so much energy and sleepless nights to make papers, you know." I had assisted Kumar dai on his asylum case as an interpreter for the last two years, but I was unable to attend his merit hearing that morning.

When I asked him to recount for me his courtroom experience, Kumar dai responded eagerly with a long, comic story about how the judge did not seem to care much about his suffering in Nepal and instead was interested in knowing if he was paying taxes for the last seven years. Panting and talking at the same time, Kumar added, "The last time I was this nervous was when I took the SLC examination in Nepal more than thirty years ago!"[6] It was as though his words lagged behind his thoughts, running in different directions. "This asylum thing," he would often say to me, "is not less difficult than sitting for the SLC exam, you understand? You have to forget about everyone and everything for a year or so to prepare for the exam, and still there is no guarantee that you will pass." I was overjoyed that he had passed the examination with flying colors, indeed.

Later that evening, I went to the Indian restaurant near New York University (NYU) where Kumar dai worked. As per his instruction, I arrived right after the lunch traffic ended and before he had to prepare for dinner. He seemed thrilled to see me. The restaurant was quite empty except for one or two customers, regular ones from NYU, according to Kumar dai. As we sat in a booth near the kitchen, I initiated the conversation. "Many congratulations to you, dai."

"Thank you. To you, too!" he said in English. "Aba ke?!" (Now what?!) He took a long, deep breath.

"I do not understand." I was unsure how else to respond to his habit of asking a rhetorical question, followed by a sigh. He went on: "I taught English in Siraha for twenty years before I had to leave my hometown for Kathmandu in 1998. There also I taught English until I came here in 2002. Now in the name of English, this is all I do." He tilted his head up and toward the direction of the open dining room space. His hand followed his head almost involuntarily. "Sir, would you like to sit by the window, I say to customers every day."

The customers in the restaurant must have overheard him, for they turned around and smiled at us. Kumar dai got up. "Check?" he raised his right hand, and as though holding a pen with his index finger and thumb, he made a scribbling gesture in the air. "Ekai chin, la" (Just a second, okay), he said to me and walked toward the front of the restaurant to attend to his regular customers.

As soon as he came back, I asked him, "So how did the hearing go this morning? What questions did the judge ask?"

"The hearing?" he rolled his eyes and continued, shaking his head, "It is such a big show. . . . two years of running around and going to the law firms, retelling my story to seven different lawyers, and the last month of preparing for all those questions and answers during prep sessions . . . the number of times I received death threats . . . was it over the phone or letters in the mail sent by the Maoists . . . the detailed description of the physical attack I suffered twice when I refused to donate money to the Maoist political party in our village. . . ." He said it all in one breath. It was as though the events from ten years ago in his life were flashing in front of him and he was trying to capture every bit of it in words. Then, shaking his head gently, he continued, "You know that the judge asked me nothing."

"Nothing?" I repeated.

"Well, the judge did ask me a lot of questions. He wanted to know whether or not I was filing taxes all these years that I have been living and working in this country," he said sarcastically and continued, "You know all this time I had to take off from work to run around the law offices for the last two years, I could have made more money and sent it home to my wife and children." He started talking about his family in Nepal.

"Next year, I will be fifty. My life is not going to change for the better in this country just because I will have made papers tomorrow. All I hope is to bring my family here and give my children a better future. My son is in middle school and my daughter is almost twenty-one. Hamro dukkha ta asylum payera pani sakindaina, bahini. Yo kaagaz banaunu bhaneko ta jeevan bharko bandhan ho . . . niskina nai nasakine. . . ." (Our suffering does not end even after getting asylum, sister. This paper making is like a lifelong bondage . . . difficult to escape from. . . .)

It is impossible to know whether Kumar dai was particularly referring to his experience of suffering in Nepal or if he was making a general commentary about Nepalis' suffering in the United States, with which I was becoming increasingly familiar. The word *our* is used here precisely to communicate this ambiguity. What is clear is that Kumar dai, like many former and current Nepali claimants I worked with, was articulating the suffering and anxiety caused by seeking asylum, even after being granted asylum. Given that he received a favorable decision, his asylum narration does not matter anymore. But Kumar dai seemed particularly disappointed with the merit hearing—the judge was not interested in his suffering story, which he had learned, memorized, and "worked hard" on for over a year. It was, like he said, "not less difficult than sitting for the SLC examination."

Like Purnima, Kumar dai also reflected on his experience with the asylum process as "making paper" always in relation to work, albeit in different ways. They both spoke of constant anxiety and fear of uncertainty as the condition of working hard for papers when they recounted their suffering work and performances in (re)narrating their stories of seeking asylum. "Narrating" the asylum story in itself was hard work that they encountered. For Purnima, the process of switching from one suffering claim to another and self-representing during asylum-seeking work in an entirely different way from the previous ten months that she had been actively guided and instructed to retell her suffering experiences now encompassed hard work. Kumar dai's frustration resulted from not being asked questions related to his actual asylum claim and persecution account that he had worked hard on and memorized over the period of two years. For both, work entailed learning about the asylum process—what and how to narrate an asylum story—from learning the language of asylum to memorizing minute details of their claim to practicing and performing the oral delivery of their story with precision and coherence during merit hearings. Still there is no way of knowing if and when this work will actually pay off. For both Purnima and Kumar dai, the "work of making papers" did pay off in terms of transforming their legal status, but it did not necessarily end their anxiety about both—making more papers and working hard. According to Kumar dai, the end of making paper is only a beginning of being trapped in the endless cycle of paperwork, as he said once in a passing, "Ke farak parthyo ra jasto lagcha kahile kahin. Yetikai baseko bhaye pani. Yehi kaam garinthyo." (I sometimes wonder what difference it would have made had I chosen to remain undocumented. I would have lived just like this. I would be doing the same work.) Purnima, too, continued to grapple with the real purpose of her labor and time put into asylum-seeking work that might conflict with her chances of remaining employed.

Indeed, claimants often describe a continuum of dukkha related to "making paper," in which the anxiety of asylum documentation left them with the feeling of a void to cope with or reminded them of more paperwork to be done in the future. Like the paperwork that facilitates people's migratory trajectories (Gomberg-Munoz 2010b) or the exchange of work documents, say in the case of Californian migrant farmworkers (Horton 2015), that bind people in a type of moral economy, making asylum papers reminds people of more paperwork to be done in the future for sponsoring family members, as Kumar dai reflected. In this sense, the collective suffering—insinuated by Kumar dai's comment on "our suffering"—must be understood in the context of an immigration system in which legalization, while necessary for the family reunification process (see Boehm 2012, 53–70), is also about a transitory status inseparable from claimants' recruitment into the workforce.

TEMPORALITY AND ANTICIPATORY LOGIC

This kind of realization of suffering that interchangeably slips between one's account of asylum documentation and an articulation about working in the United States is not uncommon. Indeed, the narrative switch is so smooth that it is often the distinction between the two that seems somewhat forced and not the other way around. This is not to suggest people's lack of awareness about the consequences of their actions. Rather, it is to acknowledge that by identifying one's suffering with the suffering of others, people positioned themselves within and alongside the discourse on labor integration inseparable from the legalization process.

This theme can be explored in my follow-up meeting with Tshering, sometime after his inconclusive testimony. He begins with an asylum hearing gone awry:

Nothing went right that time. I could not even remember my apartment address in Queens and my telephone number. I almost forgot my English date of birth that I had memorized for three years. I kept repeating my address in Mustang and in Kathmandu. I even gave my Nepali year of birth. When I said 31 March 2033, my lawyers looked at me with confusion. Still I had no idea what I had done wrong. I just could not remember right answers. I had worked one of the longest shifts at the grocery store the night before and had three hours of sleep the night before. I could not pay attention to what was being asked in the court. The court interpreter felt bad for me too, I think. So many people helped me make papers in Kathmandu to come here.

Tshering's account of suffering is about anxiety experienced during and after the courtroom hearing gone wrong. If he does not receive a favorable decision on his case, he will not be summoned for another hearing. Depending on his legal representatives, he can appeal his case to the Board of Immigration Appeal (BIA) and wait several months before the BIA either approves or denies his appeal.[7] If the appeal is denied, chances are Tshering will be deported.

Tshering was waiting to hear from his lawyers on the appeal that had been submitted. He had previously shared with me his long and difficult work schedule, which started every morning at 3:00 a.m. and ended around noon. He worked as a deliveryman, driving a truck and delivering baked goods for grocery stores, and in the evenings, he worked in an Indian restaurant. One day, I met him after his morning shift to talk about the appeal. Unlike the last time we met in the law firm to interpret the important date and details about his upcoming appeal, there was no date approaching for Tshering. However, he was more nervous about the absence of a specific date. He talked about the date in question, and how he would feel much better if he knew when to expect the news. After a while, the absence of a particular date and his everyday waiting itself framed our entire conversation without our ever explicitly talking about it. A bit awkwardly, I tried to initiate the conversation in the direction of the asylum appeal process:

TINA: As the lawyers said last month . . . there is still a chance that the BIA could overturn the judge's verdict . . . and if they do not, the judge will not be allowed to ask questions that are outside his expertise . . . like your medical reports or questions about the first asylum decision. . . .

TSHERING: Before I only had one suffering: I was worried that I did not have paper. I thought I would not be able to give a better future to my daughter, you know. But now I can neither tell my family that I am coming back home nor explain why it is taking so long to make paper to bring them here. I am stuck in the middle. I work more hours now than I did before because I do not know when I will have to stop working and will not be able to send money home . . . well, it is also because I cannot sleep peacefully. Every minute that I am not working, I am worrying about my paper and talking about it to everyone . . . see what I mean. Today is my day off, and here we are . . . talking about my asylum. This paper-making work is so much harder than what I do every day. At my work, I do not have to think or worry. I just do it. I have a work schedule, and I know when to get there and what time I will get off. Not like making paper. I don't know what have I really gained from all this? The funny thing is I am still unsure if I can provide a better life for my family with or without paper.

TINA: So going through the asylum process does not really make a difference?

TSHERING: It does. It makes you more anxious, and your suffering multiplies. Like I said, not having paper is only one problem . . . going through the asylum process, working hard to make paper, and living every day with the anxiety of not knowing whether and when you will actually have paper in hand is a source of multiple suffering.

TINA: Multiple suffering like what?

TSHERING: Well, I cannot promise my family that I can bring them here. But at the same time, I cannot explain in a way they understand what I am going through here. They do not know my worries. Until I have paper, I cannot go to Nepal and see my family. Sometimes I try not to worry too much and just think to myself that life is uncertain so as long as I am alive I will work here and send money home to my family. If they [the US state] do not give me paper and I am sent back, maybe that will be a blessing . . . it will be an end of all this hassle. But when I try not to worry or care so much, I think of my family and feel sad for them . . . for us. My family in Nepal and I have suffered so much to send me here to work and make paper. After living here and working every day like a donkey for almost seven years, what will I do if I go back? Still this waiting for paper makes you feel miserable one minute, happy next minute . . . nervous one day and fearless the day after . . . it is like you are on a swing moving forward and backward, flying high and falling low constantly. Then you start wondering if your life will be drastically different even if you have paper. This business of making paper has taught me a lot about life in America and suffering.

In the very beginning, we met at the human rights agency, where I interpreted for him, and then periodically afterward in the law firm for numerous interviews and documentation of his account of political persecution in Nepal and for intense prep sessions before his courtroom hearing. Tshering and I had discussed his asylum claims several times. This was, however, the first time he admitted that making paper was difficult work, and to make things even worse, he increasingly became doubtful of having a better life for himself and his family after, ironically, being closer to "making paper." Tshering felt that he did not have much control over the direction of his life while "making paper." He did not want to burden his family with his uncertain status or explain to others in his social network. His solution to the problem was to work more hours to escape from the mental work he was putting into making paper, which now hangs in a limbo.

Waiting is further articulated by Tshering as a problem and solution to continued and, oftentimes, expedited participation in labor precariousness. The wait is then another dimension of suffering—whether being initiated into asylum documentation, such as Priya, expected to be part of the protracted witness preparation, like that of Purnima, or awaiting a decision after the asylum hearing, as in Tshering's case—and a peculiar zone of containment that people experienced. The form of labor-time described by claimants to be outside the legal realm did not simply mirror but also overwhelmingly blurred with asylum-seeking work. Purnima's anxiety around not being a dependable worker or Tshering's active participation in long working conditions do not simply reflect but also arise from indefinite investment of their labor and time into the asylum process. People grapple with asylum-seeking work and its world as an insight into and reality of, in Tshering's words, "life in America."

While these accounts illuminate the process of "inhabiting precarization" in asylum-seeking work, they also allow us to reevaluate the actual labor-time and value that the precarious claimant-workers produce through and that are productive of precarity itself. The value of precarity lies precisely in its unspecified nature—it is not something that could be measured in the time spent or that could be accurately predicted. The production of precariousness in asylum-seeking work might thus be an example of the renewed orientation to precariousness and labor precarity to which Mole (2010) and Millar (2014) both refer.

The anticipatory logic in asylum seeking, however, does not mean that value would be exclusively future-oriented. As the accounts show, the time spent to realize one's participation in precariousness, that is, the time that asylum seeking takes, can be understood as the labor-time needed to produce the value of labor-power, both acquired by claimants through their subjective transformation and productive of the conditions of possibility for their own subordination in the process (Marx [1885] 1956) as claimant-workers. Thus, the time spent is just as, if not more, critical in the production of precarious selves and collectives as the future-oriented sensibility in constructing a peculiar workforce that mobilizes subjectivity or the rationale of those interpreting their lives by inhabiting solely in the present (Millar 2014) conditions of precariousness.

The emphasis on temporality in the production of precariousness in asylum seeking, as in the entangled past and present, directs our attention to the production of precarity that demands a specific labor-time spent in seeking asylum. Once this subjective labor of (re)orienting oneself toward inhabiting precarization is well underway, asylum-seeking work is seen to have a symbolic, if undefined and intangible, value in the present, as Tshering's unresolved case forces us to recognize.

DISCUSSION

These self-reflexive accounts showcase the types of suffering claimant-*workers* that people become upon immersing themselves in asylum-seeking work. In particular, they demonstrate challenges people face during the asylum documentation process and are able to overcome, allowing each to carry on their working lives and asylum-seeking work—emerging as individuals with full capacity for self-disciplining, subjective transformation, and flexibility through their own participation in labor subordination. Crucially, these accounts demonstrate people's critical engagement with asylum seeking as work, albeit precarious, in and of itself. The varied explanations for their immersion and sustained entanglement in the asylum process do not necessarily culminate in qualitative transformations of their legality or livelihood. Yet the continued participation in precarious labor within and outside asylum-seeking work activates and produces precariousness that is not entirely unanticipated. Asylum-seeking work does not guarantee status regularization, but it does not completely foreclose it either. There is no reason to assume that initiating the asylum process results in a positive outcome. There is no reason either to assume that the internal contradictions, including the self-disciplining practice of fitting into paradoxical subjectivities or facilitating one's participation in asylum documentation and labor precariousness, would go unrewarded, as in the case of Tshering or Purnima.

For claimants, asylum seeking within the legal realm of human rights organizations, private law firms, and asylum offices became the site of necessary labor. The separation between *"working* to make paper" and *"making paper* to work" completely disappeared. The activities of the everyday outside of "making paper" are not just working to survive in the United States and support families in Nepal; everyday work becomes increasingly about learning and performing innovatively, which will have direct consequences on people as claimant-*workers*. This is not a category confusion. It is the condition of late modernity and late liberalism, in which one learns to productively deploy identities that are not only contingent but also frequently contradictory and absurd.

While those like Kumar dai, who went through the asylum process, communicated ambivalence in terms of what is gained and lost as they anticipated suffering related to more paperwork to be done, individuals in the thick of the asylum process like Tshering expressed sheer frustration created by protracted legality. The indefinite waiting period upon embarking on the asylum documentation caused yet another type of suffering connected to asylum paperwork for my claimants. Narrating asylum claims itself was a type of suffering work that all the claimants encountered and unanimously complained about. In fact, the work entailed learning about seeking asylum—what to tell and how to narrate their suffering story—from learning the language of asylum to memorizing details of "past persecution" to practicing and performing the oral delivery of their suffering testimonies with precision and coherence. There is no way of knowing if and when the work of seeking asylum will actually end. Claimants continue to grapple with *real* work and/of making paper that has contributed to their experience of, as in the words of Tshering, "multiple suffering" or in Purnima's reflection of being "an amusement" to others around her. The participation in the asylum documentation, in other words, enables people to reinvent themselves in ways suitable, albeit not so much to their own benefit, to suffering and continuing working in the United States.

In light of these accounts, my ESL student-interlocutors' suffering articulations and silences, which had initially directed me to their language needs and livelihood options, now seemed incomplete. Their rationale to remain in the low-wage service sector, management of their workplace grievances, and dependence on relatives, friends, and close associates in and outside Adhikaar for social security had to be reassessed in light of "the work of making paper" some had participated in while others had not. Their explanation of *making paper* as a work-related issue—much like learning to speak "good" English—had informed their decisions to continue searching for better livelihood options and participating in a precarious labor economy, simultaneously. Digging deeper into their silences masked by suffering articulations and language concerns seems urgent. In the final chapter, I examine the contemporary survival strategies inseparable from precariousness, divergent and collective censorship practices through ESL sessions, migration trajectories and life histories of several of my student-interlocutors, and ongoing engagements with activists and community organizers at Adhikaar. These different conversations specifically point to the ways in which censorship delineates, ironically, survival of a perennial "suffering community" in the liberal state.

six / The Paradox of Visibility and Collective Censorship

SURVIVAL STRATEGIES

In a spontaneous moment of reflection brought on by a particularly difficult Sunday at Adhikaar, this is how Narbada didi described her work to me: "Bahini, maile bees barsa Nepal ma human rights ra social justice ko kaam garera kapaal phulako hun. Human rights ra social justice bhaneko nai aruko dukha bechne pesha ho." (Sister, my hair has become gray by working in the field of human rights and social justice for twenty years in Nepal. The profession of human rights and social justice sustains itself by selling the suffering of others.) After a long pause, she continued, "Yahaan America ma jhan tehi huncha." (Here, in America especially, it is the same thing.)

Narbada didi's short and poignant commentary—delivered between English classes and workers' rights information sessions for migrants and asylum seekers to an audience of just one listening ethnographer—captures the intangible and morally intricate landscape of suffering within which the knowledge practice of the Nepali community and the inseparable working lives and legalization experiences of people are embedded. That suffering had emerged as a way for organizing lives and survival strategies of fellow Nepalis in the city was something Narbada didi had been declaring since the time I joined Adhikaar. She was now deliberately connecting "selling suffering" to the work of community organizing, advocacy, and "the profession . . . social justice . . . in America."

In the final chapter of this book, I return to the central paradox with which I began this ethnography: the interconnection between suffering narrations and legalization experience, interchangeably used but seldom readily acknowledged among my Nepali interlocutors; yet suffering was deemed central to the emergence and survival of the community and, especially, the work of Adhikaar's grassroots activism and mobilization of Nepali New Yorkers. I also return to dialogical ethnography and the discussion that ensued about suffering among ESL student-interlocutors, community organizers, and activists to demonstrate the opportunities and challenges presented by suffering visibility in the reimagining of grassroots migrants' rights activism. The chapter further grapples with the analytic consequences of the paradox of visibility for interrelated studies of the US interior immigration enforcement, immigrant rights activism, and migrant-community formation in the contemporary political moment. These indicate that the paradox of suffering visibility is neither an analytic puzzle to be explained away nor peculiarly a liberal political problem to be solved. Rather, it is an institutionalized socio-historical outcome of various legislations and temporalization of a low-wage migrant workforce that are now productive of a troubled politics, whereby migrant communities and the liberal state are enmeshed.

The paradox prevails primarily because it is coproduced by the tension between durable forms—language, legal bureaucracy, and interior immigration enforcement configurations—and the shifting opportunities and resources offered by the grassroots migrant rights programs and pro bono asylum-assistance provisions in the liberal state. Another reason for the prevalence of the paradox of suffering is that it continues to be productive of a moral repository and meaning-making process, both perceptible and symbolic, for socialization and the intersubjective transformation of people coming together to build a community. These were the key concerns of previous chapters. A third interpretation of this paradox is the question of survival of an emergent community. This is the focus of this chapter, in which the practical considerations of identifying and being identified as a "suffering migrant community" outside the asylum context and the ongoing pro-immigrant political activism are incorporated from the liberal frame, to explore the enduring production and implication of this paradox—from consciousness raising to collective censorship. This brings me back to the beginning of this book to draw together debates on suffering and its *uses* for the Nepali migrant community, asylum legalization and precarious production, and persistent silence. I proceed by highlighting how articulations of suffering in the greater migrant community yield in the paradox of visibility: suffering variations delineate emergence and transformation of migrants' social and labor activities, with interpretive possibilities and indeterminacy at its crux, but the political subjectivity and anticipatory logic embedded in the liberal framework matter for its form, content, and meaning making.

In the wake of immigration rights activism and political change across the sanctuary cities in 2006, the "immigrant question," which expanded to consider what constituted a "suffering asylum seeker," reopened in new and critical ways. In order to address the question in any meaningful way, its key assumptions, concepts, and new boundaries must also be understood with more clarity. If an asylum-seeking migrant is to be identified by his/her suffering embodiment, interpretability, and performance, what can pro-immigrant advocates and grass-roots activists do about uninterpretable and tangential suffering accounts that exceed the legitimacy of victimhood (as in the case of Tshering's courtroom hearing or Purnima's recategorization as a victim of domestic violence during the asylum documentation), since in these cases, self-identification of the claimant as a "paradoxical victim" continues to impact the operational logic of asylum in the liberal state? If immigrant rights movements and grassroots migrant advocacy are defined by supporting a select few to legalize, and providing asylum assistance on the basis of credibility, for instance, but not in their ideologies about what counts as suffering (as we saw in the asylum credibility-establishing work Lisa engaged in for Priya's case), how might we understand the relationship between those they assist and engage on a daily basis? For disagreements within the liberal state about how different kinds of immigrant rights and political activism materialize on the ground affecting the historical narrative and endurance of representational politics is not new.[1]

Despite the treatment of 2006 pro-immigrant marches as a point of radical historical break for the emergent migrant rights activism, the sociopolitical continuities run through the suffering visibility for most working-class migrants today as pro-immigrant activism has primarily brought into the limelight the suffering associated with cross-border asylum and legal violence, everyday illegality, and criminalization. As private citizens and immigrant rights supporters of asylum seekers and undocumented migrants speak out against the restrictive immigration and asylum policies and their legal and infrastructural reconfiguration and codification, it will continue to be important to see and evaluate the ways in which they end up upholding the logic and the politics of the "migrant suffering script." More important, as representatives, advocates, and activists working with and among different migrant communities speak on behalf of "asylum seekers' suffering" and its distinctiveness, it will be important to trace the legal-political process along which the "suffering subject," as it is understood today, was an outcome of a particular sociopolitical construction and institutionalization of an ad hoc asylum as an interior immigration enforcement.

As these struggles for immigrant and asylum seekers' rights advocacy make their way through the lobbies of private law firms and human rights agencies, through waiting rooms of asylum offices and detention centers, through the immigration and asylum bureaucracy and into the courtrooms, echoing their demand for the state to (re)categorize, order, and reinscribe the "suffering-subject" logic, it will be critical to note how such demands are coproduced, how the paradoxes of suffering invisibility endorse the ongoing legal-juridical arbitrariness and subjectivity in the liberal state. As Wendy Brown (1995) has noted, the narrow legal language and political process of rights-based debate in liberal societies inevitably rely on "social hurt" or "woundedness." As Aihwa Ong has contended, drawing on Cambodian migrants and refugee experiences, the "everyday citizenship in America" is based on material "effects of the multiple rationalities [state and nonstate institutional bureaucratic procedures] that directly and indirectly prescribe techniques for living for independent [neoliberal] subjects who [must] learn to govern themselves" (2003, 15). In a logic evocative of the conceptual traps that Brown warns about, the paradox of suffering serves similar yardsticks for undocumented migrants and asylum claimants. And not unlike the neoliberal contradictions inherent in the "cultural self-making" practices among Cambodians in the 1990s, Nepalis' collective consciousness as a "suffering community" draws on censorship practices.

The transformation of suffering accounts into a domain of liberal governance—legislated by changing immigration laws and asylum policies, codified into bureaucratic documentation, interpreted by immigration lawyers and human rights advocates, upheld by the discretionary power of judiciaries, among others—has arguably been one of most significant disciplining tactics of "migrant" and "refugee" populations worldwide in the last decade. However, there is little detail about the specific ways these strategies materialize on the ground, at grassroots migrant-community organizing and mobilizing. For instance, how do legislative changes and ever-expanding "asylum credibility" or coconstruction of suffering testimonies permeate the everyday social life of people in the community? What kinds of suffering stories are constructed by and circulated among those who are affected by the interior immigration enforcement and asylum politics and have most to say about cultivating *habitual suffering*? These questions have tended to be answered by anthropologists studying contemporary immigration and asylum in the United States (and Europe) in generalities: violence, deportation, (il)legalization, truth regimes, and political subjectivity. In part, this is because studies focus on accounts of migrants and asylum claimants' individualized or collective experience in response to immigration enforcement practices and asylum politics. Even studies that critique US immigration history, interior enforcement structure, or oppressive legal discourses do so by attending to the administrative and bureaucratic workings of the state affecting migrants, or as Coutin calls it, "ethnography of a legal process" (2003, 23). In part, however, this is a "suffering visibility" problem—transformations about migrant lives and subjectivities (i.e., labor and legal regularization) are so much a part of how a migrant or asylee subjectivity is constructed through the liberal logic of suffering and what resistance against or adherence to that logic looks like. It is difficult to not equate the visibility of a given population as a form of politics.[2] Unlike the case of Tibetan refugee asylum-claimant communities of New York City who saw their dual identification as "refugees" and citizen-subjects in the United States as practicing "politics of refusal" to engage in liberal or "international norms of citizenship" (see McGranahan 2018), my student-interlocutors and claimant-interlocutors did not romanticize their legally precarious situation as disengagement from liberal politics of refusal; instead, their persistent silence and suffering around uncertain and protracted illegalities yielded what they understood as survival practices. The far-reaching consequence of suffering visibility, in addition to raising questions about immigrant activism and migrant community-in-the-making, is that answers often point to dynamics engaging the liberal state: violence, subjectification, resistance, citizenship, and exclusion. The liberal state is therefore acknowledged as the ideological center for any potential transformation, and the scholarship on migrants', refugees', and asylees' lives and legalization continues that "integration" into socioeconomic, political, and civic institutions as the putative path to long-term stability, livelihood, and security despite all evidence suggesting otherwise.

When transformation is the only accredited account, enduring suffering and its multiple and incompatible iterations become awkward and irrelevant details, and when they take on larger dimensions, they are attributed to exceptional cases or, in the language of US asylum, they are able to "overcome extraordinary circumstances." Here, I retrace suffering narrations among my ESL student-participants that yielded a collective silence—whether in the form of censorship or of disruption—in the way of transformation of the Nepali New York community. As registered in earlier chapters, there exists a considerable variation between ESL student-interlocutors, community organizers and activists, and ethnic leaders in the way they described, related, and gradually participated in the meaning-making process of a "suffering community." More important, the social and political contexts of Nepal and the United States informed their migration trajectories, and what direction their labor took upon arrival in the United States depended largely on changing immigration legislation and legalization restrictions. These variations point to the need to question, with more accuracy, the emergence and the transformation of a migrant community that depended more on the interior immigration enforcement than on the assumed adherence to constructions of shared homeland, historical memories, and sociocultural and linguistic affinities. Interpreting experiences of my ESL interlocutors at Adhikaar, I trace ambiguous acknowledgments and alignments of suffering that derive from deep interconnection—in the labor and legal organization of the interior immigration enforcement, in the assumption of a shared historical memory of civil war, in the growing efforts of Nepalis to make themselves visible and legible to the US liberal state and interpretable beyond their migration and settlement trajectories. This interconnection, however, does not tend uniformly toward convergence and different trajectories for the conceptualization of a suffering community of practice. Rather, continued variations in the production of apolitical suffering and survival strategies coexist in Nepali Queens.

"WE ARE NEW YORK"

Having been introduced to the entangled ideas about work, making paper, and suffering by my Nepali-speaking interlocutors repeatedly, I began tuning in to people's conversations around legalization at Adhikaar. After a year and a half of English-language facilitation, conversations around employment and workplace negotiation tactics gradually transformed into concerns about processing paperwork and regularizing temporary legal statuses. Pelki didi and Sanju didi would frequently break the rhythm of our discussion by sharing examples from their individual workplaces—intricate details of specific scenarios, challenges, and expectations placed upon them by their employers—while Mina didi would redirect the flow of our classroom conversation. I could then always rely on Tenzin to bring us back to our scheduled classroom discussion for the day.

Over the course of almost two years of volunteering at Adhikaar, my ESL student-participants increasingly described "making paper" in relation to becoming suffering refugees and asylum seekers, with several noting that the lack of English-language proficiency might have enabled, ironically, their participation in legalization efforts even as it produced and prolonged their dukkha. Sanju didi's experience fits this pattern. She had recently acquired a green card before

FIGURES 13 AND 14 English for Empowerment class at Adhikaar. Photograph courtesy of Sonam Ukyab.

attending the ESL class and nanny-training workshops at Adhikaar (figures 13 and 14), but hers was hardly a smooth transition from an undocumented status to a documented one. Instead, the uncertain twists and turns upon migrating to the United States and processing paperwork exerted pressure to remain in an exploitative employment; she had not seen her children for almost a decade.

At the time I interviewed her, Sanju didi had been living in the United States for nine years. She was born in Bhutan in the late 1960s, and her family fled to Darjeeling in North India during the Bhutanization process initiated in the late 1980s where Bhutanese of Nepali origin and Nepali-speaking minorities were being persecuted.[3] The dominant narrative goes: Nepali-speaking Bhutanese nationals living in southern Bhutan for generations were systematically disenfranchised, categorized as "illegal migrants" by the Drukpa majority through a series of citizenship legislations, and deprived of many civil rights; many apprehended by the Bhutanese authorities were charged for their political activities and labeled "terrorists" and "antinationalists," which resulted in a mass extradition of people who resettled in Darjeeling, Sikkim, and Nepal.[4] After living in India and working in restaurants for a couple of years, she and her husband moved back to their ancestral home in Helumbu and opened their own restaurant. The civil war in Nepal in the mid-1990s, however, disrupted their lives, making it difficult to sustain their livelihood. By then Sanju didi and her husband had two children; they both started looking for better employment possibilities in Kathmandu and overseas. They migrated to the United States in 1999 on tourist visas, as her husband's brother had been living with his family in Queens for a little over five years. The two brothers worked at a fast-food restaurant chain in New Jersey, while Sanju didi worked as a live-in nanny for a Jewish Iranian family in Long Island that she met through her sister-in-law's employer. During the early years of settling into the United States, Sanju didi and her husband's combined income not only supported their household in Queens but also elevated the family's aspirations to a middle-class lifestyle in Kathmandu, where their children were enrolled in a private English-language school. During the height of civil war in Nepal (2001–2), Sanju didi and her husband, like many Nepali-speaking migrants without regular status or legal documentation, started looking for options to regularize their status, in hopes of bringing their two children to America. Meanwhile, her husband lost his job due to illness, and most of the family savings went into paying the medical expenses for his recovery.

"Our dukkha," Sanju didi said to me during an ESL session, "will never go away even if we speak English." Sanju didi was referring to the first ESL class I facilitated: in an effort to initiate classroom conversation I had naively asked the student-participants why they *wanted* to learn English. More than a year of facilitating ESL conversations had gradually made me realize that their attendance at Adhikaar workshops and classes oriented them toward learning, questioning, and articulating not only their commonly shared work-related concerns but also their shared dilemma of legalization intervening into their daily activities and existential questions about suffering and survival. What Sanju didi meant was that speaking English fluently would never guarantee a permanent job, but that it might help her find a better-paying job as a live-out domestic worker. Now, in class, she pointed out that people without papers had limited options: they worked as live-in or live-out domestics regardless of the wages, especially if their employers promised to sponsor their visas. Sanju didi had kindly interpreted for me yet another layer of remaining in either a live-in or a live-out job inseparable from one's workplace situation, relationship to an employer, and types and stages of the "work of making paper" one was enmeshed in. This then encapsulated the similar predicament of several of my student-interlocutors.

A complete silence enveloped the classroom. Over the past year and a half, I had learned not to disrupt such abrupt, momentary, shared silence among ESL participants that seemed comforting, empowering even, for those identifying with the person being silent, while allowing others to witness empathetically, as we gradually redirected classroom discussions for the day.

After a while, in an attempt to change the subject, I proposed to discuss our scheduled lesson based on a handbook on "We Are New York."[5] The study materials, which depicted newly arrived migrants from different countries navigating the city, entailed short stories, images, phrases, and characters associated with one of the ten lessons. Going over the short story, reviewing vocabulary words and images, and asking participants questions related to the story allowed ESL teachers like myself to assess student-participants' levels of comprehension and English-speaking abilities.

In class that day, we started reviewing a lesson on telling time, and I introduced the usage of adverbs of frequency. I asked student-participants to construct sentences using one of the following: *always, never, sometimes,* and *occasionally.*

When no one volunteered to respond, I went around the room and asked if, and how often, they missed their families back home. When it came to Sanju didi, I asked if she missed her two children *sometimes.*

"Not *sometimes.* All the time. Please don't ask her, otherwise she will start crying again," Pelki didi interrupted, and other Hyolmo participants started laughing.

Sanju didi was now blushing. Fixing her composure, she responded: "I *never* listen to my employer these days."

When asked to elaborate on her statement, Sanju didi gave another one-liner: "I will not be able to work if I *always* listen to her."

"Why?" I asked.

"She [Sanju didi's employer] *never* trusts me and she *always* says sorry afterward."

"Why does she *always* say sorry?"

"Every time I take rest, she scolds me and says that I am not doing any work. She *always* goes out; she is *never* home when I am working. When she returns home from shopping, she only sees me resting. So, I tell her to check all the rooms and bathrooms before telling me to clean. And when she sees that I have done the cleaning, she *always* says sorry." Her voice got louder. "So I tell her, '*Never* say sorry to me! *Always* check your house.'"

Pelki didi chimed in, "Oh, Sanju didi and her employer *always* ignore each other. They don't listen to what they tell each other no more!" She started laughing, nudging Sanju didi playfully.

Sanju didi also started laughing, and so did everyone in the class. I was confused and asked why they thought it was funny to ignore each other at work.

Before I could follow up with another question, this is how Pelki didi interpreted for me: "Tina bahini, if you listen to everything our bosses tell us and the way they speak to us, you will *never* work. You will go crazy. You will leave the job immediately. Every time they [employers] have problems, they *always* take it out on us!"

"Excellent!" I exclaimed. "I mean . . . good use of both *never* and *always* in your response, Pelki didi," I quickly added.

As *always*, the classroom had transformed into a space for participants to share their grievances and generalized understanding of ongoing and multiple suffering. By then I had become accustomed to migrant sociality that periodically shifted between collective identification as silent migrants and suffering workers.

That same Sunday after class ended, I met up with Sonam didi for our first interview. Although she had been in my class for two consecutive sessions and I had interviewed most of her peers from the same village in Helumbu, her quiet and reserved demeanor had prevented me from approaching her. Since she barely shared her work experiences or commented on her legalization experience with me and other ESL participants, I thought it inappropriate to broach the topic. I was well aware by this point that if I requested an interview, many participants would not have refused, which made it even more difficult to ask. Seeing her laugh freely, for the first time, somehow made it easier for me to approach her.

A friend of Sanju didi's, Sonam didi was also from Helumbu and, at the time of the interview, had been working as a live-out nanny for a Jewish Indian family for the last four months. Working as a live-in domestic had been an arrangement born out of necessity for Sanju didi, given her pending paperwork. Her employer's sponsorship held out a distant promise—reuniting with her children one day. Working as a live-out nanny represented for Sonam didi, so it appeared, a newly acquired privilege: transcending drudgery and silent suffering in someone else's house. Her employment situation did not entail a codependent relationship with her employer, like that of Sanju didi. Unlike the majority of the ESL participants, furthermore, Sonam didi and her husband were both US citizens. Sonam didi migrated to the United States with her husband in 1996. She mentioned that she was especially grateful that she found work as a live-in domestic for an Indian family in the city immediately after their arrival; she stayed with the family until 2004. When asked why she had particularly sought employment with an Indian family and the reason for working as a live-in for almost a decade, she explained in the following way: "Although we are from Helumbu, my husband and I grew up and worked as laborers in Arunachal Pradesh [in northern India] for most of our lives."

At this point, I must have appeared puzzled, because Sonam didi further clarified, "As day laborers working at construction sites along the highways."

I nodded and started scribbling in my notebook.

Sonam didi continued:

My husband and I worked as day laborers in India, and after a few years we saved and opened our own tea stall along the same highway where we used to work. But you know Indians don't like us there. They sometimes come and drink tea and leave without paying. They will just bang the table after finishing their meals and leave. We would be scared to ask for any money afterward. After a while, we came back to Nepal and found work at a factory.[6] There my husband got an opportunity to come to the US. His boss in the carpet factory helped us get papers to come here. It was difficult to leave my sons in Nepal, but we had to do it for them . . . for their better future.

Sonam didi requested a glass of water, but as I got up, she kept talking, almost to herself. "Since my older son had been sick and was suffering from physical disability, we wanted to bring both of them here. I stayed with my job [as a live-in nanny] for eight years. It was my Indian boss who helped us apply for our green cards."

She continued, "Soon after we made papers in 2001, we brought our sons to America. But things became even more difficult. We had not seen them for such a long time. . . . They both finished their high school here; we were very happy. But my older son's health deteriorated. In 2004, we moved to Virginia, where our relatives live, thinking that it would be easier for my disabled son rather than in New York City. He died in 2007."

I sat back down and stopped writing. I looked up and followed her eyes, which were already looking back at mine. Our eyes interlocked. I simply gazed at my own reflection in her eyes, unable to look away, for they now seemed to be communicating what I could only interpret as pain and suffering. Yet her speech did not falter, even for a second. It sent chills down my spine as she continued talking about the family's dilemma—whether to return to Nepal, where they would have extensive support to take care of the ailing son, or to stay in the United States, where they could neither afford superior medical treatment nor continue to rely on the generosity of her newly arrived, working-class relatives in Virginia, despite finally having made papers. I listened empathetically without displaying (so I thought) any visible emotion or expression—neither of sadness nor sympathy.

In that moment, I felt as though I was involuntarily mimicking her expression. I could no longer grasp the magnitude of each word coming out of her mouth. For she kept talking in a matter-of-fact tone, recounting a chronological series of events that happened during and after the passing of her son. I was no longer caught up in expressing appropriate emotion, response, or facial expression; I was glued to hers. The entire time she was calm and had a stoic voice and a composed aura accompanying her speech. I neither broke the rhythm nor understood her suffering. All I could sense was the conversation slipping away beyond my control and hers. Rather, we were both arrested in that momentary, tumultuous mixture of intersubjective encounter with vastly separating emotional states, aided by her words, delivered in vivid details, coherence, and accuracy.

All of a sudden, my mind started wandering off, making me wonder why she was telling me this story. And as though reading my mind, Sonam didi smiled gently and declared, "Yes, that is why I had to leave my job with the Indian family in 2004. We went back to Nepal in 2007, never to return to the US, although we had already made papers. But we returned to the US in 2008 for our younger son. He is now twenty. After his brother died, he wanted to join the US Army or Marine, one of them. But my husband and I have convinced him to go back to school. He took his GED this year and started taking some classes at BMCC." She smiled with relief.

"I will get some water for you." I got up and went into the kitchen, where Narbada didi was waiting to talk to me.

"Tapainko kura kani sakiyo didi sanga"? (Is your conversation with the older sister done?) Narbada didi inquired when she saw me. "Tyo office ma hamro staff meeting hundai cha 2 baje, bahini." (We are having our staff meeting at 2:00 p.m. in that office, younger sister.)

Processing what had just emanated from my conversation with Sonam didi and unable to quickly switch off, I simply tilted my head from left to right, indicating to Narbada didi that I will wrap up my meeting.

"Tapain ko kura sakiena bhane hami arko office ma baschaun ki ta? Bhaihalcha" (If your conversation is not finished then, perhaps we can meet in another room? That is OK.), Narbada didi quickly added, probably seeing my vacant expression.

"No, we will be done before two, Narbada didi." With this response, I went back inside the office. I had already been meeting several of the ESL participants outside Adhikaar by this time, so I decided to schedule a follow-up interview with Sonam didi.

Sonam didi must have overheard my conversation with Narbada didi, for as soon as she saw me enter the room, she gathered her belongings and got up from her seat.

I handed her the glass of water. She thanked me and started walking out of the office as she drank the water. I followed her to the kitchen sink, where she started washing the glass.

"Please don't worry about it. I will do it." I tried to take the glass from her.

Holding on to the glass and pushing me gently, she said, "Hoina, hamro ta baani nai cha ni, bahini. Tapainle hamro dukkha suni dinu bhayo bhayo tyahi nai dherai thulo bhaisakyo." (No, it is already part of our habit. You listened to our suffering; that is already a lot.)

I followed her to the gate and waved at her. She left Adhikaar that Sunday afternoon, and I did not see her again. When I inquired about her whereabouts, Helumbu participants mentioned that she had not been keeping well and was worried about her son discontinuing his studies.

Under the IIRAIRA immigration reforms, legalization activities and labor both appeared less stigmatized, although considerable political anxiety remained about the implications of changing relations of migrant (il)legality in a state whose administration based its legitimacy on liberal reforms for migrants with temporary legal statuses. Migrants who had lived and worked in the city through the post-9/11 backlash period worried that the very activities at one political moment that were encouraged as central to the economic growth and stability of a newly settled community might now be deployed to condemn them as criminal aliens. Meanwhile, the constant criticism of forms of low-wage, undocumented work that migrants performed that had previously gone unscrutinized, even unacknowledged, in public spaces and political platforms destabilized a liberal moral discourse on labor and illegality as twinned aspects of migrants' existence.

For both Sanju didi and Sonam didi, like many student-interlocutors and working-class Nepalis outside New York State, their arrival in the United States in the 1990s was managed through a quota system that included family reunification schemes, limited student visas, and restrictive numbers of sponsorships by US citizens. Sanju didi's and Sonam didi's arrivals coincided with the passage of IIRAIRA in 1996, where "spaces of nonexistence" came under direct scrutiny, making employment of undocumented migrants' labor possible and governable. As Coutin has observed, "IIRAIRA . . . created a new temporality: illegal time" (2003, 31). The act retroactively imposed "180 days of illegal time"—a legal probationary period—for people without documentation physically present in the country. As a result, the locus of interior immigration enforcement shifted from state representative and INS officials to private citizens—"employers, college admissions officials, social workers, public housing officials"—who were taking an active role in surveilling the status of migrants they employed and interacted with on a regular basis (11).

Yet Sanju didi's and Sonam didi's experiences do not fit a typical legalization experience and labor regularization strategy among undocumented migrants. Sanju didi's family, originally from Bhutan, had lived as refugees in India before moving back to northeast Nepal, and Sonam didi and her husband lived and worked in India as low-wage Nepali migrant workers. They both acknowledged that their past experience in India and cultural familiarity had been useful in obtaining employment in Indian households in New York. In the case of Sonam didi, the employer eventually helped regularize her and her husband's status so she could continue working for them for most of her life in the United States. These cultural and linguistic linkages, though they may have helped them secure employment upon their arrival, did not alleviate their legal precarity. Although having spent significant years of their childhood and adulthood in India, neither of them had Indian citizenship. More important, neither sought asylum in the

United States, despite their "refugee" status in India and the family's experience of past persecution in Bhutan (in the case of Sanju didi), which would have made them eligible to file an asylum claim, for there were no legal pathways that recognized Nepali-speaking migrants as potential refugees and asylum seekers in the decade preceding 9/11. However, this changed for the majority of people arriving after 2001.

"NEW LIFE CAFÉ"

By associating aspects of labor integration with the more readily naturalized category of migrant illegality and asylum credibility, the US state to a greater extent depoliticized migrant labor at exactly the moment when it was being challenged and restructured by the series of immigrant rights mass mobilizations of 2006.[7] This rendered workplace grievances and claims undeniably tied to the undocumented-ness of people's lives by making the working-class migrants seem evidently uneducated and vulnerable. Yet the acceptance of socioeconomically marginalized positions, like those of my ESL interlocutors and members at Adhikaar, was less concerning compared to the visibility of undocumented migrants.

Like Sanju didi and Sonam didi, Phurba didi is also from Helumbu. A plump woman in her early thirties, Phurba didi was born in the late 1970s in Nepal, where her parents had relocated after living in India as Tibetan refugees for two decades. Phurba didi got married in the late 1990s and, a year later, got pregnant. Because of their difficult financial situation, she and her husband, like many others from the region, started looking for livelihood possibilities outside Nepal. Phurba didi's husband left for the United States in 2000, and the following year she also found work in South Korea in a garment factory, stitching socks and jeans.[8] In 2007, Phurba didi and her son came to New York to join her husband, whose asylum application was successful and who was working as a cab driver. She lived with her husband and son in Woodside, Queens, and worked as a live-out housekeeper for an Indian family on the Upper East Side. Since she had lived and worked in Seoul for four years, she often compared her life in Seoul and the city.

"I used to miss my son. He was only one year old when I left him with my parents in Nepal. Those four years in Korea were very difficult," she shared with the class one Sunday.

When asked to explain what she meant by *difficult*, she said, "Well, you don't have to clean people's bathrooms and wash dishes. . . . The factory work was difficult because *we* had to work like machines, but I had friends working with me. The factory provided housing and food in Korea, so we did not have to make papers. But here [in the United States], I work alone in my boss's house and see my family and friends on weekends . . . like today."

"Yasto ke bahini, America ma dukkha kaagaz nabhayera; Korea ma dukkha kaagaz bhayera" (It is like this, younger sister, in America you suffer if you do not have papers; in Korea you suffer because you have papers), Lhamu didi jumped in.

Lhamu didi, who was born in Mustang and grew up in Pokhara, northwest of Kathmandu, also arrived in the United States in 2007. She had been living in the city for two years at the time she joined Adhikaar. She had also worked in Seoul for several years before migrating to the United States to join her husband, who had been working in the construction industry in the city for the past ten years. She now lived in Brooklyn with her two teenage sons, fifteen and seventeen years old. She recently joined my ESL class and was meeting the Helumbu participants for the first time. Because she was an employee at a Korean-owned nail salon on the Upper East Side, her workplace situation and reasons for learning English were different from those of live-in and live-out nannies at Adhikaar.[9] Commenting that while her previous work experience in Korea helped her obtain the parlor job, her *kaagaz* (work permit) in Korea was tied to her specific employers, thus limiting her mobility and making it impossible to change employers.

"Yahan ta afulai man parena bane arkai kaam, arkai sahu, khoznu hunchan kyare ta hoina?" (Here, if you do not like [your current job], you can seek a different job, different boss, isn't that correct?) Lhamu didi looked around the room for assurance without asking anyone in particular.

"Sure, you can find a different job, different boss if your husband has a job and can pay for housing and food. Not everyone's situation is like yours." Mina didi was the first to respond in her usual dry, matter-of-fact, sarcastic yet playful tone.

"Kaam man napare ni tyahi sahuni ko ma basnu parya thiyo hamro ta . . . kagaaz nabhayeko karan le uti bela . . . jasarai arule ajabholi kaagaz banaunchan" (Even though we did not like our work, we had to remain with the same boss . . . because our papers were *not* made . . . in the way others make paper nowadays), Sanju didi said as she gestured toward Sonam didi, who nodded in agreement.

"Tyo kaagaz ko kura mahile bujhen didi, tara sahu sanga paisa badhaidinus bhanna ta milchan kyare ni yahan . . . ani—" (I get the issue about paper, older sister, but I have heard that you can request your boss to give you a raise here . . . and—), Lhamu didi insisted.

"What if your boss says she will find someone else who will do the same work for the same pay? You know how hard it is to even ask for a raise? I have been trying for the last six months . . . waiting for the right time to bring up the issue. But I am scared that I might get fired if I say anything," Mina didi cut off Lhamu didi.

"Can you all speak in English so we can get back to class?" Tenzin interjected, looking somewhat agitated.

"Tapain ko samasya hamro jasto hoina rahecha ni, didi" (Your problem is not like ours, older sister), Phurba didi said to Lhamu didi softly.

I, however, was caught up in an animated discussion among my participants about the fear and dilemmas they face in workplace negotiations and problems with legal paperwork that workers' rights workshops could not necessarily resolve. For a moment I forgot all about keeping up with our scheduled classroom topic—WANY's lesson titled "New Life Café"—on that crisp Sunday morning in March. As always, however, our conversation had taken on a life of its own. By the second half of the two-hour session, participants took it upon themselves to discuss issues relevant to their working lives, making paper, and surviving.

Phurba didi and Lhamu didi's experiences of labor and legal precarity, like those of the majority of Nepalis arriving after 2001, especially in the years following the 2006 immigrant rights mobilization, were different from those of people arriving in the 1990s, for this was an era where the interchangeability of migrant "illegality" with migrant criminality had become naturalized and extensively justified in the surveillance of undocumented migrant communities.[10] And to counter the then prevailing discourse, media images, and representations of undocumented migrants and working-class communities of color, as criminals and "terrorists," communities' participation in their collective representation as a "nonterrorist" undocumented workforce, contributing to the US economy, played a central role in the sociopolitical visibility and construction of new migrant subjectivities: suffering and resilient, undocumented but resourceful (Gomberg-Munoz 2010b; see also Gonzales 2011, 2016). As such, many, like Phurba didi and Lhamu didi, recounted their experience of hardship and socioeconomic marginalization—though employed in different low-wage labor industries—through the lens of being migrant workers elsewhere, hence the comparison of restrictive mobility imposed by the Employment Permit System (EPS) in Korea with the presumably agentive choices of seeking employment upon arrival in the city despite lack of work documentation or pending legality. Yet their choices, as well as those of Sanju didi, Pelki didi, Sonam didi, and other ESL participants, had much to do with divergent interior immigration enforcements between the 1990s and early 2000s and the specific expansion of federal immigration enforcement into state laws and local-level governance after 2006. The proposed Comprehensive Immigration Reform Act of 2006 produced a specific form of legal precarity, expanding temporalization of low-wage undocumented migrants into several legal categories through the new H-2C visa system.[11] It redefined the state's conception of the relationship between the undocumented migrant workforce already present within its borders and deportability. Specifically, the increased visibility of the presence of an undocumented migrant workforce facilitated the expansion of interior immigration enforcement provisions through workplace raids in the 2006 pro-immigrant mass mobilization period.

The restructuring of the comprehensive immigration reform law in 2006 undermined the legal framework of the 1990s, and of the early 2000s, that had produced and managed the un/documented migrant workforce for decades. The system that had presided over a production of legal and ambiguous semilegal statuses, including working-class migrant families whose members were both naturalized US citizens and newly arrived migrants belonging to "a range of temporary or permanent interim statuses," now sought to reduce ambiguous legalities through worksite enforcement and temporalization of people's "illegal" presence.[12] Like Sanju didi or Sonam didi, most of these individuals had been working in the low-wage labor sector and living on meager earnings: most men in restaurants and grocery stores, and some as cab drivers, while women overwhelmingly as live-in and live-out maids and nannies in the tristate area. Some, like Sonam didi and Lhamu didi, considered themselves fortunate to have been hired by generous and understanding employers who assisted them in regularizing their statuses. Others, like Sanju didi, shared their stories of years of struggle to find employment despite arriving in the United States as long-term residents with papers. Meanwhile, those arriving without papers in the post-2006 era, like Lhamu didi or Phurba didi, who found employment in ethnic enclaves but needed to explore legalization options to regularize their temporary legal statuses, had sprung up only in the last decade.

If, in the decades following IIRAIRA reforms, the liberal state created necessary loopholes for constructing temporary migrant legalities that seemingly undermine illegality, the decade following post-2006 pro-immigrant mass mobilization political processes worked to reify them through enhanced interior enforcement in migrant workplaces and effective policing of activities within migrant communities. Providing space for and enabling community-based activism and grassroots migrant centers like Adhikaar to provide new immigrants with social support and language interpretation services meant not only effective disciplining of marginalized migrant communities but also outsourcing federal immigration enforcement to local law authorities and state-level ones, increasing funding allocation to state and local enforcement.[13] Indeed, using the migrant community's labor, energy, and resources to restructure and expand the liberal state governance technologies has succeeded precisely because of the commonsensical logic of interconnecting migrant labor regularization and legal temporalization through facilitation into the layered dynamics of a given migrant community.

People arriving in the post-2006 period hesitated to share their ongoing legalization experiences, at least until they acquired a green card or became naturalized US citizens. Phurba didi and Lhamu didi would seem to be exceptions to this logic, given their quite vocal and forthcoming attitude about the importance of "making paper." Perhaps because Phurba didi's husband had already obtained asylum by the time she entered the country as a green card holder, her legalization experience was less difficult than she cared to divulge. In discreetly remarking to Lhamu didi that her problem was not like those of more recent migrants, Phurba didi gently discouraged her from further inquiring into kaagaz banaune—even though she had never explicitly asked ESL participants about their experiences of legalization. Alternately, Lhamu didi might have simply been inquiring into employment opportunities that did not demand proper work documentation or legal status. Whatever the reason, Lhamu didi's innocent inquiry created uneasiness among a majority of the ESL participants, provoking Sanju didi to admit somewhat sarcastically that more recent migrants had to work for "the same boss . . . because [their] papers were *not* made . . . in the way others make paper nowadays."

As people offered these self-reflexive critiques and worked out their dilemmas of increasing labor precarity, competing understandings of "making paper" and multiple interpretations of suffering seeped into our classroom discussion. At the same time, the legibility and *interpretability* of this emergent community depended on people's adherence to the dominant narrative of "migrant suffering" in contemporary America. Far from being an over simplistic dichotomy between agency and victimhood, the suffering template expanded into and relied on people's capacity and self-disciplining techniques enabling their visibility as a vulnerable and desirable mass of low-wage, temporary workers. On the one hand, the widespread usage of suffering as the seemingly objective outcome of one's participation in labor subordination meant that people knew exactly how they were being interpreted and, in turn, needed to represent a homogenous disposition and language fitting into some kind of formulaic interpretation of a marginalized migrant community. On the other hand, their different migration trajectories and experiences of legalization during different political moments make impractical a logic of shared suffering, whether as a collective definition or of particular significance associated with livelihood struggles, workplace conditions, and temporary legalization options.

Many felt anxious about their intertwined lives and temporalized legality as a type of dukkha experienced only upon arrival and socialization in the United States. Nepalis arriving in the mid- to late 1990s, many of whom could have filed for asylum, like Sonam didi or Sanju didi, did not learn about the process let alone know of or receive direct legal assistance and, therefore, typically relied on their employers' goodwill and generosity. They attended English classes to assume productive roles as workers. As a result, "making paper" was seldom considered a first choice, or a desirable option, even by those eligible for asylum, like Sonam didi or Sanju didi, who qualified for a "refugee" status. Despite their having lived in the United States for three or more years, the need to secure a sustainable livelihood provided impetus for Sanju didi, Sonam didi, Lhamu didi, and Phurba didi to explore status regularization while working as domestics. The domestic-work industry, while providing readily accessible employment for many of the ESL participants, was not without its own problems. From the perspectives of the ESL interlocutors, the prospect of not finding employment or losing their current job posed as much of a risk as remaining undocumented, despite having lived and worked without proper documentation. Or, rather, they regarded employment and status regularization interchangeably and as coconstitutive of work, suffering, and survival since their arrival.

So far, discussions of suffering and survival strategies in the Nepali community have focused on the lives of my student-interlocutors, migration trajectories and shared workplace grievances in ESL classroom sessions, and their particular experience of labor and legalization. However, Adhikaar activists, community organizers, and fellow volunteers also have strategic use for stories of "migrant suffering" and survival. Specifically, their anecdotes and explanations around practices of censorship demonstrate how their work with Nepali migrants and refugees have emerged in dialogue with the changing interior immigration enforcement and asylum politics. My discussion with Luna during the editing process of the Jankari (information) research report titled "Snapshots of the Nepali-Speaking Community in New York City: Demographics and Challenges" provides an instructive example of how these dynamics materialized on the ground.

BETWEEN COLLECTIVE CONSCIOUSNESS AND CENSORSHIP

The Jankari report, published in December 2010, was an initial attempt by Adhikaar to document the growing Nepali migrant community in New York City as well as to showcase the organization's outreach, mobilization, direct service, and advocacy around social justice and workers' rights for newly arrived members of the Nepali New York community. One of the objectives was to bring awareness to the larger community regarding the specific needs of Nepali migrant workers. Second, and subsequently, by making it public it was also educating nonprofits, immigrant rights organizations, and public institutions that either worked or anticipated working with Nepali-speaking migrants. The data was based on three hundred surveys administered over the last three years and twelve qualitative interviews reflecting the diversity of the population in New York City. Survey questionnaires had captured basic information on the then makeup of the community (based on age, gender, ethnicity, language, and occupation), followed by some detailed accounts of types of direct services and facilities people used and several anecdotal references on their experience of encountering public institutions and city services, such as schools, hospitals, immigration offices, police, and other government offices. A large part of the report also provided information on people's occupation back home, employment history since their arrival, and overall (dis)satisfaction with their current jobs. This section of the report offered various snippets and vignettes to highlight the downward social mobility that the majority of Adhikaar's members experienced.

The report was based on community research, which started two years prior my engagement with the Adhikaar's activists, fellow board members, community members, volunteers, and organizers. By the time I learned of the project, the report was in the last stages of the writing and prepublication phase—past data collection, coding, interpretation, and analysis—and I was invited to mainly assist with the final edits. Because of my own immersion and research in the community within and outside Adhikaar, it was not surprising that Luna and fellow board members asked for my input prior to its publication. I knew the main purpose of publishing the report then. I was not specifically looking for in-depth interpretation or analysis of complex questions about people's experience of seeking employment and legalization marked by lived dilemmas and contradictions.

At the same time, I was a bit perplexed and disappointed to find the report's oversimplified rendering of people's reasons, responses, and silences on those questions. After a long deliberation, I decided to share these concerns in my editorial feedback. Given the report's imminent launch at the New School University's campus, which a longtime Adhikaar supporter had kindly offered to sponsor, I was uncertain how it would be received. To my relief, I got a phone call from Luna immediately after I sent in my comments.

LUNA: I agree with your observation that the report provides very little information on the actual difficulties of migration and settlement trajectories of many of our community members, including the issue of underemployment and exploitative conditions that people continue to work in. You are absolutely right about . . .

[Her voice trailed off on the other end before picking up again.]

the need to question reasons for people not reporting incidents of discrimination either at workplaces or during their encounters with state authorities and city officials beyond merely reporting its occurrence. . . .

[Quoting my written comment, she continued.]

"Or people unwilling to provide specific answers to their unemployment situations" cannot simply be stated as having a "close link between work and prestige in the Nepali community" as the report does.

[I did not interrupt her until she finished reciting back my feedback on the report, which I also had with me.]

TINA: I realize the report is already in its final stage of production and my feedback has less to do with editing. . . . I am asking difficult questions not only about Adhikaar's roles but also about our own participation and ongoing engagement with the community members, none of which have simple answers. Yet, in not raising some of these concerns about why many Nepali migrants are placed in such a disadvantaged position in the first place, are we not neglecting structural issues? We both know that being unable to speak English fluently or having irregular immigration status are not the primary reasons why they continue to experience downward social mobility. It is a logical, normative response, yes. But it is not the truth from what we see at Adhikaar. "Truth is quite simple," I am told by my ESL student.

I could hear myself quoting Mina didi, emulating her tone even, as I uttered those words. Luna did not disagree. She wondered to what extent the final report should have a separate commentary section to address issues of structural inequalities and legal violence governing people's lives in the country. More important, she worried how that might impact Adhikaar's popularity among its wealthy Nepali and non-Nepali philanthropists. When asked for clarification about potential "impacts," she responded in the following way: "You have been facilitating English classes. Does the language training we provide at Adhikaar guarantee people's mobilization for future activism and organizing skills? English speaking is a basic requirement to survive in this country that you and I take it for granted. So far Adhikaar has been successful in mobilizing workers and taking them to the rally in Albany last year. But how many of those forty Nepalis involved in the process and the rally do you think understood the actual reason and purpose for doing so? Maybe four or five."

A momentary silence entered our conversation, then offering a concrete example, she continued: "Let's talk about the participation of Nepali Domestic Workers within the DWU [Domestic Workers United], for instance. It is hardly consistent, as many of the participants do not know of its history, existence, or purpose. Those who do know the purpose can hardly enter the debate or understand the cause that actually exists to help working class migrants of color like themselves."

I interjected.

TINA: Let's go back to English-language classes. Do you think it is necessary for people to learn the language other than being able to survive in this country? Would you say it is still key for their engaged participation or for them to become politicized then?

LUNA: Absolutely. Maybe there are only four or five who understand why they are going to Albany or participating in the DWU rally every now and then. But every year, the number of participants has increased, and so has the number of those who understand the cause for and commitment to these activities occurring in the public spaces.

[...]

As an ethnic intermediary, I am in a privileged position to translate and interpret for many. But I've been placed in a relatively powerful position and to be battling for their cause have raised unsettling and difficult questions with no easy answers. But should I stop doing what I do because of these personal dilemmas? Absolutely not.

The conversation quickly turned to our own relatively privileged social positions. Luna explained how this was not the way to sustain a grassroots, migrant-workers' rights organization like Adhikaar. "In order for a community-based organization like Adhikaar to exist, there needs to be more than just passionate energy of individuals. It won't be sustainable in the long run. It is only good for the first two or three years before people get burnt out. There needs an effective system to ensure organization's sustainability."

Her dilemma is perhaps shared by many cultural intermediaries, "native insiders," and interpreters—me included—who have taken up causes for members of the community with whom we do not share the specificity of migration trajectory, integration experience, and daily legalization battle. According to Luna, running an organization like Adhikaar required support from people who were loyal to the cause but could also function in a workplace environment. "People with a larger vision who are both self-motivated and independent workers," she emphasized. She explained that the past few years have been a learning experience in terms of understanding not only the needs and services of community members but also how those needs then needed to be translated, interpreted, and packaged appropriately to long-standing supporters, activists and advocates, private individuals and institutional donors, and public funding agencies throughout the city and the tristate area.

To me, she was echoing De Genova again: "By asserting their physical and bodily presence, these migrants thereby affirmed the ineradicably and incorrigibly insistent character of their very material needs, desires, capacities and dispositions" (2009, 450). I thought a lot about our conversation that evening.

The importance of considering the question of suffering, survival, and censorship together struck me with clarity one evening in the midst of a nanny-training workshop at Adhikaar in January 2011. Reema was one of the key facilitators at the workshop and responded to my question about what it might mean to have realistic options for people with temporary legal statuses to negotiate wages and benefits at workplaces. She told me with a warm smile, "Bahini, haven't you figured it out already? *That* is *one* of the reasons why our community members are employed in this sector [domestic work]." Turning to the workshop audience—many of the student-participants from ESL classes, including mine—she continued in Nepali, "An employer will only ask to see your documents if he/she is looking to replace you or has no longer need for domestic help." She was not alone in instructing people about their relatively advantageous positions without directly acknowledging their temporary legal status.

In her usual upbeat tone, Narbada didi chimed in, "Saathiharu ho, America ma junai sukai kaam ko pani mahatwa dinchan. Phohor uthaune wa bathroom safa garne wa table pusne hos, kunai pani naramro wa laaj ko kaam hoina. Yo matra eutai des hun ki jahan manche afno kaam bata ramro maanincha ra yahan afno pahichan wa mahatwa afno pariwar, saathiharu, kaamdar beech banauchan—yo Ameriki samudaya ma. Maile bhannu ta parne hoina, tara yahan aja aunubhayeka didi bahini haru ko aa-afnai samsya ra dukkha chan . . . tara hami sir uthayera, mehenata gari kaam garera baancheka chaunai ta?" (Friends, in America, every work and profession is valued. There is no shame or negativity associated with collecting trash or cleaning bathroom or wiping tables. And this is also the country where people continue to take pride in what they do to establish their worth among their friends, family, colleagues—in the US society. I do not have to mention, but all of us sisters gathered here today have our own stories of struggle and suffering . . . but aren't we surviving here, working hard with dignity?)

Nepali migrant workers, among them my ESL student-interlocutors, participated in what I had, until then, come to see as collective silence around legalization activities. However, Reema's remark of whether I had not yet learned the real reason for Nepali migrants' employment in the domestic labor sector or Narbada didi's speech of suffering practicalities similar to the ones she delivered now seemed fraught and exaggerated. For there was a kind of acknowledgment that people's struggle and suffering had also led to the survival of the emergent Nepali New York community. Moreover, in explicitly encouraging people to focus on work-related activities and to verbalize grievances, Narbada didi was participating, ironically, in a particular kind of censorship around the labor *of* legalization that mattered most for regular Adhikaar attendees and community members. Narbada didi was further tacitly encouraging that attendees partake in that censorship for the community's survival.

Here, surviving is intended to avoid dwelling in the actual in-betweenness of participants' legal statuses, yet people's narratives of overcoming hardship at workplaces constructed them as suffering workers surviving despite all odds.

Survival is a dynamic process, much like suffering, continuously transforming and contingent on a given context. It is a deeply personal and individualized experience; yet, at the same time, it is a collective and cultivable practice. I suggest that the balance between the two is created through intersubjective relations requiring not an exact articulation but acknowledgment of its multiple manifestations. The individuals composed a community of "suffering migrants and asylum seekers," to use Narbada didi's phrase, regardless of their actual legal status. People in the community are not always familiar with one another's legalization experience or the specificities of their suffering stories. Neither do they have knowledge of the specific reason of suffering in relation to "making paper." Moreover, they effectively practice censorship surrounding details of their asylum-seeking work. And yet, they were not alone in their suffering accounts. They assumed that the others in their social networks understand, without having to verbalize their suffering, since they all participate in similar legalization and labor activities, one way or another. Not having to share the specific content of one's suffering with others, while still acknowledging the generally shared experience, facilitated a kind of collective reflexivity that allowed for a meaning-making process contingent on everyday survival practicalities.

People like Luna, Reema, or Narbada didi were involved because of their vision, passion, and continued fight for social justice for people they encountered and worked with on a daily basis. Yet each had a distinct rationale about what that entailed and how it needed to be addressed based on their own background, experience, and position within and outside the migrant community. Each had thought long and hard about personal challenges, professional compromises, difficulties, and dilemmas brought on by their role as cultural interpreters and intermediaries—translating the world of social justice and human rights, particularly those relevant to workers' rights–based orientations to facilitate migrants' survival strategies, intermediating the lives of people they encountered on a daily basis to make legible and interpretable suffering to the liberal state for the sustainability of the community's work. Still each seemed ambivalent of their role and discussed indefinitely the limits and the possibilities offered by it.

The diversity and internal conflict within the grassroots organization informing their divergent priorities and practices notwithstanding, there was a shared acknowledgment for a more balanced and careful tactic of migrant mobilization work among Adhikaar activists and community organizers given the undocumented-ness and legal limbo statuses of the majority of the members they served. They were conscious of the far-reaching and potentially detrimental consequences that a certain kind and scale of suffering visibility could bring for people in the greater migrant community.[14] Among these included the disambiguation of suffering visibility from asylum-seeking work, so there always existed the possibility for deniability of "the work of *making paper*" performed by those they provided direct service to and assisted with employment-related matters.

Redirecting conversation to workplace scenarios about one's daily hardship and survival tactics, the paradox of the migrant and asylum suffering script and the accompanying categories provoked anxiety, yet it also allowed both community activists and members to tacitly participate in a collective censorship. At the same time, to relegate these practices to the domain of migrant resistance or resilience would be to miss *why* they were cultivated in the first place and had gradually shaped people's perceptions, practices, and performances as well as consciousness of *what* legality does: specific ways to legalize as a site for socioeconomic hardships and survival strategies. Participation in censorship, as a survival strategy and practice, much like the self-imposed isolation among Latin American day laborers in Northern California that Juan Thomas Ordóñez documents (2016), gestures toward enduring and expected roles within a specific community and enables subjective transformations and potentials as they become legible and interpretable. Censorship, in other words, is key to the contemporary migrant community formation and, more accurately in the case of Nepalis, a "suffering community" is brought into existence through censorship and survival practices. Hypervisibility around labor precariousness and ambivalence toward temporary legalities are key mechanisms of the community through which Nepalis incorporated mainstream suffering discourses around the categories of "refugee" and "asylum seeker" and displayed subjective rationales to participate in censorship. If inhabiting the normative expectation of a "suffering claimant"—even while participating in the coconstruction of previously unavailable oppositional categories of suffering migrants and claimant-*workers*—informed norms, behaviors, and dispositions of migrants, then participating in censorship around a range of legalization activities ensured survival of the community itself (figure 15).

Luna and Narbada didi primarily saw themselves as cultural interpreters not only sharing their skills and knowledge, or to use Luna's phrase, "raising awareness," with other community members but also deciphering the inner workings of the US labor laws and interior immigration enforcements for the community members. They are active and engaged participants producing knowledge about the community given their social positions with relatively secured legal existence. It is perhaps this dynamic relationship—their own legality and work becoming

FIGURE 15 Adhikaar at Walk for Nepal, New York City, 2012.
Photograph courtesy of Sonam Ukyab.

deeply entangled, internalized, and significant—not unlike the undocumented work performed by claimant-*workers* in legal-institutional spaces, that enables both identification with and differentiation from those they encountered, assisted, and developed relationships with over a long period.

Luna, Narbada didi, and fellow community volunteers all acknowledged the problem of censorship around legalization, given that the organization's mission was to interrogate, unfold, and address the "real" suffering and hardships confronting its members and the kind of activism work to be promoted that had emerged from their daily encounters. Their awareness of becoming designated and accidental cultural facilitators, interpreters, and representatives speaks volumes about the absence of the liberal state (broadly conceived through administrative, judicial, and bureaucratic institutions) engagement, welfare support, and resource allocation to migrant communities in one of the biggest immigrant cities. Rather than a problem confounding a large-scale analysis, the absent presence of the liberal state was the constitutive ground for cohesive community-building, particularly for those effortlessly inhabiting spaces of intermediations as interpreters, researchers, and organizers. Coming together as representatives of an emergent community, their differently situated positions and dilemmas arising from their positions notwithstanding, the collective identification in themselves was valuable for Adhikaar's ongoing social justice work and migrant workers' rights activism. The process of awareness raising and consciousness ultimately constructed the community as entailing particular kinds of vulnerable workers through their relationship to labor and legality; it made them a visible mass of silently *surviving* migrants in the city, as Narbada didi had pointed out to me long before I started fieldwork or understood its significance for the survival of the Nepali New York community.

Conclusion

THE "MIGRANT [AND ASYLEE] SUFFERING" SCRIPT

It is a given that the ever-changing scripts in liberal democracies have complicated legibility or the functionality of a particular "migrant suffering" story. Rather than seeing asylum as status regularization and materialization of long-standing socioeconomic and political insecurities in the United States and several Western democracies, recent studies suggest that the explosion of migrants', refugees', and asylum seekers' accounts provide a political platform and form of authentic work through which individuals contest and claim their own voice in the public space (Blitz 2017; Ataç, Rygiel, and Stierl 2016).

Although the problematic narration, representation, and politicization of the "migration and refugee crisis" has been critiqued, the growing attention to cases of "real" refugees and asylum seekers has only deepened the reinforcement of spectacular suffering (Ramsay 2019; De Genova and Tazzioli 2016; Knight and Stewart 2016). Observing the marked separation between conceptual and legal categorization of "refugees," "asylum seekers," and "economic migrants" with policy implications, scholars repeatedly show the limitations posed by administrative categories to account for the diversity of people, their social realities, reasons for migrating, claiming refugee status, and seeking asylum. Many list individualized stories of seeking and failing to obtain asylum and chronicle harrowing tales of peoples' migratory journey in vivid details and descriptions (see Cabot 2014). Advocates of the latter pay particular attention to geographical routes and geopolitical trajectories to conceptualize notions of "limbo" status and the constrained mobilities of migrants and asylum seekers (Cabot 2012; Tuckett 2016). Increasingly, anthropological studies of refugees and asylum are based on collaboration among advocates, activists, and scholars, on the one hand, and "people on the move" themselves showcasing their own accounts of suffering, on the other (see, for instance, Cabot 2016; Selim et al. 2018). Even as an author challenges a stereotypical profile of an asylum seeker and promises to paint a more complex picture of ever-changing migration trends and asylum regimes, the characterization and categorization of a given population as resilient and economically productive dominates much of this scholarship. People's own accounts of suffering are heralded as a powerful example of universal humanity, reframed through familiar frames of victimhood, only to be represented as "real" refugees or "credible" asylum seekers. Voices, videos, and compilations of social media uploads by people about their tragic circumstances get held up as signs of individual agency and a shift from normative politics to transformative, radical potentials, despite evidence pointing to the increasing unlikelihood of actual changes materializing for many on the ground. Even more puzzling than how suffering recognition might have ironically contributed to "categorical fetishism" (see Crawley and Skleparis 2018; Long 2013) is how it has been operationalized in popular and scholarly work.

The visibility and privileging of migrant suffering therefore signify structural dynamics and are productive of the diversification of temporary (il)legalities. Ethnographic focus on either a certain population's visibility and experiences as "refugees and asylum seekers" or concern with the ahistorical production of suffering within the legal-juridical spaces of their asylum claims without attention to parallel, broader accounts of *habitual suffering* circulated within migrant communities risks overlooking the sociopolitical order in which specific kinds of "suffering tales" (see Good 2011a; see also McKinley 1997), and not others, might be occurring in significance and *why*. It also risks overlooking the conditions shaping contemporary relations between suffering, survival, and censorship in liberal democracies.

At a time when shifts in migrant and asylum legalization are compounded with obvious socioeconomic consequences in the organization and management of different populations around the world, as has been the case for United States in the context of pre- and Trump-era immigration and asylum policies, attending simultaneously to temporary legalities and suffering across different population has critical political and scholarly implications. The growing visibility and spectacle of undocumented migrants' and asylum seekers' suffering speeches in the public platform and social media is heralded as a sign of radical and transformative politics (Nicholls 2013; Bal and Hernández-Navarro 2011; Squire 2011). This public discourse equating suffering recognition with the political viability of the proliferation of temporary, increasingly bureaucratized, and ever narrowly constructed categorizations of "migrants, refugees and asylum seekers" has also seeped into recent scholarship, privileging rather than questioning the normative political identities and the conditions that create them (Martinez-Schuldt and Martinez 2019).

SUFFERING TRANSFORMATIONS AND VISIBILITY

Some of the drastic consequences of the transformation of suffering accounts and the production of migrant or asylee subjectivities in the contemporary moment have been institutional interpretations and techniques of visibility: among them, Malkki has forcefully argued that the knowledge production about refugee-ness in the wake of World War II displacement, the rise of humanitarian and international interventions, and the administration of the UN conventions by refugee agencies in collaboration with nation-states, by detaching political histories of displacement and suffering from institutional history, discourse, and scholarship that sustained the assumed coherence of "the refugee" and of "refugee studies," jointly constituted "refugees and exile" (1995b). Fassin, making a wider point and an incisive critique about discourse, truth, and asymmetrical development of institutional translation, argues that "the precarious truth of asylum" is an intrinsic part of the new configuration of refugee recognition regimes tied to immigration enforcement and asylum, "emphasizing suffering more than it does rights" (2013, 39). For Ticktin, the transformation and visibility of suffering, migrants applying for work permits or appealing for the illness clause in particular, into the sphere of the liberal state amounts to the "production of new forms of subjectivity and inequality" (2011, 127).

This project began from a different supposition and aims at a different objective: the socioeconomically disadvantaged ESL student-interlocutors, the naturalized citizens and green card–holding community activist-interlocutors, the undocumented migrants seeking status regularization through employment, and the claimant-*workers* incorporated in the asylum documentation and the witness preparation all acknowledged or anticipated incommensurable degrees of suffering. In their daily activities, discourses, and survival strategies, they had all experienced it to some extent in the spaces of encounter between the state, the wider South Asian migrant community, and the ongoing legalization matters related to their lives. To this effort, they all had made a conscious decision between observing silence surrounding *habitual suffering* and making certain claims legible to the liberal state, new possibilities through participating in the "work of making paper" and the coconstruction of suffering testimonies, fitting into the suffering script, and becoming visible. Yet Priya's successful asylum interview did not mirror Tshering's failed asylum, despite months of coconstructing credible suffering testimonies at the private law firms, nor did Tshering's experience match Mina didi's suffering articulations, despite similar investment in the process of preparing, memorizing, reciting, and fitting into the changing frame of victimhood. Notwithstanding these variations, individualized expressions, articulations, and iterations, people in the community found reasons to invest in suffering as a basis for its transformation and continued survival in a sphere of liberal recognition. The substance of this project has focused on particular forms this investment has taken and how, despite institutional incoherence, misrecognition, and misinterpretive outcomes in legal and judicial procedures, suffering accounts served as a platform from which the community members, including ESL student-interlocutors, organizers, and activists at Adhikaar, mobilized dukkha to a central place in their language of (in)visibility and gaining legitimacy.

A (SILENTLY) SUFFERING COMMUNITY

At the beginning of this project, Narbada didi's claim that Nepalis' lives in America should be understood to be primarily about "surviving . . . by selling suffering, silently" was revealed to me in two seemingly distinct spaces: (1) the joint experience of asylum-seeking work, or "making paper," and suffering testimonies among claimant-interlocutors in the law firms and asylum courtrooms and (2) the experience of exploitative labor conditions and racialization through language of suffering among ESL-interlocutors at Adhikaar community center and the greater Nepali community in Queens. The simultaneous suffering visibility and temporary legal statuses were all the more curious when we consider that by 2012, the time I wrapped up pending asylum interpretation assignments and interviews with claimant-interlocutors, asylum provisions were only beginning to expand their eligibility and credibility-determination criteria. Today, asylum law is where US immigration law and interior enforcement reside, and the visibility and performance of "migrant suffering" is a key criterion by which potential asylum claimants are judged. The rise and the tangible effect of asylum legalization as an interior immigration enforcement in the lives of Nepali migrants and asylum claimants have been detailed in this book through the expression of "the work of making paper" and suffering—from locating resourceful individuals in their personal and professional social networks and the community center to participating in protracted and apprenticeship-like conditions of asylum bureaucracy, documentation, testimonial coconstruction, interpretation, and witness preparation, the disciplining effect of asylum was instrumental in shaping their labor lives and legality. This disciplining was put into practice by the intermediary roles of social and institutional actors in human rights agencies, private law firms, and immigration courtrooms and asylum offices. Insofar as the incorporation of people into asylum legalization materialized primarily through the prolonged encounter with private citizens, including pro bono lawyers and human rights advocates, they were perceived as facilitators of immigration and asylum law among people in the greater Nepali community.

This book has traced one long process of the socio-existential and mundane experience of migration and legalization through which everyday suffering is consistently overlooked, produced anew through asylum seeking, and exacerbated for others regardless of having obtained asylum; it has contested assumptions that migrant "integration" or asylee and refugee "resettlement" alleviates suffering for both individuals and the communities to which they belong and located the multilayered interpretations and interjections of suffering in the migrant community that end up ensuring, paradoxically, their participation into long-term marginalization in the liberal state. For Jason De León, the immigration enforcement system is effective precisely because of the indeterminate and unidentifiable objects, institutional apparatuses, and ever-changing agents: "The Border Patrol can draw on the *agency* of animals and other non-humans to do its dirty work while simultaneously absolving itself of any blame connected to migrant injuries or loss of life" (2015, 42).[1] De León offers a revised way of thinking about migrant suffering as a complicated process of deliberate and routinized violence that resulted from the last two decades of immigration and border enforcement practices and the "production of [migrant] trauma"—a generalizable characteristic of structural violence (27). He has brought into the limelight the pervasiveness of this "indirect" violence that materializes through *habitual suffering* or internalization of suffering through people's stories of everyday survival (i.e., the techniques, patterns, usage, and contradictions inherent in migrant material culture) during border crossing that often go unreported, unremarked even, by those who experience or anticipate experiencing the various effects of border enforcement technologies and must continue to navigate dangerous terrain as they succeed (or fail) to make their way to the low-wage exploitable labor markets in the United States.

Nepali Queens, and especially Adhikaar community center, is gradually coming into existence as a migrant space for verbalizing labor grievance yet observing shared silence around (il)legalization and at the same time a key space for migrant grassroots organizing and activism, also emerging as a site for suffering communities, and it functions in much the same way as the "border crossing communities and the diversity of individuals involved in the process" that De León documents (2012, 491). In Nepali Queens, however, the multifaceted and routinized suffering articulations accentuate the internalization process, enabling an individual's socialization into and collective self-identification as a suffering community of practice—an unplanned consequence of the joint interior immigration enforcement and asylum policies containing low-wage surplus labor within the US borders. De León further contends the result of "indirect" violence or "the result of federal policy" (i.e., Border Patrol's enforcement for border crossing communities) is rethinking of undocumented migration and migrant suffering: "This rise in deportations of long-time undocumented residents and young adults raised in the United States indicates that immigration enforcement policies are now creating a *new* type of undocumented migration stream that is fundamentally different from previous generations in terms of life histories, as well as general awareness and preparedness for a desert crossing" (2012, 482).

The substance of this project has worked to illuminate deep roots of similar types of indirect violence and unplanned consequences of the federal policy of interior immigration enforcement governing communities of migrants and asylum claimants, a legal production of new migrant and asylee subjectivities, as well as a community's knowledge of and response to mitigating suffering. The centrality of the case of Nepalis has served to reiterate the ways in which interior immigration and legalization systems, rather than the (assumption) of shared migration trajectory, experience of displacement, or narrative of nationalized past or political history, produce and control migrant suffering imaginaries, narratives, and socialization of communities within the US state borders.

Epilogue

I last visited Queens in July 2019, a year before the COVID-19 pandemic disrupted lives and livelihoods around the world.[1] The Nepali New York migrant communities, like other emergent and/or marginalized communities in the city, were already experiencing increased surveillance, policing, and immigration enforcement, including regular crackdowns on migrant neighborhoods, community spaces, and small businesses employing undocumented migrants. Rising unemployment and cost of living and expedited gentrification of several Queens neighborhoods—Jackson Heights included—exacerbated by continued negligence and inadequate access to quality health care, had driven many migrants out of the city; several families relocated to upstate New York and neighboring states.

I remember being nostalgic and anxious as I walked along Roosevelt Avenue and witnessed shuttered Nepali- and Tibetan-owned businesses and restaurants—including Rato Bhale—on that late afternoon in July. Sitting on an empty bench in a deserted community park, where I once could hardly pass without bumping into my ESL students, fellow volunteers, and community members, I heard Mina didi in my head: "So, have you found what you were looking for? Still writing and *interpreting* our stories?"

That bizarrely quiet Sunday in Jackson Heights made me anxious. I hurriedly made my way toward Woodside Avenue. As I stepped into the Adhikaar office, I felt a sense of relief momentarily. For I met Narbada didi, who was the only "old" staff I knew in a sea of unfamiliar, friendly faces—new community organizers, a team of young activist-interns, and volunteers. The community center itself had gone through a transformation, expanding its modest open-space first floor into a two-story house with cubicles and a lounge. Yet as I browsed the walls of Adhikaar, admiring photos, newspaper clippings of recognition, public awards, and certificates for advocacy and organizing work, I felt the same gush of energy and idealism I had felt as a young volunteer, facilitating ESL classes on Sundays, participating in workers' rights workshops, and engaging volunteers and community members. I knew those accolades and warm smiles hid the untold stories and struggles of many working men and women. It was as though I was transported back in time; I realized then that a part of me had never quite left. That moment, too, was short-lived.

Narbada didi updated me on the dire situation of the community members in the city: "Pahile, haami sabai lai bolnu parcha, afno adikaar magnu parcha, ra afno dukkha bhannu parcha bhanthyaoun. Tara aja bholi, hamra saathi-bhai harulai kehi kaam napare ghar baahira naniklinus, nachinne manche le dhoka knock gare nakholnus, kasaile kaagaz dekhau bhane haamilai khabar garnus . . . yesta yesta salah dinu parne bhayeko cha. Ahile ko awastha ta pahile bhanda naramro cha, bahini." (We used to encourage people to talk, demand their rights, and share their suffering stories. But these days, we ask our community members not to leave their houses or neighborhood unless to go to work, not to open doors to strangers, to notify us [Adhikaar] if people ask you to show papers [legal documents] . . . these are the kinds of advice we are having to give out to members. Sister, the situation of our community is worse than before.) Like a bittersweet homecoming, I was reminded how much the community center as well as the greater Nepali-speaking communities in and outside NYC had transformed in the last five years. I had missed some of the important activities that had occurred in the lives of my interlocutors. According to Narbada didi, the latest fight for the reinstatement of the temporary protected status (TPS) holders had been Adhikaar's most important advocacy work.[2] Shortly after the 7.8 magnitude earthquake in April 2015 and May 2015 in Nepal, Nepalis had become eligible for TPS, which the DHS, under the Trump administration, had announced to terminate in 2018.[3] Although the Nepali-speaking community had fought back—joining the Honduran TPS holders—with a class action suit demanding prevention of the termination and redesignation of the TPS status, the community's future remains uncertain.[4]

More important perhaps, Nepali migrants' suffering visibility and related survival strategies were once again gaining traction in both Nepali diasporic consciousness and popular American imagination. This visibility, however, had gone from grassroots activism, advocacy, and lobbying in Congress related to migrant workers' rights to mobilizing community members and lobbying for legislation to create a pathway to citizenship and permanent residency and, more recently, the HR6 (American Dream and Promise Act of 2021).[5] The scale and mode of activism and advocacy had undergone significant changes. Yet the centrality of the dual practices of suffering and survival had remained intact.

Glossary

NOTE: Nepali belongs to an Indo-Aryan language family and is written in Devanagari script. This glossary uses the transliteration from Devanagari to the Roman script and focuses on the colloquial usage and meaning of the words within the context of the contemporary Nepali-speaking communities in the United States.

adhikaar rights

bahini younger sister; kinship term used to address younger (female) person
banaune to make, to create
bolne to speak

dai older brother; kinship term used to address older (male) person
didi older sister; kinship term used to address older (female) person
dukkha suffering, pain, hardship, struggle; often expressed in opposition to *sukkha*

hamro ours
Hyolmo or *Yolmo* people from the eastern and northern Himalayan regions of Nepal; Hyolmo is also Tibeto-Burman language

jankari information
jeevan life

kaagaz paper; term used for official documents and bureaucratic paperwork
kaam work, often referring to physical or manual labor; can be used in contrast to *jaagir*, which implies formal and professional employment

Maobadi Maoists

saathiharu friends, colleagues, supporters

sahu-ji employer, shop owner; its colloquial usage has a hierarchical connotation

samudaya community

sukkha happiness, joy, contentment; often expressed in opposition to *dukkha*

Notes

INTRODUCTION

1. The conceptualization of the Himalayan diaspora in scholarly work is as diverse as the "Himalayan region" itself, often encompassing northern Nepal, Bhutan, Tibet, China, and North India, including Ladakh and Sikkim. Notwithstanding the important discussion on questions of homeland, belonging, and identity in the Himalayan diaspora, throughout this book I use *Himalayan* and *Nepali diaspora/Nepali-speaking migrants* interchangeably given that my Nepali-speaking interlocutors came from various parts of Nepal, Bhutan, Tibet, and North India.

2. Unlike many anthropologists studying the asylum-seeking experience of Nepali-speaking claimants as well as those from the Himalayan region in the United States (McGranahan 2012; Gallagher 2018; Hindman 2013), I did not enter the asylum scene as an expert witness during asylum hearings nor as a country condition reporter on the political situation of Nepal. Rather, I was expected to play the part of an informant—an informed insider—to lawyers at the human rights agencies, private law firms, and asylum offices. Clearly, the varying degree of relationships with lawyers and legal experts contributed to ever-changing positionalities I ended up occupying, inadvertently, throughout fieldwork. The irony presented by this continuous switching from being an ethnographer researching among Nepalis to becoming an interpreter translating and, essentially, speaking for (and on behalf of) claimants was too viscerally discomforting and surreal to simply dismiss my own accidental insertion into a convoluted asylum-seeking process.

3. The ambivalence around asylum legality features quite sharply in my study of Nepali claimant-interlocutors' experience of status-regularization from the story that Susan Coutin (2003b) tells with respect to El Salvadorans, mainly because seeking asylum is more than "legalizing moves" that would put them on the pathway to becoming legal permanent residents. Another reason is that Coutin's is a story told from the vantage point of "the spaces of [legal] nonexistence" or, as she aptly describes, "an ethnography

of a legal process rather than of a particular group" (2003b, 23), while mine is of a particular group's struggle, survival strategies, and suffering exacerbated by legalization—asylum seeking as one of many aspects of "legalizing moves"—and labor incorporation.

4. I do not subscribe to the assumed "neutrality" of one's positionality in ethnographic research, let alone that of a participant-interpreter. However, it is important to highlight the relatively less influential role of an interpreter compared to those who write country-condition reports or appear in the immigration court as a country-condition expert. I never worked as a court-appointed interpreter for any of the asylum cases for which I interpreted and turned down offers to work on or become part of several highly sensitive asylum cases. My concern was not that my "objective" viewpoint would somehow be compromised. Rather, I simply worried that my partial knowledge and lack of understanding of the specific claims might end up adversely impacting the claimants entangled in the process for years.

5. I use pseudonyms for all my interlocutors, colleagues, and peers across the Nepali migrant community and asylum institutional spaces in New York City.

6. The phenomenological scholars (Desjarlais 1992, 2003; Jackson 1998; Throop 2010; Mattingly and Garro 2000; Robbins 2013) are invested in the concept of suffering primarily in relation to existential questions. In particular, they insist on the limits of interpreting suffering as narrated and as a coherent experience. They point to the problematic binary distinction between experience as narrated versus narrative of lived experience in the Western anthropological understanding of suffering. There can be no narrative, for Mattingly and Garro, without an actual lived experience—a past that can be recalled in a given context in anticipating an imaginable future with an "intrinsic 'toward which we are heading'" quality. Joel Robbins (2013) has called for a renewed ethnography of suffering that goes "beyond the suffering subject" without resurrecting "the suffering slot" in anthropology. Alternatively, the scholars of "social suffering" (Kleinman, Das, and Lock 1997; Antze and Lambek 1996; Scheper-Hughes 1998) are concerned with the reductive tendency of the ethno-psychological interpretation of human suffering, when experience-distant, that delegitimizes or even denies its moral significance. In particular, they point to the increasing use of the medical and psychiatric discourse on suffering that does not so much claim a "new discovery" as it provides the template to frame and comprehend trauma and the emergent self (and identity) produced from the intersection of modern political, economic, and sociocultural realities. Their argument is based on the conceptualization of suffering as, first and foremost, a subjective experience necessarily requiring language as a medium for verbal and communicative expression.

7. These have interrogated the institutional organization, bureaucratic management, and production of "refugee or asylum" subjectivity, including the standard elicitation of a "trauma story," a routinized medical checkup for physical or psychological marks,

and the process of political subjectification. Miriam Ticktin, in *Casualties of Care* (2011), has shown in the case of French asylum governance that it is a conglomeration of "humanitarian interventions" or the "regimes of care" as part of the transnational organizations and private agencies, rather than the state per se, involved in the management of people seeking asylum.

8. On this reopened discussion, see "Comments" section, including Sylvain Perdigon, "*As'lem*, Forms of Life, Uncertain Otherwise" and Miriam Ticktin, "*As'lem*: An Ethical Diagnosis of the Contemporary," in Fassin, Wilhelm-Solomon, and Segatti 2017.

9. The "illness clause," as Ticktin documents, was used by undocumented migrants in France to legalize their irregular status within the context of growing anti-immigration sentiments.

10. Bringing together the concept of "biological citizenship," introduced by Nicholas Rose and Carlos Novas, and Clifford Geertz's notion of "involution," Ticktin characterizes this paradox as a form of "biological involution," whereby undocumented migrants in France participate in "a spiraling biological self-exploitation, which continues despite diminishing returns" (2011, 212).

11. After 9/11, a widespread backlash against migrant communities was reported across major cities and states throughout the United States, including New York, often followed by increased workplace immigration raids; policing and surveillance of working-class, racialized migrant communities; and detention of undocumented and documented migrants of color. For studies focusing on South Asian working-class migrant neighborhoods and communities, see Verma 2008; see also Puar and Rai 2004.

12. In 2009, out of 779 Nepali asylum applicants, only 172 were granted asylum. In 2010, 231 (out of 829) applicants received asylum, and in 2011, 323 (out of 871) claimants were granted asylum. US Department of Homeland Security, Office of Immigration Statistics, *2010 Yearbook of Immigration Statistics*, August 2011, www.dhs.gov/xlibrary /assets/statistics/yearbook/2010/ois_yb_2010.pdf. In 2012, out of 44,170 asylum applications, roughly 11,978 were granted asylum at the immigration courts in the United States. Daniel C. Martin and James E. Yankay, "Refugees and Asylees: 2013," *Annual Flow Report*, August 2014, www.dhs.gov/sites/default/files/publications/Refugees_ Asylees_2013.pdf. Nepali applicants were among the top eight nationalities to have filed for and been granted asylum: out of 750 asylum applicants received by the US Department of Justice, 403 were granted asylum. What is significant about this number is that Nepal was the only country from which more than 50 percent of the applicants were granted asylum. While asylum applicants from countries like China (10,985), Mexico (9,206), El Salvador (2,991), Guatemala (2,895), India (1,703), Honduras (1,257), and Ecuador (847) exceeded Nepali applicants (750), the number of people granted asylum from these countries was less than 50 percent, except from China (5,383).

13. Like the construction of "community" itself, voices within it invariably consist of

multiple perspectives, displaying a wide range of experiences and radically opposing dominant points of view. Without assuming an internally cohesive group and notion of belonging, people may, and often do, subscribe to the idea of the Nepali migrant community as newly arrived members from the Indian subcontinent.

14. Anthropologist Nicholas De Genova (2005) argues that ethnography poses a critical pedagogical potential—all ethnographic contexts inherently dialogical, necessarily open to contestations, and therefore, political from the outset. Channeling Paulo Freire's seminal work *Pedagogy of the Oppressed,* De Genova argues that dialogical ethnography has transformative potential that is "oriented not to fixing the differences between ethnographic interlocutors but rather to intersubjectively collaborating in the meaningful mediation of the world" (25). In this way, he explains, "Ethnographic practice potentially becomes more candidly what it has always been—an exercise in *learning,* and more important, one which is not merely one-sided, instrumental, and extractive" (28, emphasis in the original).

15. There is little disagreement today that ethnography as an anthropological rite of passage influenced and was, in turn, shaped by the institutionalization of disciplinary frames, tools, and knowledge production in Euro-American academia. Its "exemplary status," however, has been undergoing scrutiny in the last four decades (Clifford 1983). Anthropologists, drawing on particular strands of postcolonial, postmodern, and literary criticism theories prevalent in the postwar United States, proposed that the promise of anthropology lay in its service "as a cultural critique of American society" (Marcus and Fisher 1986) intricately connected to research and literary experimentation conducted outside the "dominant West." Giving rise to what is now known as the "crisis of [ethnographic] representation" era, the exclusive focus on anthropological knowledge production became fixated on textual representation of people and places constituted as "non-West." While enabling a "reflexive turn" in ethnographic writing, however, many ethnographies simply remained trapped in this internal, rather American-centric, debate on "the politics and the poetics of ethnography," deepening the institutionalization of the disciplinary frameworks for knowledge production. Others less interested in this insular debate have, however, addressed the inseparability of anthropological knowledge production from "institutionally embedded social relations of domination and subordination" inherent in the concept of ethnography (De Genova 2005, 20; Trouillot 2003; Gupta and Ferguson 1992). These anthropologists, also drawing on and inspired by postcolonial theory, showed that anthropological knowledge production relies upon and reinforces the "asymmetry in the dialectic of world power," whereby the tools, categories, and framing devices are reproductive of colonial and neocolonial relational dynamics (Asad 1973, 17; Abu-Lughod 1991; Harrison 1997; Smith 1999).

16. Nicholas De Genova argues that a sustained postcolonial critique of anthropo-

logical research must go beyond merely acknowledging "epistemological subjugation inherent in [its] textual representation" (2005, 20). He contends, "The practice of ethnographic research . . . poses what appears to be an intractable problem: it is the singular means of formal social research that enables a production of the textured knowledge of human perspectives and structures of feeling in the present that emerges only through extended engagement with the everyday lives, labors, and struggles of living people, yet it seems to be simultaneously an inherently objectifying methodology" (19).

17. Writing refusal(s) into ethnographic description—then theorizing it—rather than intervening in any "radical" way, Audra Simpson (2007) has shown how disengagement from the dominant anthropological ways of knowing and producing knowledge opens up its own space for a renewed engagement along with her interlocutors (whom she identifies with in multiple ways while also being uniquely positioned as a "researcher in her own community"). Much like Simpson's positionality, and political stance to consider refusal (to participate in ethnographic research) not as an analytical end but a redirection of conversations previously unexplored, I found myself following my interlocutors' cues on their silent participation as a suffering community.

ONE *Locating Nepali New Yorkers*

1. For contemporary works on the Himalayan diasporic cultural formation, see Gellner and Hausner 2018; Subba and Sinha 2017; Hutt 1997; Shrestha 2022.

2. There exists a vibrant debate on the distinction between the concepts of "diaspora" and "migrant" and related conceptual frameworks, namely (post)colonialism, temporality, affect, and belonging to highlight its global reach and continual transformation beyond its specific location. Scholars of the South Asian diaspora (Shukla 2003; Axel 1996) have long highlighted how the categories of "migrant" or "overseas South Asian communities" are a result of indentured labor organized and managed by colonial institutions and administration. Notwithstanding this important debate, however, I interchangeably use "diaspora" and "migrant" here to recenter suffering accounts of people that cross these conceptual boundaries, even challenge them.

3. I follow historian Paul Kramer's suggestion of using "imperial" as "an interpretive category . . . [that] cuts across" prior divisions between "a late-eighteenth-century transition from 'colony' to 'nation'" and "a late-nineteenth-century shift from 'continental' to 'overseas' empire" and thereby invites "new periodizations and richer questions about [imperial] continuity and change" (2011, 1354).

4. Narayan Khadka discusses the fact that the primary objective of the US aid was to counter communism from spreading to Nepal and to the Indian subcontinent, given its geographical proximity to China, and the growing "Russian and Chinese Communist interest in the Himalayan periphery of Nepal" (2000, 79–80).

5. "The U.S. government stated that 'it might not be in the interest of stability in the present international situation to do anything to weaken the Rana regime in Nepal.'" Policy suggestion by the US ambassador Loy W. Henderson on November 13, 1950 (cited in Khadka 2000, 79–80). On change and continuity of American liberalism and postwar liberal political organizations, see Brinkley 1995; Hamby 1973, 56–213, 299–301.

6. Werner Levi describes the mixture of apprehension and gratitude with which the Nepali state received eighty million rupees in aid to be used in agriculture, education, and health. It was also the year, Levi observes, that the American library in Kathmandu was established as an extension of the American "foreign operations mission" (1957, 238).

7. Praised for its enterprising liberal internationalism, the Fulbright Program has historical roots in and institutional relationship to the making of American "nationalist globalism." Sam Lebovic (2013) situates the political orientation, organizational agenda, and attitudes of the Fulbright Program as bleeding into, rather than a product of, Cold War international politics.

Exalted within the United States as "the embodiment of Kennedy's genuine determination to respond to the needs of Third World nations on their own terms," the Peace Corps gained prominence at home and in the international arena, reinforcing US political influence around the world (see Cobbs 1996, 80). The Peace Corps program recruited and facilitated the transplantation of US civilian volunteers, rather than diplomats and officials, throughout the world. The first set of seventy Peace Corps youth volunteers arrived in Nepal in 1962.

8. Susan Coutin discusses the official, if polarizing, debate of the 1990s resulting in an unprecedented number of naturalization applicants and adoption of restrictive immigration policies, simultaneously (2003a).

9. The launching of the "Citizenship USA" drive at the advent of the Clinton presidency and the material process of reorganizing migrant legality—the inclusion of "one million [racialized] legal permanent residents" into the US nation-state—meant liberal politics produced and legitimated the politicization surrounding the demographic shift (Carcasson and Rice 1999).

10. For a comprehensive study of the social and political history of the Maoist armed conflict, see Hutt 2004; Thapa and Sijapati 2004.

11. Ironically, along with international media came international military and humanitarian assistances for initiating collateral and multilateral dialogue between the Nepali government and the Maoist rebels, who were then listed as "terrorists." For an overview of the significant sequence of events leading to the US security officials' arrival in Nepal in 2004 and the emergence of US-India military assistance to manage "counterterrorism," see John Mage, "The Nepali Revolution and International Relations," *Monthly Review*, May 18, 2007, https://mronline.org/2007/05/18/the-nepali-revolution -and-international-relations/. The events leading up to numerous cease-fires in 2002,

2003, and 2006 and the establishment of the interim government in 2007 resulted in the United Nations–backed mission in Nepal (UNMIN), to assist with drafting of a new constitution. In collaboration with several local and international nongovernmental organizations (NGOs), including the International Crisis Group (ICG), Nepal had its parliamentary, Constituent Assembly, election in 2008 with a formidable US military presence.

12. USIP, "Transitional Justice in Nepal: A Look at the International Experience of Truth Commissions," United States Institute of Peace briefing, September 2007.

13. Susan Coutin conceptualizes "the spaces of nonexistence" as physical "domains [within the United States] occupied by legal non-subjects" who are socially and politically active but lack legal status (2003b, 27). She details areas of such nonexistence—from undocumented residencies to unregistered employment denying people minimum wage labor to myriad forms of services and facilities requiring legal documentation—that potentially "subvert the power of immigration law" (28). Ambivalence around asylum legality features quite sharply in my study of Nepali claimants' experience of status regularization from the story that Coutin tells with respect to El Salvadoran asylum seekers. One of the crucial reasons for this is that Coutin's is a story told from the vantage point of "the spaces of [legal] nonexistence" or, as she aptly describes, "an ethnography of a legal process rather than of a particular group" (23), while mine is of a particular group's struggle, survival strategies, and suffering existence exacerbated by experience of legalization—asylum seeking simply as one of many—and labor incorporation.

On May 1, 2006, across major US cities, millions of people participated in protests over growing anti-immigrant sentiments and wider immigration debate, primarily instigated by the proposal of the Border Protection, Antiterrorism, and Illegal Immigration Control Act (HR 4437), also known as the Sensenbrenner bill, in the House of Representatives on December 16, 2005. The eight-week-long nationwide marches were the most recent visible mass mobilization and organizing of racialized, working-class, un/documented migrant communities. Begun as a series of demonstrations in Chicago in March 2006, the May Day protest, also known as "a day without immigrants," urged people to participate who were mostly undocumented migrants, employed in the low-wage labor sector, who had boycotted work for the day. The objective of the protest, above many things, was to draw attention to the significant economic contribution of undocumented migrants to the US society.

14. See De Genova's (2007) concise discussion of the development, legal content, and evolution of the term *enemy aliens* since the passage of the Enemy Aliens Act of 1798, serving different political purposes, most specifically "during wartime to detain, deport, or otherwise restrict the liberties of any person . . . who is a citizen of a state with which the United States is at war" and most recently the George W. Bush administration's

deployment of the term *terrorism*, which significantly "improvised a rather more appropriately ambiguous and elastic category with which to preemptively justify the indefinite detention of some of its terrorism 'suspects'—without formal charges and without any semblance of due process of law: they have been labeled 'enemy combatants'" (429).

15. The then-president of the National Capital Immigrant Coalition Jaime Contreras's oft-cited speech delivered in Washington, DC, is used to evoke the political sentiment of the movement: "I have a message for all the politicians in Congress and . . . our president. Today we march, tomorrow we vote!" Long before it became central to Obama's election campaign, the slogan "Sí se puede!" (Yes, we can!) was chanted by protesters in the 2006 demonstrations all over the major US cities. See, for instance, "Newly Energized, Undocumented U.S. Immigrants Plan More Protests," *USA Today*, April 11, 2006, www.usatoday.com/news/nation/2006-04-11-immigration-boycott_x .htm.

16. Benjamin Johnson, "Manage Immigration as a Resource, Not an Enforcement Matter," New America Media, September 7, 2006, https://www.americanimmigration council.org/research/managing-immigration-resource.

17. See Benita Heinskanen (2009) for the polarized media interpretation of the immigrant mobilization protests: Lou Dobbs, "Radical Groups Taking Control of Immigrant Movement," *CNN*, May 2, 2006, www.cnn.com/2006/US/05/01 /dobbs.immigrantprotests/index.html; Jerome Corsi, "May Day Protest Organized by Communists," World Net Daily, May 3, 2006, www.wnd.com/2006/05/36002/

18. The SB 1070 bill passed in Arizona in 2010, which armed state law enforcement to police and criminalize undocumented migrants employed without proper documentation and imposed penalties on employers for hiring, is one such example. See also, for instance, Nicholls 2014.

19. For details, see Asian American Federation, "Profile of New York City's Nepalese Americans," Asian American Federation Census Information Center, 2019, https:// aafederation.org/wp-content/uploads/2020/12/2019np.pdf. It is important to note that this number indicates documented Nepali residents and does not reflect the actual number of Nepali undocumented migrants (considered to be much higher than the report reflects) residing in NYC with families, some holding a range of temporary legal visas.

TWO *Language of Suffering, for Survival*

1. "Encore Presentation: Interview with Barack Obama," transcripts, *Larry King Live*, CNN, March 24, 2007, https://transcripts.cnn.com/show/lkl/date/2007-03-24/ segment/01.

2. Initially introduced by the US government as the "Basic Pilot Program" in 1997 to prevent undocumented migrants from obtaining formal employment, E-Verify is the digitization of Form I-9 that employers file on behalf of their employees on a voluntary basis. By 2007, Immigration and Customs Enforcement required the mandatary filing and reporting by businesses and employers. Besides E-Verify, another immigration policy designed to reduce and criminalize undocumented migrant workers is 287(g) agreements. While 287(g) agreements train local police to act as immigration agents (Pham and Van 2010; Bohn and Santillano 2017), E-Verify is deployed to curb direct access to employment for undocumented migrants and not necessarily as a deportation tool. See also Sarah Horton's "Ghost Workers," where she brings attention to how the routine workplace raids have become a normalized procedure for criminally charging undocumented migrants: "In 2008 alone, Immigration and Customs Enforcement (ICE) arrested more than 960 unauthorized migrants for such document-related offenses, charging them with 'aggravated identity theft' and 'Social Security fraud'" (Dowling and Inda 2013, 17, cited in Horton 2016, 13).

3. My use of the term *nativism* here is derived from Nicholas De Genova's formulations of "native-ism: right to citizenship based on 'native' claims to the land and 'US exceptionalism'" and "the shared premises derive from U.S. nationalism itself" uniting, rather than separating, the liberals versus the conservatives or the Democrats versus the Republicans, or left-wing versus right-wing politics (2005, 56).

4. Ana Gonzalez-Barrera and Jens Manuel Krogstad, "U.S. Deportation of Immigrants Reaches Record High in 2013," Pew Research Center, October 2, 2014, www .pewresearch.org/fact-tank/2014/10/02/u-s-deportations-of-immigrants-reach-record -high-in-2013.

5. Jeff Vandam, "For a People Overlooked, a Lens at Last," *New York Times*, April 29, 2007, www.nytimes.com/2007/04/29/nyregion/thecity/29stre.html; see, for instance, Anh Do, "A 'Hidden' Community of Nepalese Migrants Fights to Remain in U.S.," *LA Times,* April 17, 2019, www.latimes.com/local/lanow/la-me-ln-nepal-migrants-tps -trump-immigration-20190417-story.html.

6. Federal funding for adult English as a Second language (ESL) began with the launching of the Economic Opportunity Act of 1964, "toward the elimination of the inability of all adults to read and write English" (Center for Applied Linguistics 2010). Subsequent legislation supported language instruction programs for "migrants and refugees." The introduction of the Workforce Investment Act of 1998 through the US Department of Education further required states receiving federal adult education funds to assess local ESL programs' performance and outcomes using a range of assessment schemes approved by the National Reporting System (NRS). By the early 2000s, ESL and other similar adult secondary and basic education programs were administered through local school districts, community colleges, prisons and correctional facili-

ties, and community-based organizations. See, for instance, National Center for ESL Literacy Education 1998; Moss and Ross-Feldman 2003; Peyton 2005; US Department of Education 2005.

7. On the linguistic anthropological concept of language use, Michael Silverstein (1985) proposed "the total linguistic fact," identifying four aspects: form, use, ideology, and domain; see also Duranti 1997; Mertz 2007. Hymes (1972) and Silverstein (1985) focus on the user's point of view.

On speaking Hindi, given the rise, popularity, and consumption of the North Indian film industry, or Bollywood, in Nepal since as early as the 1960s, it comes as no surprise that the majority of Nepalis comprehend and/or are proficient in Hindi.

8. I do not read English speaking ability itself, in terms of linguistic aptitude or skill, as a potential source of social transformation or a uniform experience of upward mobility for its speakers. Rather, I describe and analyze the specific ways Nepali interlocutors interpret and explain—and the particular mode of relating that information—their "need" to access English, which do not reveal a dominant, straightforward narrative of migrant integration into US society, negotiating and navigating the labor industry. In this sense, my engagement with the literature on language racialization and contemporary migration to the United States points to an apparent paradox: scholars criticize the rhetoric of "lack of skill in English as an index of 'backwardness' and 'irrationality'" (cited in Dick 2011, 231) but leave unchallenged the underlying supposition that acquisition of English should be indexed as "skill," if and when acknowledged in ethnographic works (Urciuoli 2008 and De Genova 2005 are noteworthy exceptions), and the subsequent indexing of work performed by non-English-speaking migrants as "unskilled."

9. See, for instance, studies focusing on the causes and consequences of language socialization, after Schieffelin and Ochs (1984), and racialized identity formations among 1.5- and 2nd-generation migrant youth. For some key works on migrant language use, include studies focusing on code-switching, "language crossing," and bilingualism as attempts to resist socialization into "standard English" or participation into racialization process, see Rampton 2005; Zentella 1997; Urciuoli 1996; Lippi-Green 1997; Woolard 2004; Shankar 2008; Heller 2007; Mendoza-Denton 2008; Reyes and Lo 2009.

10. De León appropriates the archaeological concept of "use wear" to go beyond interpretive and symbolic analyses of migrant suffering and, instead, trace the embodied, visible, and material forms of suffering sustained by people crossing borders in the Sonoran Desert of Arizona.

11. See, for instance, Lomnitz and Hammel 1977; Mahler 1995; Gomberg-Munoz 2010a; Alarcón and Heyman 2013. For studies highlighting the migrant moral economy, see Menjívar 2001; Horton 2015.

12. My use of the term *ethnicization* follows Bonnie Urciuoli's understanding of a "marked" identity construction against generic white, middle-class, English-speaking Americans, often conflated with class mobility. See, for instance, Shalini Shankar's (2008) study on consumption practices among "Desi" or South Asian American youth in Silicon Valley, which illuminates this conflation of ethnicity and class, indexing value in ways that conceal or, at least, successfully disrupt socioeconomic disparities within a predominantly upwardly mobile Indian ethnic community. Rampton's (2005) work among migrant multiethnic youth in the United Kingdom demonstrates that performances of ethnicity achieved through non-English language use, or "crossing," besides being stigmatized or practiced as resistance, contribute to the broader politics of difference, which can be disadvantageous to its users.

13. Ronald Schmidt (2002) challenges the binary created by the proponents and opponents of an English-only language policy controversy and suggests instead the ideological linkage between language policy and the social processes of racialization. Notable exceptions, besides De Genova (2005), on racialization and migrant English-language usage include Ramos-Zayas 2011.

14. Scholars studying the ethnic and racial formations of South Asians in the United States and "South Asian" identity as a political construct employ a wide range of analytical categories, including ethnicity (Rudrappa 2004; Koshy 1998), religion (Kurien 2001), class (Das Gupta 2006; Prashad 2001), gender and sexuality (George 2005; Puar 2004), questions of home and belonging (Shukla 2003; Khandelwal 2002; Radhakrishnan 1996), and youth subculture (Sharma 2010; Maira 2002; Shankar 2008).

15. Ben Rampton (1995) argues that language "crossing" among migrant multiethnic youth in the United Kingdom is an identifiable pattern of stylized linguistic performance that borrows certain words and features from other languages in the course of a single utterance in English.

16. Here, Kumar dai was referring to the generally known fact among Nepali migrants and asylum claimants, the possibility of obtaining a work authorization document 150 days after one's asylum application is filed and undergoing review for decision. This is, however, no longer the case; in September 2019, the Trump administration, in consultation with the DHS, proposed a delay in authorizing and processing work permits for asylum seekers to 365 days. Melissa Cruz, "Changes to Work Permit Eligibility Leave Asylum Seekers without a Job," Immigration Impact, January 13, 2020, https://immigrationimpact.com/2020/01/13/work-permit-changes-asylum-seekers/#.XobhJi-cZxg.

THREE *Logic of "Claimant Credibility"*

1. The I-589 form, available online, is endorsed jointly by the Department of Homeland Security (DHS) under the US Citizenship and Immigration Services (USCIS) and the US Department of Justice. It is one of the first legal documents introduced to asylum claimants by lawyers, who insist on its centrality in asylum credibility consideration.

2. The scholarship investigating the role of asylum advocates as well as decision makers as powerful intermediaries shaping asylum systems in the United States and Western liberal democracies, though in its nascent stage, is steadily growing. See, for instance, Gill 2009; Gibb and Good 2013; Jubany 2017; Bohmer and Shuman 2018.

3. Anthony Good has written extensively on what is meant by credibility in the asylum courts and how it is employed by legal practitioners, often drawing on the UNHCR document: the "basic requirement is that the asylum seeker's account should be 'consistent and plausible,' and 'not run counter to generally known facts'" (UNHCR 1992, 204, cited in Good 2011b, 4).

4. Williksen 2004; McKinnon 2009; Good 2011b; for asylum eligibility determination, see Sweeney 2009 and Cabot 2013; for the role of corroborators and experts in asylum, see Good 2007; Fassin and d'Halluin 2007; for analyses of courtroom hearings, see Fletcher 2006; Good 2009, 2011b; Kelly 2012; Sorgoni 2019; on the topic of moral judgment in asylum, see Kobelinsky 2015.

5. Naomi Paik (2017) compares the dual contexts of neoliberalism and criminalization within which the sanctuary movement evolved to argue that the movement's continued deployment of liberal framework "risks reproducing the exclusions it has sought to dismantle." For Paik, adopting a more "radical framework" as that of the "prison abolition movement" could potentially salvage the movement's strategy and cause. Ananya Roy (2019) also argues that drawing on the abolitionist history, rather than the current liberal frame of inclusion employed, by the sanctuary movement would radically transform its political future. She advances the notion of *hospitality*, instead, in rethinking and (re)strategizing the sanctuary movement's political orientation.

6. Given that US asylum came of age in the wake of "the sanctuary movement" and advocacy around refugees and claimants from Central America, an understanding of asylum legality relies significantly on the region's political history, internal conflicts, and socioeconomic conditions. Their "legalizing moves" (Coutin 2003b) became a reference point for legal scholars, asylum advocates, immigration judges, and policy makers concerned with asylum categorization, more generally. As Central Americans were a homogenized and racialized group of asylum seekers and low-wage migrant workers, the specific terms of the 1980s controversy that had led to the visibility of Central Americans in the first place receded in the background. Even though current

media and scholarly attention highlight familiar issues related to the plight of Central American asylum seekers in the United States thirty years ago, their asylum-seeking experiences have emerged in a different though interconnected political context. See, for instance, Ananya Roy's argument about the specificities of this distinction: the "sanctuary movement of the 1980s [was] a departure from liberal inclusion," whereby the sanctuary movement's "civil initiative . . . as mobilizations against American imperialism" in Central America is contrasted with the *new* sanctuary movement's "practices that consolidate the police power of the state" (2019, 8–9). See also Heyman, Slack, and Guerra 2018; Yarnold 1990.

7. IARLJ, *Assessment of Credibility in Refugee and Subsidiary Protection Claims under the EU Qualification Directive*, 2013, www.refworld.org/docid/557028564.html; CREDO, "Credibility Assessment in Asylum Procedures," expert roundtable, Budapest, Hungary, January 14–15, 2015, http://helsinki.hu/wp-content/uploads/CREDO-training -manual-2nd-volume-online-final.pdf.

FOUR *Testimonial in the Asylum Backstage*

1. Alessandra Gribaldo argues that in the case of domestic violence proceedings in Italy, a female claimant is pressured to fit into the category of a "paradoxical victim" through her own testimony that entailed a particular admission and socialization into broader norms and notions of victimhood (2014, 748).

2. Cited in Ridgley 2008; Jennifer Ridgley discusses how decades of criminalization of immigration has situated it as primarily a "law-and-order issue" and the one increasingly governed by federal law. See also Kanstroom 2004.

3. Gilberto Rosas (2016) discusses the legacy of IRCA in facilitating and sustaining immigration enforcement through policing practices not only in the southwestern US borders but also within migrant communities under the federal initiatives, such as "Secure-Communities," a program implemented by the United States Immigration and Customs Enforcement (ICE) that brings together federal, state, and local law enforcement agencies to police immigrant communities, across sanctuary cities and states.

4. The "defensive asylum process" refers to claimants already in the removal proceedings, who are seeking asylum from an immigration judge. An immigration judge hears both an applicant's claim and concerns and claims raised by the DHS, Immigration and Customs Enforcement attorney—representative of the US government in courtroom hearings.

"Affirmative asylum process" refers to asylum seekers who directly file for asylum— submit Form I-589, Application for Asylum and for Withholding of Removal—with the USCIS without legal representation. Individual asylum officers evaluate applicants' claims and oral testimonies and look for "credibility of their claims." The seven steps for this process are outlined under the heading of "The Affirmative Asylum Process" in United States Office of International Affairs, *Affirmative Asylum Procedures Manual*, February 2003, www.refworld.org/docid/42d7bc3021.html.

5. A 2010 report points out that the one-year deadline resulted in denials on the basis of a technicality. It offered the following suggestions for the administrative agencies to address the issue even before the deadline is repealed: "DOJ and DHS should revisit regulations governing exceptions to the deadline, create additional training materials and guidance on the deadline, issue precedential decisions interpreting the deadline . . . and monitor the adjudication of asylum cases involving the deadline." National Immigrant Justice Center, Human Rights First, Penn State Law, "The One-Year Asylum Deadline and the BIA: No Protection, No Process," *An Analysis of Board of Immigration Appeals Decisions 2005–2008* (2010). Similar deadlines were introduced for other immigration benefits, including applications for family reunification for refugees to be filed within two years of the principal applicant's arrival in the United States. "8 C.F.R. § 207.7. Derivates of Refugees," Aliens and Nationality of Code of Federal Regulations, 2011, www.ecfr.gov/current/title-8/chapter-I/subchapter-B/part-207/section-207.7.

6. For critical literature on asylum testimony that has challenged the problematic elicitation of "trauma story" in trial hearings, ranging from unequal narrative production to problems related to communicative and interpretive modes, see Jacquemet 2009, 2011; Maryns 2005; Inghilleri 2012; Pöllabauer 2004. This growing body of literature highlights the creation of what anthropologist Juan Thomas Ordóñez has called the "state of confusion" throughout the asylum determination, documentation, and adjudicative procedures (2008).

7. For Sophia Rainbird (2014), although asylum seeking may not drastically transform people's lives, testimonies offer "agentive capacity" for claimants, if temporarily, in the country they are filing asylum. Accounting for the arrested phase, or "silence," during testimony in court to be a site for "full potentiality" in terms of the logic of the liminality as theorized by Victor Turner, Rainbird argues that the efficacy of testimony is less about overcoming "a marked point of liminality . . . entrapped by their asylum status, bound to the State" than of "striv[ing] to move on to a future in which an existential understanding of self can be attained" (460).

8. My usage of *field* is here derived from Bourdieu's (1977) notion of legal habitus (practice-oriented behavior).

9. Cristiana Giordano has shown in the case of Italy that the process of translating testimony of a female trafficked migrant into legal language involves a rehabilitation mechanism through which the claimant is pressured into confessing and committing to being socialized into what is assumed to be the "'Italian way of being' of the female citizen" (2008, 589).

10. Bourdieu (1977) has underlined in his theory of practice how the macro-structural constraints are brought into face-to-face social interaction through the *habitus* of learned "dispositions": the most effective and controlling dispositions referring to assumptions widely accepted as commonsense. In this way, even the arbitrary performance gets interpreted as natural—the process Bourdieu describes as symbolic violence because of the dominating role it plays.

FIVE *Production of Claimant-Workers*

1. See, for instance, Grace Yukich (2013), who describes the "model movement strategy" that constructs and employs some people as "model cases" to distinguish from others in the marginalized communities, reinforcing the negative stereotypes of undocumented immigrants as often undeserving of legal services, especially residency and citizenship.

2. See De Genova and Peutz 2010; Kanstroom 2012; Nyers 2003. See De Genova for a compelling argument that the contemporary US deportation law must be understood within the context of long-standing historical political processes of removal of different populations that relied on "race-based policies, [where] its doctrines [were] honed through the successive efforts to remove or exclude indigenous populations (the 1830 Indian Removal Act), freed slaves (the 1850 Fugitive Slave Act), Chinese Laborers (the 1882 Chinese Exclusion Act) and other 'racially ineligible' groups (the 1924 Johnson-Reed Immigration Act) from the U.S. body politic" (2018, 23).

3. Cecilia Menjívar, also drawing on anthropologist Victor Turner's (1969) concept of "liminality," highlights the "betwixt-and-between" stage that Central American immigrants go through while legalizing their statuses in the United States. She argues that "legal citizenship in the United States is no longer easy to attain, and even permanent residence has proven an elusive dream for many" (2006, 1003).

4. Channeling Bourdieu's theory of *habitus*, Jokinen notes that this process of "inhabiting precarization" (2016, 88) is about multiple ways of becoming "worker and subject," whereby overlapping subject positions evoke characteristics of ambivalence, disorientation, anxiety, even paranoia.

5. The political organization was classified under the international "terrorist" list by the United States between 2008 and 2012. For a brief history of the formation of the organization, political demands, leadership, and activities, see South Asian Terrorism Portal, Institute for Conflict Management, "Janatantrik Terai Mukti Morcha," 2001, www.satp.org/satporgtp/countries/nepal/terroristoutfits/jtmmj.html.

6. SLC, School Leaving Certificate, is a national examination that people take after finishing tenth grade or high school in Nepal. Without passing SLC exam, one cannot

get admission to colleges. Having passed SLC is also a symbolic marker of a person leaving his/her sheltered familial life and being on his/her way to entering the civil life and assuming civil responsibilities—by joining college or getting a job, settling down, and getting married. One can often hear people beyond the age of thirty in Kathmandu speak of their "SLC time" and waiting for their results to be published in the newspaper as a period of both nervousness and heightened excitement and an important turning point of their youth. The metaphor used by Kumar dai is to express the similar anxiety and the arrested sense of time and social life that people refer to when discussing their days of preparing for and taking the exam and waiting for the result.

7. If the appeal is approved, one of three things can happen, according to his lawyers: (1) the BIA can overturn the judge's verdict, which is extremely unlikely; or (2) the BIA finds fault with the judge's assessment of the evidence presented on the case and appoints a different judge to reschedule another merit hearing, which is somewhat likely; or (3) the BIA appoints the judge to schedule another hearing, but the judge will not be allowed to ask questions outside his/her judicial expertise, which primarily includes the critical evaluation of medical experts' reports in Tshering's case.

SIX *Paradox of Visibility and Censorship*

1. Lisa Lowe (1996) explores the historical, political, and cultural processes through which Asian Americans participate in the American political spheres to challenge the institution of US citizenship as well as to consider collaborative political practices bringing together racial and ethnic minorities on the topic of immigration laws and policies.

2. For rapidly growing scholarship on visibility as form of politics and resilience, see Schreiber 2018; Vesely, Letiecq, and Goodman 2017; Marez 2016; Lemus-Way and Johansson 2020.

3. A process of Bhutanization, also known as Drukpanization, was introduced in the 1980s by the king of Bhutan as a reaction to the growing Lhotsampa population and in the guise of unifying the country under the Druk religion, culture, and language. By 1989, around a hundred thousand ethnic Nepalis were expelled from Bhutan and lived in parts of North India and Nepal as refugees and stateless. For a comprehensive social history and consequences of this policy in the region, see, for instance, Rose 1977; Evans 2010; see also Rizal and Yokota 2006. Amnesty International, "Bhutan: Human Rights Violations against the Nepali-Speaking Population in the South," December 1, 1992, www.amnesty.org/en/documents/asa14/004/1992/en.

4. For a study of this contested sociopolitical history between Nepal and Bhutan, and narratives of evicted Nepali refugees, in particular, see Hutt 2005.

5. Recently retitled "We Speak NYC," it was a widely used resource, formerly known as "We Are New York" by activists, volunteers, and ESL facilitators at Adhikaar during the two years I was there. First introduced in 2009 by the New York City Mayor's Office of Immigrant Affairs, the WANY program featured ten episodes and study materials to help adult English-language learners, primarily newly arrived migrants, to orient their daily lives in the city and improve their "language skills, learn about their rights, and access City services." This program is part of the immigrant rights movements of "Sí Se Puede" and "We Are America," preceding Obama-era immigrant politics. See, for instance, NYC Media, "We Speak NYC," accessed November 13, 2022, www.nyc.gov/site/media/shows/we-speak-nyc.page.

6. The carpet factory—late '80s and early '90s—was part of the growing cottage industry exporting rugs all over the global North; the rise and the fall of garment factories in Kathmandu provided impetus for internal migration and employment for many from outside the country's capital.

7. "My Name Is Eddie," accessed November 13, 2022, http://wespeaknyc.cityofnewyork.us/wp-content/uploads/2018/11/READER-WS1_SS18_B3_EDDIE_NLC_F_web_single.pdf.

8. Nepali labor outmigration to South Korea began in the 1980s and 1990s, when the Korean government's economic restructuring caused medium-size domestic manufacturers to scale down their wages and recruit workers from South and Southeast Asia, including Nepal. However, in the period between the implementation of the Industrial Trainee System (ITS) in 1993 and the Employment Permit System (EPS) in 2004, migrant recruits were undocumented and employed in highly precarious and labor-intensive manufacturing industries. See Gray 2006.

9. At the time I was conducting fieldwork in the city, the nail salon was an emergent labor industry where Nepali women were seeking and finding employment, and a handful of Nepalis also owned them in Queens and Manhattan. Since 2014, Adhikaar has started running nail salon workers' rights campaigns and health and safety awareness and training programs.

10. There is no dearth of scholarly evidence on policing of working-class, undocumented migrants and marginalized communities in the post-9/11 era: Maira 2004; Puar and Rai 2002; Volpp 2002; Cainkar 2005.

11. The H-2C visa system identified undocumented migrants as belonging to three legal categories: (1) earned legalization, (2) mandatory departure and reentry, and (3) all others. For the specific description of these legal categories as part of the broader interior immigration enforcement practices under "The Comprehensive Immigration Reform Act of 2006," or S.2611, see National Conference of State Legislatures, *Summary: Comprehensive Immigration Reform Act of 2006*, accessed November 13, 2022, www.ncsl.org/Portals/1/documents/immig/immigS2611.pdf.

12. Susan Coutin argues that the distinction between "official and unofficial versions of immigration law" contributed to the proliferation of several ambiguous statuses, including student, tourist, guest worker, and legal permanent resident as means and "differing degrees of inclusion and exclusion" (2003b, 51).

13. The State Criminal Alien Assistance Program (SCAAP) authorized federal funding for incarceration of unauthorized immigrants between FY 2010 and 2012. For a comprehensive report of the funding breakdown, see National Conference of State Legislatures, *Immigrant Policy: Comprehensive Immigration Reform Act of 2006,* accessed November 13, 2022, www.ncsl.org/research/immigration/comprehensive-immigrationreform-act-of-2006-summ.aspx.

14. On diverse tactics employed by undocumented youth organizations on the issue of deportation, for instance, see Patler 2017; Terriquez, Brenes, and Lopez 2018; see also Nicholls 2013.

CONCLUSION

1. Jason De León, on "Prevention through Deterrence" strategy: "No one individual is responsible for it . . . it often occurs out of sight, many portray it as 'natural,' and it can easily be denied by state actors and erased by the environment" (2015, 27).

EPILOGUE

1. For studies that highlight new forms of vulnerability in the Nepali New York community due to the COVID-19 pandemic, see the following: Nawang Tsering Gurung, Ross Perlin, Mark Turin, Sienna R. Craig, Maya Daurio, and Daniel Kaufman, "Himalayan New Yorkers Tell Stories of COVID-19," *Nepali Times,* June 6, 2020, 8–9; Craig et al. 2021; Perlin et al. 2021.

2. US Citizenship and Immigration Services, "Temporary Protected Status," accessed November 13, 2022, www.uscis.gov/humanitarian/temporary-protected-status. On September 14, 2020, in Ramos et al. v. Wolf et al., no. 18-16981, the US Court of Appeals for the Ninth Circuit prohibited DHS from terminating TPS for El Salvador, Haiti, Nicaragua, and Sudan. Nepali nationals were added as one of the beneficiaries under the TPS designations. In collaboration with the US Immigration Policy Center (USIPC) and the Center for American Progress (CAP), *Adhikaar* conducted survey research and published a report on the situation of Nepali TPS holders. See, for instance, Tom Wong, Anna Coleman, Pabitra Benjamin, Aakriti Khanal, and Silva Mathema, "Nepali TPS Holders Make Significant Contributions to America," October 19, 2020, www.americanprogress.org/issues/immigration/reports/2020/10/19/491812/nepali-tps-holders-make-significant-contributions-america. See Mountz et al. 2002.

As the title suggests, the report highlights contributions of Nepali TPS holders to the US economy and the society at large—a case for extending the TPS deadline and continued eligibility. Drawing on the survey conducted (between June and August 2020) across several US states, the report concludes that the "lives of 14,800 Nepali TPS holders hang in the balance" while "legal and policy decisions loom in the courts and federal government." It also briefly outlines the negative impact of the COVID-19 pandemic on TPS holders, including job loss, economic insecurity, and eviction threats, among others.

3. Chris Fuchs, "U.S. Plans to End Protected Status Granted to Nepalis after 2015 Earthquake," NBC News, April 26, 2018, www.nbcnews.com/news/asian-america/u-s -plans-end-protected-status-granted-nepalis-after-2015-n869401.

4. Bhattarai v. Nielsen, 3:19-cv-00731-EMC, ND California (March 12, 2019), www .aclusocal.org/sites/default/files/aclu_socal_bhattarai_20190312_stipulation_stay.pdf; Royce Murray, "Ninth Circuit Court Allows Trump's Plan to End Temporary Protected Status to Go Forward," Immigration Impact, September 14, 2020, https://immigration impact.com/2020/09/14/tps-ramos-decision/#.X3dpUWhKg2x.

5. 2021 Dream and Promise Act UWD Recommendations, "American Dream and Promise Act of 2021," accessed November 13, 2022, www.congress.gov/bill/117th -congress/house-bill/6/text.

References

Abu-Lughod, L. 1991. "Writing against Culture." In *Recapturing Anthropology: Working in the Present*, edited by R. G. Fox, 137–62. Santa Fe, NM: School of American Research Press.

Alarcón, Amado, and Josiah McC. Heyman. 2013. "Bilingual Call Centers at the U.S. Mexico Border: Location and Linguistic Markers of Exploitability." *Language in Society* 42: 1–21.

———. 2014. "From 'Spanish-Only' Cheap Labor to Stratified Bilingualism: Language, Markets and Institutions on the US-Mexico Border." *International Journal of the Sociology of Language* 227: 101–17.

Allison, Anne. 2012. "Ordinary Refugees: Social Precarity and Soul in 21st Century Japan." *Anthropological Quarterly* 85 (2): 347–70.

Antze, Paul, and Michael Lambek. 1996. *Tense Past: Cultural Essays in Trauma and Memory*. New York: Routledge.

Asad, Talal. 1973. *Anthropology and the Colonial Encounter*. London: Ithaca Press.

Ataç, Ilker, Kim Rygiel, and Maurice Stierl. 2016. "Introduction: The Contentious Politics of Refugee and Migrant Protest and Solidarity Movements: Remaking Citizenship from the Margins." *Citizenship Studies* 20 (5): 527–44.

Axel, Brian Keith. 1996. "Time and Threat: Questioning the Production of the Diaspora as an Object of Study." *History and Anthropology* 9 (4): 415–43.

Bailey, Benjamin. 2001. "Dominican-American Ethnic/Racial Identities and United States Social Categories." *International Migration Review* 35 (3): 677–708.

Bal, M., and M. Á. Hernández-Navarro. 2011. *Art and Visibility in Migratory Culture: Conflict, Resistance, and Agency*. Amsterdam: Rodopi.

Batalova, Jeanne, Sarah Hooker, and Randy Capps. 2014. "DACA at the Two-Year Mark: A National and State Profile of Youth Eligible and Applying for Deferred Action." Washington, DC: Migration Policy Institute. www.migrationpolicy.org /research/daca-two-year-mark-national-and-state-profile-youth-eligible-and -applying-deferred-action.

Beneduce, Roberto. 2015. "The Moral Economy of Lying: Subjectcraft, Narrative Capital, and Uncertainty in the Politics of Asylum." *Medical Anthropology* 34 (6): 551–71.

Bhuyan, Rupaleem. 2008. "The Production of the 'Battered Immigrant' in Public Policy and Domestic Violence Advocacy." *Journal of Interpersonal Violence* 23 (2): 153–70.

Bletzer, Keith V. 2013. "Mexican Trans-migrants and Their Experience on Both Sides of the Border: Intimacy and Distance through Use of Deictic Referents." *Open Anthropology Journal* 6: 1–10.

Blitz, Brad. 2017. "Another Story: What Public Opinion Data Tell Us about Refugee and Humanitarian Policy." *Journal on Migration and Human Security* 5 (2): 379–400.

Bloemraad, Irene, and Kim Voss. 2020. "Movement or Moment? Lessons from the Pro-immigrant Movement in the United States and Contemporary Challenges." *Journal of Ethnic and Migration Studies* 46 (4): 683–704.

Blommaert, Jan. 2001. "Investigating Narrative Inequality: African Asylum Seekers' Stories in Belgium." *Discourse and Society* 12 (4): 413–49.

Boehm, Deborah A. 2012. *Intimate Migrations: Gender, Family, and Illegality among Transnational Mexicans*. New York: New York University Press.

Bohmer, Carol, and Amy Shuman. 2015. "Cultural Silences as an Excuse for Injustice: The Problems of Documentary Proof." In *African Asylum at a Crossroads: Activism, Expert Testimony, and Refugee Rights,* edited by Iris Berger, Tricia Redeker Hepner, Benjamin Lawrence, Joanna Tague, and Meredith Terretta, 41–162. Athens: Ohio University Press.

———. 2018. *Political Asylum Deceptions: The Culture of Suspicion*. Cham, Switzerland: Palgrave Macmillan.

Bohn, Sarah, and Robert Santillano. 2017. "Local Immigration Enforcement and Local Economies." *Industrial Relations: A Journal of Economy and Society* 56 (2): 236–62.

Bonilla-Silva, Eduardo. 2006. *Racism without Racists: Color-Blind Racism and the Persistence of Racial Inequality in the USA*. 2nd ed. Lanham, MD: Rowman & Littlefield.

Bourdieu, Pierre. 1977. *Outline of a Theory of Practice*. Cambridge: Cambridge University Press.

Brinkley, Alan. 1995. *The End of Reform: New Deal Liberalism in Recession and War*. New York: Vintage Books.

Brown, Wendy. 1995. *States of Injury: Power and Freedom in Late Modernity*. Princeton, NJ: Princeton University Press.

Bruslé, Tristan. 2012. "What Kind of Place Is This?" *South Asia Multidisciplinary Academic Journal*, no. 6. https://doi.org/10.4000/samaj.3446.

Butler, Judith. 1997. *The Psychic Life of Power: Theories in Subjection*. Stanford, CA: Stanford University Press.

Cabot, Anna. 2014. "Problems Faced by Mexican Asylum Seekers in the United States." *Journal on Migration and Human Security* 2 (4): 361–77.

Cabot, Heath. 2012. "The Governance of Things: Documenting Limbo in the Greek Asylum Procedure." *Political and Legal Anthropology Review* 35 (1): 11–29.

———. 2013. "The Social Aesthetics of Eligibility: NGO Aid and Indeterminacy in the Greek Asylum Process." *American Ethnologist* 40 (3): 452–66.

———. 2016. "'Contagious' Solidarity: Reconfiguring Care and Citizenship in Greece's Social Clinics." *Social Anthropology* 24 (2): 152–66.

Cainkar, L. 2005. "Space and Place in the Metropolis: Arabs and Muslims Seeking Safety." *City & Society* 17 (2): 181–209.

Canizales, Stephanie. 2015. "American Individualism and the Social Incorporation of Unaccompanied Guatemalan Maya Young Adults in Los Angeles." *Ethnic and Racial Studies* 38 (10): 1831–47.

Carcasson, M., and M. F. Rice. 1999. "The Promise and Failure of President Clinton's Race Initiative of 1997–1998: A Rhetorical Perspective." *Rhetoric and Public Affairs* 2 (2): 243–74.

Center for Applied Linguistics. 2010. *Education for Adult English Language Learners in the United States: Trends, Research, and Promising Practices.* Washington, DC: Center for Applied Linguistics.

Chauvin, Sébastien, and Blanca Garcés-Mascareñas. 2012. "Beyond Informal Citizenship: The New Moral Economy of Migrant Illegality." *International Political Sociology* 6 (3): 241–59.

Clifford, James. 1983. "On Ethnographic Authority." *Representations*, no. 2: 118–46.

Cobbs, Elizabeth. 1996. "Decolonization, the Cold War, and the Foreign Policy of the Peace Corps." *Diplomatic History* 20 (1): 79–105.

Coutin, Susan. 2003a. "Cultural Logics of Belonging and Movement: Transnationalism, Naturalization, and U.S. Immigration Politics." *American Ethnologist* 30 (4): 508–26.

———. 2003b. *Legalizing Moves: Salvadoran Immigrants' Struggle for U.S. Residency.* Ann Arbor: University of Michigan Press.

———. 2010. "Exiled by Law." In *The Deportation Regime: Sovereignty, Space, and the Freedom of Movement*, edited by Nicholas De Genova and N. M. Puetz, 351–70. Durham, NC: Duke University Press.

Craig, Sienna. 2020. *Ends of Kinship: Connecting Himalayan Lives between Nepal and New York.* Seattle: University of Washington Press.

Craig, Sienna, and Nawang Tsering Gurung. 2018. "The Khora of Migration: Everyday Practices of (Well) Being and Belonging between Mustang, Nepal, and New York City." In *Global Nepalis: Religion, Culture, and Community in a New and Old Diaspora*, edited by David Gellner and Sondra Hausner, 271–302. New Delhi: Oxford University Press.

Craig, Sienna, Nawang T. Gurung, Ross Perlin, Maya Daurio, Daniel Kaufman, Mark Turin, and Kunchog Tseten. 2021. "Global Pandemic, Translocal Medicine: The COVID-19 Diaries of a Tibetan Physician in New York City." *Asian Medicine* 16 (1): 58–88.

Crawley, Heaven, and Dimitris Skleparis. 2018. "Refugees, Migrants, Neither, Both: Categorical Fetishism and the Politics of Bounding in Europe's 'Migration Crisis.'" *Journal of Ethnic and Migration Studies* 44 (1): 48–64.

Dahlvik, Julia. 2017. "Asylum as Construction Work: Theorizing Administrative Practices." *Migration Studies* 5 (3): 369–88.

Das Gupta, Monisha. 2006. *Unruly Immigrants: Rights, Activism and Transnational South Asian Politics in the United States*. Durham, NC: Duke University Press.

De Genova, Nicholas. 2002. "Migrant 'Illegality' and Deportability in Everyday Life." *Annual Review of Anthropology* 31 (1): 419–28.

———. 2005. *Working the Boundaries: Race, Space, and "Illegality" in Mexican Chicago*. Durham, NC: Duke University Press.

———. 2007. "The Production of Culprits: From Deportability to Detainability in the Aftermath of 'Homeland Security.'" *Citizenship Studies* 11 (5): 421–48.

———. 2009. "Conflicts of Mobility, and the Mobility of Conflict: Rightlessness, Presence, Subjectivity, Freedom." *Subjectivity* 29: 445–66.

———. 2018. "The Deportation Power." *Radical Philosophy*, no. 203: 23–27.

De Genova, Nicholas, and N. M. Peutz. 2010. *The Deportation Regime: Sovereignty, Space, and the Freedom of Movement*. Durham, NC: Duke University Press.

De Genova, Nicholas, and M. Tazzioli, eds. 2016. *Europe/Crisis: New Keywords of "the Crisis" in and of "Europe."* Zone Books Online. http://nearfuturesonline.org/europe crisis-new-keywords-of-crisis-in-and-of-europe.

de Graauw, Els, Shannon Gleeson, and Xóchitl Bada. 2019. "Local Context and Labour-Community Immigrant Rights Coalitions: A Comparison of San Francisco, Chicago, and Houston." *Journal of Ethnic and Migration* 46 (4): 728–46.

De León, Jason. 2012. "'Better to Be Hot than Caught': Excavating the Conflicting Roles of Migrant Material Culture." *American Anthropologist* 114 (3): 477–95.

———. 2013. "Efficacy and Impact of the Alien Transfer Exit Programme: Migrant Perspectives from Nogales, Sonora, Mexico." *International Migration* 51 (2): 10–23.

———. 2015. *The Land of Open Graves: Living and Dying on the Migrant Trail*. Berkeley: University of California Press.

Desjarlais, R. R. 1992. *Body and Emotion: The Aesthetics of Illness and Healing in the Nepal Himalayas*. Philadelphia: University of Pennsylvania Press.

———. 2003. *Sensory Biographies: Lives and Deaths among Nepal's Yolmo Buddhists*. Berkeley: University of California Press.

Dhingra, Pawan. 2007. *Managing Multicultural Lives: Asian American Professionals and the Challenge of Multiple Identities*. Stanford, CA: Stanford University Press.

Dick, Hilary Parsons. 2010. "Imagined Lives and Modernist Chronotopes in Mexican Non-migrant Discourse." *American Ethnologist* 37 (2): 275–90.

———. 2011. "Language and Migration to the United States." *Annual Review of Anthropology* 40: 227–40.

Dowling, Julie, and Jonathan Inda, eds. 2013. *Governing Immigration through Crime*. Stanford, CA: Stanford University Press.

Doyle, G. 2002. *The USA Patriot Act: A Legal Analysis. CRS Report for Congress*. Library of Congress, April 15.

Duranti, A. 1997. *Linguistic Anthropology*. New York: Cambridge University Press.

Evans, Rosalind. 2010. "The Perils of Being a Borderland People: On the Lhotshampas of Bhutan." *Contemporary South Asia* 18 (1): 25–42.

Fassin, Didier. 2001. "The Biopolitics of Otherness: Undocumented Foreigners and Racial Discrimination in French Public Debate." *Anthropology Today* 17 (1): 3–7.

———. 2012. "Truth Ordeal: Attesting Violence for Asylum Seekers." In *Humanitarian Reason: A Moral History of the Present*. Berkeley: University of California Press.

———. 2013. "The Precarious Truth of Asylum." *Public Culture* 1 (69): 39–63.

Fassin, Didier, and Estelle d'Halluin. 2005. "The Truth from the Body: Medical Certificates as Ultimate Evidence for Asylum Seekers." *American Anthropologist* 107 (4): 597–608.

———. 2007. "Critical Evidence: The Politics of Trauma in French Asylum Policies." *Ethos* 35 (3): 300–329.

Fassin, Didier, and Richard Rechtman. 2010. *The Empire of Trauma: An Inquiry into the Condition of Victimhood*. Translated by Rachel Gomme. Princeton, NJ: Princeton University Press.

Fassin, Didier, Matthew Wilhelm-Solomon, and Aurelia Segatti. 2017. "Asylum as a Form of Life." *Current Anthropology* 58 (2): 176–83.

Fletcher, Aubra. 2006. "The Real ID Act: Furthering Gender Bias in U.S. Asylum Law." *Berkeley Journal of Gender, Law and Justice* 21: 111–32.

Foucault, Michel. 1982. "The Subject and Power." *Critical Inquiry* 8 (4): 777–95.

Gallagher, Katherine. 2018. "Traversing Boundaries: Anthropology, Political Asylum and the Provision of Expert Witness." *Studies in Law, Politics and Society* 74: 115–32.

Gellner, David, and Sondra Hausner, eds. 2018. *Global Nepalis: Religion, Culture, and Community in a New and Old Diaspora*. New Delhi: Oxford University Press.

George, Sheba. 2005. *When Women Come First: Gender and Class in Transnational Migration*. Berkeley: University of California Press.

Gibb, R., and Anthony Good. 2013. "Do the Facts Speak for Themselves? Country of Origin Information in French and British Refugee Status Determination Procedures." *International Journal of Refugee Law* 25: 291–322.

Gibney, Matthew. 2006. *Ethics and Politics of Asylum: Liberal Democracy and the Response to Refugees*. Cambridge: Cambridge University Press.

Gill, Nick. 2009. "Presentational State Power: Temporal and Spatial Influences over Asylum Sector Decision Makers." *Transactions of the Institute of British Geographers*, new series, 34 (2): 215–33.

Gillon, Steven. 1987. *Politics and Vision: The ADA and American Liberalism, 1947–1985*. New York: Oxford University Press.

Giordano, Cristiana. 2008. "Practices of Translation and the Making of Migrant Subjectivities in Contemporary Italy." *American Ethnologist* 35 (4): 588–606.

Golash-Boza, Tanya. 2015. *Deported: Immigrant Policing, Disposable Labour, and Global Capitalism*. New York: New York University Press.

Gomberg-Munoz, Ruth. 2010a. *Labor and Legality: An Ethnography of a Mexican Immigrant Network*. Oxford: Oxford University Press.

———. 2010b. "Willing to Work: Agency and Vulnerability in an Undocumented Immigrant Network." *American Anthropologist*, new series, 112: 295–307.

Gonzales, Roberto G. 2011. "Learning to Be Illegal: Undocumented Youth and Shifting Legal Contexts in the Transition to Adulthood." *American Sociological Review* 76: 602–19.

———. 2016. *Lives in Limbo: Undocumented and Coming of Age in America*. Berkeley: University of California Press.

Gonzales, Roberto, Basia Ellis, Sarah A. Rendón-García, and Kristina Brant. 2018. "(Un)authorized Transitions: Illegality, DACA, and the Life Course." *Research in Human Development* 15 (3–4): 345–59.

Good, Anthony. 2007. *Anthropology and Expertise in the Asylum Courts*. New York: Routledge-Cavendish.

———. 2009. "The Taking and Making of Asylum Claims: Credibility Assessments in the British Asylum Courts." In *Keynote Lecture, Seeking Refuge: Caught between Bureaucracy, Lawyers, and Public Indifference*, ESRC-funded Conference, School of Oriental and African Studies, London. 2009.

———. 2011a. "Tales of Suffering: Asylum Narratives in the Refugee Status Determination Process." *West Coast Line*, no. 68: 80–89.

———. 2011b. "Witness Statements and Credibility Assessments in the British Asylum Courts." In *Cultural Expertise and Litigation: Patterns, Conflicts, Narratives*, edited by Livia Holden, 94–122. London: Routledge.

Gray, K. 2006. "Migrant Labor and Civil Society Relations in South Korea." *Asian Pacific Migration Journal* 15 (3): 381–90.

Gribaldo, Alessandra. 2014. "The Paradoxical Victim: Intimate Violence Narratives on Trial in Italy." *American Ethnologist* 41 (4): 743–56.

Griffiths, Melanie. 2012. "Vile Liars, and Truth Distorters: Truth, Trust, and the Asylum System." *Anthropology Today* 28 (5): 8–12.

Gupta, A., and J. Ferguson. 1992. Beyond "Culture": Space, Identity, and the Politics of Difference. *Cultural Anthropology* 7 (1): 6–23.

Gurung, Nawang, Ross Perlin, Daniel Kaufman, Mark Turin, and Sienna R. Craig. 2018. "Orality and Mobility: Documenting Himalayan Voices in New York City." *Verge: Studies in Global Asias* 4 (2): 64–80.

Gurung, Shobha Hamal. 2009. "Nepali Female Migrants and Informalization of Domestic Care Work: Service or Servitude?" *Journal of Workplace Rights* 14 (3): 375–96.

Gurung, Tashi W., Emily Amburgey, and Sienna R. Craig. 2021. "Unsettling the American Dream: Mobility, Migration and Precarity among Translocal Himalayan Communities during COVID-19." *Development and Change* 52 (6): 1277–300.

Hamby, Alonzo. 1973. *Beyond the New Deal: Harry Truman and American Liberalism.* New York: Columbia University Press.

Hangen, Susan. 2018. "Transnational Politics in Nepali Organizations in New York." In *Global Nepalis: Religion, Culture, and Community in a New and Old Diaspora*, edited by David Gellner and Sondra Hausner. New Delhi: Oxford University Press.

Harrison, Faye. 1997. *Decolonizing Anthropology: Moving Further toward an Anthropology for Liberation.* 2nd ed. American Anthropological Association.

Heinskanen, Benita. 2009. "A Day without Immigrants." *European Journal of American Studies* 4 (3): 1–16.

Heller, M. 2007. *Bilingualism: A Social Approach.* New York: Palgrave Macmillan.

Heyman, Josiah, Jeremy Slack, and Emily Guerra. 2018. "Bordering a 'Crisis': Central American Asylum Seekers and the Reproduction of Dominant Border Enforcement Practices." *Journal of the Southwest* 60 (4): 754–86.

Hindman, Heather. 2013. "Social Service Provider Perceptions of 'Nepali-ness' among Asylum Seekers and Refugees in Austin, Texas." *European Bulletin of Himalayan Research* 43: 103–19.

Hoftun, Martin. 1999. *People, Politics, and Ideology: Democracy and Social Change in Nepal.* Kathmandu: Mandala Book Point.

Horton, Sarah. 2015. "Identity Loan: The Moral Economy of Migrant Document Exchange." *American Ethnologist* 42 (1): 55–67.

———. 2016. "Ghost Workers: The Implications of Governing Immigration through Crime for Migrant Workplaces." *Anthropology of Work Review* 37 (1): 11–23.

Humphreys, Michael, and Tony J. Watson. 2009. "Ethnographic Practices: From 'Writing-up Ethnographic Research' to 'Writing Ethnography.'" In *Organizational Ethnography: Studying the Complexities of Everyday Life*, edited by Sierk Ybema,

Dvora Yanow, Harry Wels, and Frans Kamsteeg, 40–55. London: Sage Publications.

Hutt, Michael. 1997. "Being Nepali without Nepal: Reflection on a South Asian Diaspora." In *Nationalism and Ethnicity in a Hindu Kingdom: The Politics of Culture in Contemporary Nepal*, edited by David N. Gellner, J. Pfaff-Czarnecka, and J. Whelpton, 101–44. Amsterdam: Harwood Academic Press.

————. 2004. *Himalayan People's War: Nepal's Maoist Rebellion*. Bloomington: Indiana University Press.

————. 2005. *Unbecoming Citizens: Culture, Nationhood, and the Flight of Refugees from Bhutan*. Oxford: Oxford University Press.

Hymes, Dell. 1972. "On Communicative Competence." In *Sociolinguistics*, edited by J. B. Pride and J. Holmes, 269–93. London: Penguin.

Inghilleri, Moira. 2012. *Interpreting Justice: Ethics, Politics and Language*. New York: Routledge.

Jackson, Michael. 1998. *Minima Ethnographica: Intersubjectivity and the Anthropological Project*. Chicago: University of Chicago Press.

Jacquemet, Marco. 2009. "Transcribing Refugees: The Entextualization of Asylum-Seekers' Hearings in a Transidiomatic Environment." *Text and Talk* 29 (5): 525–46.

————. 2011. "Crosstalk 2.0. Asylum and Communicative Breakdowns." *Text and Talk* 31 (4): 475–98.

Johnson, Toni. 2011. "On Silence, Sexuality and Skeletons: Reconceptualizing Narrative in Asylum Hearings." *Social and Legal Studies* 20 (1): 57–78.

Jokinen, Eeva. 2016. "Precarious Everyday Agency." *European Journal of Cultural Studies* 19 (1): 85–99.

Joshi, Bhuwan Lal, and Leo E. Rose. 1966. *Democratic Innovations in Nepal: A Case Study of Political Acculturation*. Berkeley: University of California Press.

Jubany, O. 2017. *Screening Asylum in a Culture of Disbelief: Truths, Denials, and Skeptical Borders*. New York: Springer.

Kanstroom, Daniel. 2004. "Criminalizing the Undocumented: Ironic Boundaries of the Post–September 11th 'Pale of Law.'" *North Carolina Journal of International and Commercial Regulation* 29: 639–69.

————. 2012. *Aftermath: Deportation Law and the New American Diaspora*. New York: Oxford University Press.

Kelly, Tobias. 2012. *This Side of Silence: Human Rights, Torture, and the Recognition of Cruelty*. Philadelphia: University of Pennsylvania Press.

Khadka, Narayan. 2000. "US Aid to Nepal in the Cold War Period: Lessons for the Future." *Pacific Affairs* 73 (1): 77–95.

Khandelwal, M. 2002. *Becoming American, Being Indian: An Immigrant Community in New York City*. Ithaca, NY: Cornell University Press.

Khosravi, Shahram. 2016. "Deportation as a Way of Life for Young Afghan Men." In *Detaining the Immigrant Other: Global and Transnational Issues*, edited by Rich Furman, Douglas Epps, and Greg Lamphear, 169–81. Oxford: Oxford University Press.

Kleinman, Arthur. 1998. *The Illness Narratives: Suffering, Healing, and the Human Condition*. New York: Basic Books.

Kleinman, Arthur, Veena Das, and Margaret Lock, eds. 1997. *Social Suffering*. Oakland: University of California Press.

Knight, D. M., and C. Stewart. 2016. "Ethnographies of Austerity: Temporality, Crisis and Affect in Southern Europe." *History and Anthropology* 27 (1): 1–18.

Kobelinsky, Carolina. 2015. "Judging Intimacies at the French Court of Asylum." *Political and Legal Anthropology* 38 (2): 338–35.

Koshy, Susan. 1998. Category Crisis: South Asian Americans and the Questions of Race and Ethnicity. *Diaspora* 7 (3): 285–320.

Kramer, Paul. 2011. "Power and Connection: Imperial Histories of the United States in the World." *American Historical Review* 116 (5): 1334–91.

Kurien, Prema. 2001. "Religion, Ethnicity and Politics: Hindu and Muslim Indian Immigrants in the United States." *Ethnic and Racial Studies* 24 (2): 263–93.

Lazzarato, Maurizio. 1996. "Immaterial Labor." In *Radical Thought in Italy: A Potential Politics*, edited by Paolo Virno and Michael Hardt, 133–50. Minneapolis: University of Minnesota Press.

Lebovic, Sam. 2013. "From War Junk to Educational Exchange: The World War II Origins of the Fulbright Program and the Foundations of American Cultural Globalism, 1945–1950." *Diplomatic History* 37 (3): 280–310.

Lecadet, Clara. 2017. "Europe Confronted by Its Expelled Migrants: The Politics of Expelled Migrants' Associations in Africa." In *The Borders of "Europe": Autonomy of Migration, Tactics of Bordering*, edited by Nicholas De Genova, 141–64. Durham, NC: Duke University Press.

Lemus-Way, M. C., and H. Johansson. 2020. "Strengths and Resilience of Migrant Women in Transit: An Analysis of the Narratives of Central American Women in Irregular Transit through Mexico towards the USA." *International Migration and Integration* 21 (3): 745–63.

Levi, Werner. 1957. "Nepal in World Politics." *Pacific Affairs* 30 (3): 236–48.

Lippi-Green, R. 1997. *English with an Accent: Language, Ideology and Discrimination in the United States*. London: Routledge.

Lomnitz, Larissa, and E. A. Hammel. 1977. *Networks and Marginality: Life in a Mexican Shantytown*. New York: Academic Press.

Long, Katy. 2013. "When Refugees Stopped Being Migrants: Movement, Labour and Humanitarian Protection." *Migration Studies* 1 (1): 4–26.

Lowe, Lisa. 1996. *Immigrants Act: On Asian American Cultural Politics*. Durham, NC: Duke University Press.

Mahler, Sarah. 1995. *American Dreaming: Immigrant Life on the Margins*. Princeton, NJ: Princeton University Press.

Maira, Sunaina. 2002. *Desis in the House: Indian American Youth Culture in New York City*. Philadelphia, PA: Temple University Press.

———. 2004. "Youth Culture, Citizenship and Globalization: South Asian Youth in the United States after September 11th." *Comparative Studies of South Asia, Africa, and the Middle East* 24 (1): 219–31.

———. 2010. "Radical Deportation: Alien Tales from Lodi and San Francisco." In *The Deportation Regime: Sovereignty, Space, and the Freedom of Movement*, edited by Nicholas De Genova and Nathalie Puetz, 295–325. Durham, NC: Duke University Press.

Maldanado, Marta. 2009. "'It Is Their Nature to Do Menial Labour': The Racialization of 'Latino/a Workers' by Agricultural Employers." *Ethnic and Racial Studies* 32: 1017–36.

Malkki, Liisa. 1995a. *Purity and Exile: Violence, Memory, and National Cosmology among Hutu Refugees in Tanzania*. Chicago: University of Chicago Press.

———. 1995b. "Refugees and Exile: From 'Refugee Studies' to the National Order of Things." *Annual Review of Anthropology* 24: 495–523.

Marcus, George E., and Michael M. J. Fischer. 1986. *Anthropology as Cultural Critique: An Experimental Moment in the Human Sciences*. Chicago: University of Chicago Press.

Marez, Curtis. 2016. *Farm Worker Futurism: Speculative Technologies of Resistance*. Minneapolis: University of Minnesota Press.

Martinez-Schuldt, Ricardo D., and Daniel E. Martinez. 2019. "Sanctuary Policies and City-Level Incidents of Violence, 1990 to 2010." *Justice Quarterly* 36 (4): 567–93.

Maryns, Katrijn. 2005. "Displacement in Asylum Seekers' Narratives." In *Dislocations/Relocations: Narratives of Displacement*, edited by M. Baynham and A. De Fina, 185–96. Manchester: St. Jerome.

Maryns, Katrijn, and Jan Blommaert. 2001. "Stylistic and Thematic Shifting as a Narrative Resource: Assessing Asylum Seekers' Repertoires." *Multilingua: Journal of Cross-Cultural and Interlanguage Communication* 20 (1): 61–84.

Marx, Karl. (1885) 1956. *Capital: A Critique of Political Economy*. Vol. 2, edited by Frederich Engels and translated by I. Lasker. Moscow: Progress.

Massey, Douglas. 2007. *Categorically Unequal: The American Stratification System*. Russell Sage Foundation. www.jstor.org/stable/10.7758/9781610443807.

Mattingly, Cheryl, and Linda C. Garro. 2000. *Narrative and the Cultural Construction of Illness and Healing.* Berkeley: University of California Press.

Mayo, Jessica. 2012. "Court-Mandated Story Time: The Victim Narrative in U.S. Asylum Law." *Washington University Law Review* 89 (6): 1485–1522.

McGranahan, Carole. 2012. "An Anthropologist in Political Asylum Court, Part I." Human Rights Forum, *Anthropology News.*

———. 2018. "Refusal as Political Practice: Citizenship, Sovereignty, and Tibetan Refugee Status." *American Ethnologist* 45 (3): 367–79.

McKinley, Michelle. 1997. "Life Stories, Disclosure and the Law." *Political and Legal Anthropological Review* 20 (2): 71–82.

McKinnon, S. L. 2009. "Citizenship and the Performance of Credibility: Audiencing Gender-Based Asylum Seekers in US Immigration Courts." *Text and Performance Quarterly* 29 (3): 205–21.

Mendoza-Denton, N. 2008. *Homegirls: Language and Cultural Practice among Many Latinoa Youth Gangs.* Malden, MA: Blackwell.

Menjívar, Cecilia. 2001. *Fragmented Ties: Salvadoran Immigrant Networks in America.* Berkeley: University of California Press.

———. 2006. "Liminal Legality: Salvadoran and Guatemalan Immigrants' Lives in the United States." *American Journal of Sociology* 111 (4): 999–1037.

Menjívar, Cecilia, and Sarah Lakhani. 2016. "Transformative Effects of Immigration Law: Immigrants' Personal and Social Metamorphoses through Regularization." *American Journal of Sociology* 121 (6): 1818–55.

Mertz, Elizabeth. 2007. "Semiotic Anthropology." *Annual Review of Anthropology* 36: 337–53.

Millar, Kathleen. 2014. "The Precarious Present: Wageless Labor and Disrupted Life in Rio de Janeiro, Brazil." *Cultural Anthropology* 29 (1): 32–53.

Miller, Alexander. 2012. "Deportation as a Process of Irreversible Transformation." *Journal of Ethnic and Migration Studies* 38 (1): 131–46.

Mole, Noelle. 2010. "Precarious Subjects: Anticipating Neoliberalism in Northern Italy's Workplace." *American Anthropologist* 112 (1): 28–53.

———. 2012. "Haunting of Solidarity in Post-Fordist Italy." *Anthropological Quarterly* 85 (2): 371–98.

Moss, D., and L. Ross-Feldman. 2003. *Second Language Acquisition in Adults: From Research to Practice.* Washington, DC: Center for Applied Linguistics.

Mountz, Alison, Richard Wright, Ines Miyares, and Adrian Bailey. 2002. "Lives in Limbo: Temporary Protected Status and Immigrant Identities." *Global Networks* 2 (4): 335–56.

Muehlebach, Andrea. 2012. *The Moral Neoliberal: Welfare and Citizenship in Italy.* Chicago: University of Chicago Press.

Narayan, Kirin. 1999. "Ethnography and Fiction: Where Is the Border?" *Anthropology and Humanism* 24 (2): 134–47.

National Center for ESL Literacy Education. 1998. *Research Agenda for Adult ESL.* Washington, DC: Center for Applied Linguistics.

Neilson, Brett, and Ned Rossiter. 2005. "From Precarity to Precariousness and Back Again: Labor, Life and Unstable Networks." *Fiberculture Journal*, no. 5: FJC-022.

Ngai, Mae. 2003. *Impossible Subjects: Illegal Aliens and the Making of Modern America.* Princeton, NJ: Princeton University Press.

Nicholls, Walter. 2013. *The DREAMers: How the Undocumented Youth Movement Transformed the Immigrant Rights Debate.* Stanford, CA: Stanford University Press.

———. 2014. "From Political Opportunities to Niche-Openings: The Dilemmas of Mobilizing for Immigrant Rights in Inhospitable Environments." *Theory and Society* 43 (1): 23–49.

Nicholls, Walter, and Justus Uitermark. 2016. *Cities and Social Movements: Immigrant Rights Activism in the United States, France and the Netherlands, 1970–2015.* Malden, MA: Wiley-Blackwell.

Nicholls, Walter J., Justus Uitermark, and Sander van Haperen. 2019. "Going National: How the Fight for Immigrant Rights Became a National Social Movement." *Journal of Ethnic and Migration Studies* 46 (4): 705–27.

Nyers, Peter. 2003. "Abject Cosmopolitanism: The Politics of Protection in the Anti-deportation Movement." *Third World Quarterly* 24 (6): 1069–93.

O'Neill, Tom. 2007. "'Our Nepali Work Is Very Good': Nepali Domestic Workers as Transnational Subjects." *Asian and Pacific Migration Journal* 16 (3): 301–22.

Ong, Aihwa. 2003. *Buddha Is Hiding: Refugees, Citizenship, the New America.* Berkeley: University of California Press.

Onta, Pratyoush. 1994. "Dukha during the World War." *Himal Southasian* 7 (6): 24–29.

———. 1996. "The Politics of Bravery: A History of Nepali Nationalism." PhD diss., University of Pennsylvania. ProQuest (AAI 9636193). https://repository.upenn.edu /dissertations/AAI9636193.

Ordóñez, Juan Thomas. 2008. "The State of Confusion: Reflections on Central American Asylum Seekers in the Bay Area." *Ethnography* 9 (1): 35–60.

———. 2016. "Documents and Shifting Labor Environments among Undocumented Migrant Workers in Northern California." *Anthropology of Work Review* 37 (1): 24–33.

Paik, Naomi. 2017. "Abolitionist Futures and the US Sanctuary Movement." *Race and Class* 59 (2): 3–25.

Patler, Caitlin. 2017. "'Citizens but for Papers': Undocumented Youth Organizations, Anti-deportation Campaigns, and the Reframing of Citizenship." *Social Problems*, 65: 96–115.

Perlin, Ross, Nawang T. Gurung, Sienna R. Craig, Maya Daurio, Daniel Kaufman, and Mark Turin. 2021. "Who Will Care for the Care Worker? The COVID-19 Diaries of a Sherpa Nurse in New York City—स्याहार कर्मीको स्याहार कसले गर्ने? न्युयोर्क शहरको एक शेर्पा नर्सको कोभिडि-१९ डायरी." *Issues* 4.

Peyton, J. K. 2005. *Using the ESL Program Standards to Evaluate and Improve Adult ESL Programs*. Washington, DC: Center for Applied Linguistics.

Pham, H., and P. H. Van. 2010. "The Economic Impact of Local Immigration Regulation: An Empirical Analysis." *Cardozo Law Review* 32: 485–518.

Pigg, Stacey L. 1992. "Inventing Social Categories through Place: Social Representations and Development in Nepal." *Comparative Studies in Society and History* 34 (3): 491–513.

Pöllabauer, Sonja. 2004. "Issues of Role, Responsibility and Power." *Interpreting* 6 (2): 143–80.

Portes, Alejandro, and Ruben Rumbaut. 2001. *Legacies: The Story of the Immigrant Second Generation*. Berkeley: University of California Press.

Prashad, Vijay. 2001. *The Karma of Brown Folk*. Minneapolis: University of Minnesota Press.

Puar, Jasbir K. 2004. "Abu Ghraib: Arguing against Exceptionalism." *Feminist Studies* 30 (2): 522–34.

Puar, Jasbir, and Amit Rai. 2002. "Monster, Terrorist, Fag: The War on Terrorism and the Production of Docile Patriots." *Social Text* 20 (3): 117–48.

———. 2004. "The Remaking of a Model Minority: Perverse Projectiles under the Specter of (Counter)Terrorism." *Social Text* 22 (3): 75–104.

Radhakrishnan, R. 1996. *Diasporic Mediations: Between Home and Location*. Minneapolis: University of Minnesota Press.

Rainbird, Sophia. 2014. "Asserting Existence: Agentive Narratives Arising from the Restraints of Seeking Asylum in East Anglia, Britain." *Ethos* 42 (4): 460–78.

Ramji-Nogales, Jaya, Andrew Schoenholtz, and Phillip G. Schrag. 2007. "Refugee Roulette: Disparities in Asylum Adjudication." *Stanford Law Review* 60 (2): 295–412.

Ramos-Zayas, Ana. 2011. "Learning Affect, Embodying Race: Youth, Blackness, and Neoliberal Emotions in Latino Newark." *Transforming Anthropology* 19 (2): 86–104.

Rampton, Ben. 2005. *Crossing: Language and Ethnicity among Adolescents*. London: Routledge.

Ramsay, Georgina. 2020. "Time and the Other in Crisis: How Anthropology Makes Its Displaced Object." *Anthropological Theory* 20 (4): 385–413.

Reyes, Angela, and Adrienne Lo, eds. 2009. *Beyond Yellow English: Toward a Linguistic Anthropology of Asian Pacific America*. New York: Oxford University Press.

Reynolds, J. F., and M. F. Orellano. 2009. "New Immigrant Youth Interpreting in White Public Space." *American Anthropologist* 111 (2): 211–23.

Ridgley, Jennifer. 2008. "Cities of Refuge: Immigration Enforcement, Police, and the Insurgent Genealogies of Citizenship in U.S. Sanctuary Cities." *Urban Geography* 29: 53–77.

Rizal, Dhurba P., and Yozo Yokota. 2006. *Understanding Development, Conflict and Violence: The Cases of Bhutan, Nepal, North-east India and the Chittagong Hill Tracts of Bangladesh*. New Delhi: Adroit Publishers.

Robbins, Joel. 2013. "Beyond the Suffering Subject: Toward an Anthropology of the Good." *Journal of the Royal Anthropological Institute* 19 (3): 447–62.

Robertson, Thomas. 2016. "Cold War Landscapes: Towards an Environmental History of US Development Programmes in the 1950s and 1960s." *Cold War History* 16 (4): 417–41.

———. 2018. "DDT and the Cold War Jungle: American Environmental and Social Engineering in the Rapt Valley of Nepal." *Journal of American History* 104 (4): 904–30.

Rosas, Gilberto. 2016. "The Border Thickens: In-Securing Communities after IRCA." *International Migration* 54 (2): 119–30.

Rose, Leo. 1977. *The Politics of Bhutan*. Ithaca, NY: Cornell University Press.

Roy, Ananya. 2019. "The City in the Age of Trumpism: From Sanctuary to Abolition." *Environment and Planning D: Society and Space* 37 (5): 761–78.

Rudrappa, Sharmila. 2004. *Ethnic Routes to Becoming American: Indian Immigrants and the Cultures of Citizenship*. New Brunswick, NJ: Rutgers University Press.

Scheper-Hughes, Nancy. 1998. "Undoing: Social Suffering and the Politics of Remorse in the New South Africa." *Social Justice* 25 (4): 114–42.

Schieffelin, B., and E. Ochs. 1984. "Language Acquisition and Socialization: Three Developmental Stories and Their Implications." In *Culture Theory: Essays on Mind, Self and Emotion*, edited by R. Shweder and R. Levine, 276–320. New York: Cambridge University Press.

Schmidt, Ronald. 2006. "Racialization and Language Policy: The Case of the U.S.A." *Multilingua: Journal of Cross-Cultural and Interlanguage Communication* 21 (2): 141–61.

Schreiber, Rebecca. 2018. *The Undocumented Everyday: Migrant Lives and the Politics of Visibility*. Minneapolis: University of Minnesota Press.

Selim, Nasima, Mustafa Abdalla, Lilas Alloulou, Mohamed Alaedden Halli, Seth Holmes, and Maria Ibiss. 2018. "Coming Together in the So-Called Refugee Crisis: A Collaboration among Refugee Newcomers, Migrants, Activists, and Anthropologists in Berlin." *Anthropology in Action* 25 (3): 34–44.

Shankar, Shalini. 2008. *Desi Land: Teen Culture, Class, and Success in Silicon Valley*. Durham, NC: Duke University Press.

Sharma, Jeevan. 2018. *Crossing the Border to India: Youth, Migration, and Masculinities in Nepal*. Philadelphia: Temple University Press.

Sharma, Nitasha. 2010. *Hip Hop Desis: South Asian Americans, Blackness, and a Global Race Consciousness*. Durham, NC: Duke University Press.

Sherpa, Pasang. 2019. "Preserving Sherpa Language and Culture in New York." *Book 2.0* 9 (1–2): 19–29.

Shrestha, Tina. 2018. "Aspirational Infrastructure: Everyday Brokerage and the Foreign Employment-Recruitment Agencies in Nepal." *Pacific Affairs* 91 (4): 675–95.

———. 2022. "Nepali: Outmigration and Evolving Diaspora." In *Languages of Japan: Communities and Cultures*, edited by John Maher, 129–37. Oxford: Oxford University Press.

Shukla, Sandhya. 2003. *India Abroad*. Princeton, NJ: Princeton University Press.

Shuman, Amy, and Carole Bohmer. 2012. "The Stigmatized Vernacular: Political Asylum and the Politics of Visibility/Recognition." *Journal of Folklore Research* 48 (2): 199–226.

Signorini, Virginia. 2015. "Producing Memory: Narratives of Suffering in the Asylum Experience." *Subjectivity* 8: 382–408.

Sijapati, Bandita. 2010. "Nepali Transmigrants: An Examination of Transnational Ties among Nepali Immigrants in the United States." *European Bulletin of Himalayan Research* 35–36: 139–53.

Silverstein, Michael. 1985. "Language and the Culture of Gender: At the Intersection of Structure, Usage and Ideology." In *Semiotic Mediation*, edited by Elizabeth Mertz and R. Parmentier, 219–59. Orlando: Academic Press.

Silverstein, Paul A. 2005. "Immigrant Racialization and the New Savage Slot: Race, Migration, and Immigration in the New Europe." *Annual Review of Anthropology* 34: 363–84.

Simpson, Audra. 2007. "Ethnographic Refusal: Indigeneity, 'Voice' and Colonial Citizenship." *Junctures: The Journal for Thematic Dialogue* 9: 67–80.

Smith, Linda Tuhiwahi. 1999. *Decolonizing Methodologies: Research and Indigenous Peoples*. London: Zed Books.

Sorgoni, Barbara. 2019. "The Location of Truth: Bodies and Voices in the Italian Asylum Procedure." *PoLAR* 42 (1): 161–76.

Squire, V. 2011. "From Community Cohesion to Mobile Solidarities: The *City of Sanctuary* Network and the *Strangers into Citizens* Campaign." *Political Studies* 59 (2): 290–307.

Stewart, Kathleen. 2012. "Precarity's Forms." *Cultural Anthropology* 27 (3): 518–25.

Subba, Tanka B. 2008. "Living the Nepali Diaspora in India: An Autobiographical Essay." *Zeitschrift für Ethnologie* 133 (2): 213–32.

Subba, Tanka B., and A. C. Sinha. 2017. *Nepali Diaspora in a Globalized Era*. New Delhi: Routledge.

Subedi, Janardan. 1989. "Modern Health Services and Health Care Behavior: A Survey in Kathmandu, Nepal." *Journal of Health and Social Behavior* 30 (4): 412–20.

Sweeney, James A. 2009. "Credibility, Proof and Refugee Law." *International Journal of Refugee Law* 21 (4): 700–726.

Talavera, Victor, Guillermina Gina Nunez-Mchiri, and Josiah Heyman. 2010. "Deportation in the U.S.-Mexico Borderlands: Anticipation, Experience, and Memory." In *The Deportation Regime: Sovereignty, Space, and the Freedom of Movement*, edited by Nicholas De Genova and Nathalie Puetz, 166–95. Durham, NC: Duke University Press.

Terriquez, Veronica, Tizoc Brenes, and Abdiel Lopez. 2018. "Intersectionality as a Multipurpose Collective Action Frame: The Case of the Undocumented Youth Movement." *Ethnicities* 18 (2): 260–76.

Thapa, Deepak, and Bandita Sijapati. 2004. *A Kingdom under Siege: Nepal's Maoist Insurgency, 1996 to 2003*. Kathmandu: Printhouse.

Throop, Jason. 2010. *Suffering and Sentiment: Exploring the Vicissitudes of Experience and Pain in Yap*. Oakland: University of California Press.

Ticktin, Miriam. 2006. "Where Ethics and Politics Meet: The Violence of Humanitarianism in France." *American Ethnologist* 33 (1): 33–49.

———. 2011. *Casualties of Care: Immigration and the Politics of Humanitarianism in France*. Berkeley: University of California Press.

Trouillot, Michel-Rolph. 2003. *Global Transformations: Anthropology and the Modern World*. New York: Palgrave Macmillan.

Tuckett, Anna. 2016. "Moving on: Italy as a Stepping Stone in Migrants' Imaginaries." *Focaal* 76: 99–113.

Turner, Victor W. 1969. *The Ritual Process: Structure and Anti-structure*. Chicago: Aldine.

UNHCR. 1992. *Handbook on Procedures and Criteria for Determining Refugee Status under the 1951 Convention and the 1967 Protocol Relating to the Status of Refugees*. Geneva: UNHCR.

Urciuoli, Bonnie. 1996. *Exposing Prejudice: Puerto Rican Experiences of Language, Race, and Class*. Boulder, CO: Westview Press.

———. 2008. "Skills and Selves in the New Workplace." *American Ethnologist* 35 (2): 211–28.

US Department of Education, Office of Vocational and Adult Education. 2005. *Adult Education and Family Literacy Act: Program Facts*.

Verma, Ritu. 2008. *Backlash: South Asian Immigrant Voices on the Margins*. Rotterdam: Sense Publishers.

Vesely, Colleen, Bethany Letiecq, and Rachael Goodman. 2017. "Immigrant Family

Resilience in Context: Using a Community-Based Approach to Build a New Conceptual Model." *Journal of Family Theory and Review* 9 (1): 93–110.

Visweswaran, Kamala. 1997. "Diaspora by Design: Flexible Citizenship and South Asians in the US Racial Formation." *Diaspora* 6 (1): 5–29.

Volpp, Letti. 2002. "The Citizen and the Terrorist." *UCLA Law Review* 49: 1575–98.

Walters, William. 2002. "Deportation, Expulsion, and the International Politics of Aliens." *Citizenship Studies* 6 (3): 265–92.

Whelpton, John. 2005. *A History of Nepal*. Cambridge: Cambridge University Press.

White, Hylton. 2012. "A Post-Fordist Ethnicity: Insecurity, Authority, and Identity in South Africa." *Anthropological Quarterly* 85 (2): 397–427.

Williksen, S. 2004. "On the Run: The Narrative of an Asylum Seeker." *Anthropology and Humanism* 29 (2): 117–32.

Woolard, K. A. 2004. "Codeswitching." In *A Companion to Linguistic Anthropology*, edited by A. Duranti. Malden, MA: Blackwell.

Yarnold, Barbara. 1990. "The Refugee Act of 1980 and the Depoliticization of Refugee/Asylum Admissions: An Example of Failed Policy Implementation." *American Politics Quarterly* 18 (4): 527–36.

Yukich, Grace. 2013. "Constructing the Model Immigrant: Movement Strategy and Immigrant Deservingness in the New Sanctuary Movement." *Social Problems* 60 (3): 302–20.

Zarowsky, Christina. 2004. "Writing Trauma: Emotion, Ethnography, and the Politics of Suffering among Somali Returnees in Ethiopia." *Culture, Medicine and Psychiatry* 28: 189–209.

Zentella, Ana. 1997. *Growing up Bilingual: Puerto Rican Children in New York*. Malden, MA: Blackwell.

Index

Page numbers in *italics* refer to illustrations.

124–25, 133–39, 170; domestic work and, 155–56, 167; dukkha in, 47–50; English-only language policy, 199n13; ethnicization and, 199n12; and Hindi, 59–62; language crossing and, 199n15; making paper and, 153; problems with, 66; suffering documentation and, 75–76; teachers of, 50–53, 198n8; uses of migrant language and, 53–58

English for Empowerment (English as Second Language, ESL), 1, 50, *154*

ESL (English as Second Language), 1–2; Economic Opportunity Act of 1964 and, 197n6; facilitators' teaching of, 50–53; student-interlocutor of, 8, 58, 146, 149, 172, 179

ethnography, 6, 22, 148–49, 152, 189n3, 190n6, 192nn14–15, 195n12

E-Verify, 197n2

Fassin, Didier, 10–11, 78, 98, 179, 191n8, 200n4

Form I-589, 73–76, 93, 96, 201n4

Fulbright Program, 34, 194n7

habitual suffering, 21, 53–54, 58

Hindi: domestic work and, 61–66; and English language, 59–62; Nepalese and, 53, 56, 58, 198n7

Homeland Security Act of 2002, 97

H-2C visa system: immigration enforcement, 165, 205n11

human rights: Adhikaar and, 49; agency of, 5–8, 14, 86–97, 145; asylum seekers and, 81; eligibility determination and, 100, 102; Purmina and, 132–33; suffering testimony and, 99, 115–17; survival strategies and, 148–51, 173, 180–81

Human Rights First, 133, 202n5

Humphreys, Michael, 6

Hyolmo, 25, 60–61

ICE (Immigration and Customs Enforcement), 97, 197n2, 201n3

IIRAIRA (Immigration Reform and Immigration Responsibility Act), 15, 35, 96, 160–61, 165

illegality: asylum legalization and, 80, 195n13; asylum migrant labor and, 127, 161; migrant criminality and, 164; politicization of, 21, 37–39, 150, 162, 165; survival strategy and, 21

imagination: of asylum claimant, 105, 111–18; dukkha in, 31–33; of social and cultural Nepali, 44, 184; of suffering, 16, 99

immigrant: communities of, 183, 191n11; existential suffering of, 12–13, 17–21, 172–76, 198n10; immigration enforcement and, 80–82, 160–62; invisibility of, 31–33; labor of, 35, 126–28, 162, 199n16, 200n6; language of suffering and, 48–50; learning English and, 53–58, 197n6, 198nn8–9; legalization of, 39; policing of, 201n3; racialization of, 62–65, 80, 194n9, 199n13; rights activism of, 149–53; transformation and visibility of, 179–82

immigration: Adhikaar and, 2, 24; asylum migrant labor and, 126–28; changing laws and policies of, 2–3, 12–16, 70, 82–87, 96–97; Department of Homeland Security and, 96–97; pro-immigration rallies and, *40, 41*; survival strategies of, 148–53

Immigration and Customs Enforcement (ICE), 97, 197n2, 201n3

Immigration and Naturalization Services (INS), 97

immigration courtroom: affirmative asylum process in, 201n4; asylum backstage and, 99; claimant credibility and, 77–79, 93–95; cross-examination in, 45; Kumar and, 138–41; official stories that win in, 71; Purnima and, 131–37; suffering and, 115–18; Tshering and, 141–45; witness testimony in, 112–15

immigration enforcement: asylum and, 80–82; H-2C visa system, 205n11; immigrant question and, 38–41; suffering emergence and, 10–11, 17–18, 21, 29, 37, 180–82

immigration law: credible claims and, 82; enforcement of, 96–97, 151, 180, 195n13, 204n1, 206n12; lack of information of, 2–3; undocumented labor and, 39

immigration reform, 48–50, 165–66

Immigration Reform and Control Act (IRCA), 15, 96, 201n3

interlocutor: asylum credibility and, 79, 92–93; for claimant, 6–8, 44, 69, 120, 126, 152, 180; dukkha and, 47; ESL students as, 8, 58, 146, 149, 172, 179–80; and language for survival and silence, 62–66; Nepali-speaking, 14, 28, 47, 148, 153, 189n1, 189n3, 198n8; silence and, 52–53; suffering and, 148–49, 152–53; time spent by, 7, 121

International Commission for Transitional Justice (ICTJ), 36

interpretation, 5–8, 106–7, 179

interpretation, suffering, 94–97, 103–5

interpreter, 6–7, 67, 106, 173–76, 189n2, 190n4

IRCA (Immigration Reform and Control Act), 15, 96, 201n3

Jackson Heights, 1–2

Jankari Report, 168

kaagaz banaune, 13, 20, 22–26, 120–21. *See also* making paper

Kumar, 45–46, 69–70, 138–41, 199n16, 204n6

labor: of asylum migrants, 126–28, 162; of claimant-workers, 128–31, 138; community suffering and, 180–82; dukkha of, 32–34; English language and, 62–66, 198n8; IIRAIRA and, 160–61; making paper and, 136–37; migrant languages and, 53–58; precariousness of, 19, 45, 130–31, 136, 145–47, 174; regularization of, 15–18, 166

labor, low-wage: Comprehensive Immigration Reform Act of 2006 and, 165; learning English and, 53–57, 146; migrant workers and, 39, 149, 161–64; Nepali New Yorkers and, 10, 31, 182; suffering and, 166

labor activists, 38–39

labor incorporation, 5, 18, 53–54, 195n13

labor-time, 144–45

language: ESL facilitator and, 50–53, 197n6; in Nepali Queens, 66–71; speaking Hindi as, 59–62, 198n7; of suffering, 48–50; for survival, 62–66, 198n8; uses of migrant languages, 53–58, 55, 56, 198n9, 199nn12–13

legality: collective censorship and, 174; economic status and, 45; migrant labor and, 35–37, 81, 126–28, 137, 194n9; in Nepali Queens, 120. *See also* asylum legality

legalization: anxiety and risk of, 69–71;

Nepali (*continued*)
imaginaries of, 18–22; survival strategies of, 148–53, 167–68; Temporary Protective Service for, 206nn2–3

Nepali New Yorkers: diaspora of Nepali and, 31–35; dukkha as collective consciousness of, 46–47; epilogue for, 183–85, 206n1; pro-immigrant mass mobilization and, 37–46, *40*, *41*, *42*, *43*; in Queens, 66–71, 120, 123, 180–82; transnational migratory networks of, 35–37

nongovernmental organizations (NGOs), 36, 49, 194n11

paradox, experience of, 9, 12–17, 148–76, 191n10, 198n8

participant-interpreter role, 6, 22, 73, 190n4

Pelki, 25–26, 60–62, 156–57

Phurba, 162–66

precarity: asylum seeking and, 130, 144–45; of labor, 14, 34, 121, 166; suffering and, 32; the work of making paper and, 11. *See also* legal precarity

precarization, 130

Purnima, 8, 83–91, 131–37, 150

racialization, 53–58, 199n13

Reema, 26, 128–29, 171–73

refugee: asylum system and, 98, 100, 190n7; migrant suffering and, 177–79; transformation of suffering and, 179–80

Refugee Act of 1980, 15, 96

Refugee Protection Program, 100, 133

sahu-ji, 51, 61, 128

samudaya, 31

sanctuary cities, 39, 150, 201n3

sanctuary movement, 80–81, 200nn5–6

Sanju: legalization of, 153–58, 161–63; shared silence of, 52; speaking Hyolmo by, 25–26, 59–66

SB 1070, 196n18

Segatti, Aurelia, 10–11

silence: encounters of, 62–66; interlocutors and, 28–29; significance of shared, 52–53

Simpson, Audra, 29, 193n17

social suffering, 9, 190n6

sociocultural phenomena, 6, 43, 120, 137, 153, 190

Sonam, 157–61

South Asian people: domestic labor industry and, 53, 63–64; Nepali-speaking communities and, 27–35, 191n11, 199n14

South Korea, 162, 205n8

suffering: being visible and, 31–32, 44; as cultivable behavior, 18–22; documentation of, 73–80; dukkha as, 22–30, 47; interpretations of, 94–97; language of, 48–50, 198n10; migrant and asylee script for, 177–79; Nepali diaspora and, 37; silent community of, 180–82; and surviving, 1–8; testimony of, 84, 94–110; theories of, 9–18, 190n6; transformation and visibility of, 152–53, 179–80, 185. *See also* habitual suffering; social suffering

suffering imaginaries, 9, 18–22

suffering narration, 10, 12–14, 21, 44, 90, 123, 125, 148

survival strategy: asylum seeking and, 127; of Nepali New Yorkers, 8–16; speaking English as, 59; suffering and, 148–53

surviving, 1–9, 172, 176, 180